D0421497

Recruiting, Training, and Retention of Science and Technology Librarians

Recruiting, Training, and Retention of Science and Technology Librarians has been co-published simultaneously as *Science & Technology Libraries*, Volume 27, Numbers 1/2 2006.

Monographic Separates from *Science & Technology Libraries*™

For additional information on these and other Haworth Press titles, including descriptions, tables of contents, reviews, and prices, use the QuickSearch catalog at http://www.HaworthPress.com.

Recruiting, Training, and Retention of Science and Technology Librarians, edited by Patricia A. Kreitz, MLS, MS, and JoAnn DeVries, MLS (Vol. 27, No. 1/2, 2006). *Comprehensive discussion of the recruitment, training, and retention of science and technology librarians.*

Emerging Issues in the Electronic Environment: Challenges for Librarians and Researchers in the Sciences, edited by Jeannie P. Miller, PhD (Vol. 25, No. 1/2, 2004). *Examines the rapid advances in technology and scientific discovery that have changed the way sci/tech library users seek information and interact with library staff.*

Innovations in Science and Technology Libraries, edited by William Miller, PhD, MLS, and Rita M. Pellen, MLS, BA (Vol. 24, No. 1/2, 2003 and Vol. 24, No. 3/4, 2004). *"An invaluable resource.... Tells the stories of innovative libraries and librarians.... Strikes a good balance between technical specification and illustration/discussion of strategic issues.... Will appeal to a broad range of technologists, reference librarians, and managers." (Michael L. Nelson, PhD, Assistant Professor, Department of Computer Science, Old Dominion University)*

Online Ecological and Environmental Data, edited by Virginia Baldwin, MS, MLS (Vol. 23, No. 4, 2003). *Explores aspects of the online data projects developed in various fields from ecological and environmental research programs.*

Leadership and Management Principles in Libraries in Developing Countries, edited by Wei Wei, MA, MLS, Sue O'Neill Johnson, BA, MLS, MPA, and Sylvia E. A. Piggott, BA, MLS (Vol. 23, No. 2/3, 2002). *Examines case studies of innovative programs from special libraries in developing countries, with a focus on the management and leadersip skills that made these initiatives successful.*

Scholarly Communication in Science and Engineering Research in Higher Education, edited by Wei Wei, MA, MLS (Vol. 22, No. 3/4, 2002). *Examines science and technology libraries' difficulties with maintaining expensive journal subscriptions for both researchers and tenure-ready scholars; offers advice and examples of efficient improvement to make fact-finding and publication easier and more cost-efficient.*

Patents and Trademark Information: Uses and Perspectives, edited by Virginia Baldwin, MS, MLS (Vol. 22, No. 1/2, 2001). *"A lucid and in-depth presentation of key resources and information systems in this area." (Javed Mostafa, PhD, Victor H. Yngve Associate Professor, Indiana University, Bloomington)*

Information and the Professional Scientist and Engineer, edited by Virginia Baldwin, MS, MLS, and Julie Hallmark, PhD (Vol. 21, No. 3/4, 2001). *Covers information needs, information seeking, communication behavior, and information resources.*

Information Practice in Science and Technology: Evolving Challenges and New Directions, edited by Mary C. Schlembach, BS, MLS, CAS (Vol. 21, No. 1/2, 2001). *Shows how libraries are addressing new challenges and changes in today's publishing market, in interdisciplinary research areas, and in online access.*

Electronic Resources and Services in Sci-Tech Libraries, edited by Mary C. Schlembach, BS, MLS, and William H. Mischo, BA, MA (Vol. 20, No. 2/3, 2001). *Examines collection development, reference service, and information service in science and technology libraries.*

Engineering Libraries: Building Collections and Delivering Services, edited by Thomas W. Conkling, BS, MLS, and Linda R. Musser, BS, MS (Vol. 19, No. 3/4, 2001). *"Highly useful. The range of topics is broad, from collections to user services ... most of the authors provide extra value by focusing on points of special interest. Of value to almost all librarians or information specialists in academic or special libraries, or as a supplementary text for graduate library courses." (Susan Davis Herring, MLS, PhD, Engineering Reference Librarian, M. Louis Salmon Library, University of Alabama, Huntsville)*

Electronic Expectations: Science Journals on the Web, by Tony Stankus, MLS (Vol. 18, No. 2/3, 1999). *Separates the hype about electronic journals from the realities that they will bring. This book provides a complete tutorial review of the literature that relates to the rise of electronic journals in the sciences and explores the many cost factors that may prevent electronic journals from becoming revolutionary in the research industry.*

Digital Libraries: Philosophies, Technical Design Considerations, and Example Scenarios, edited by David Stern (Vol. 17, No. 3/4, 1999). *"Digital Libraries: Philosophies, Technical Design Considerations, and Example Scenarios targets the general librarian population and does a good job of opening eyes to the impact that digital library projects are already having in our automated libraries." (Kimberly J. Parker, MILS, Electronic Publishing & Collections Librarian, Yale University Library)*

Sci/Tech Librarianship: Education and Training, edited by Julie Hallmark, PhD, and Ruth K. Seidman, MSLS (Vol. 17, No. 2, 1998). *"Insightful, informative, and right-on-the-mark. . . . This collection provides a much-needed view of the education of sci/tech librarians." (Michael R. Leach, AB, Director, Physics Research Library, Harvard University)*

Chemical Librarianship: Challenges and Opportunities, edited by Arleen N. Somerville (Vol. 16, No. 3/4, 1997). *"Presents a most satisfying collection of articles that will be of interest, first and foremost, to chemistry librarians, but also to science librarians working in other science disciplines within academic settings." (Barbara List, Director, Science and Engineering Libraries, Columbia University, New York, New York)*

History of Science and Technology: A Sampler of Centers and Collections of Distinction, edited by Cynthia Steinke, MS (Vol. 14, No. 4, 1995). *"A 'grand tour' of history of science and technology collections that is of great interest to scholars, students and librarians." (Jay K. Lucker, AB, MSLS, Director of Libraries, Massachusetts Institute of Technology; Lecturer in Science and Technology, Simmons College, Graduate School of Library and Information Science)*

Instruction for Information Access in Sci-Tech Libraries, edited by Cynthia Steinke, MS (Vol. 14, No. 2, 1994). *"A refreshing mix of user education programs and contain[s] many examples of good practice." (Library Review and Reference Reviews)*

Scientific and Clinical Literature for the Decade of the Brain, edited by Tony Stankus, MLS (Vol. 13, No. 3/4, 1993). *"This format combined with selected book and journal title lists is very convenient for life science, social science, or general reference librarians/bibliographers who wish to review the area or get up to speed quickly." (Ruth Lewis, MLS, Biology Librarian, Washington University, St. Louis, Missouri)*

Sci-Tech Libraries of the Future, edited by Cynthia Steinke, MS (Vol. 12, No. 4 and Vol. 13, No. 1, 1993). *"Very timely. . . . Will be of interest to all libraries confronted with changes in technology, information formats, and user expectations." (LA Record)*

Science Librarianship at America's Liberal Arts Colleges: Working Librarians Tell Their Stories, edited by Tony Stankus, MLS (Vol. 12, No. 3, 1992). *"For those teetering on the tightrope between the needs and desires of science faculty and liberal arts librarianship, this book brings a sense of balance." (Teresa R. Faust, MLS, Science Reference Librarian, Wake Forest University)*

Biographies of Scientists for Sci-Tech Libraries: Adding Faces to the Facts, edited by Tony Stankus, MLS (Vol. 11, No. 4, 1992). *"A guide to biographies of scientists from a wide variety of scientific fields, identifying titles that reveal the personality of the biographee as well as contributions to his/her field." (Sci Tech Book News)*

Information Seeking and Communicating Behavior of Scientists and Engineers, edited by Cynthia Steinke, MS (Vol. 11, No. 3, 1991). *"Unequivocally recommended. . . . The subject is one of importance to most university libraries, which are actively engaged in addressing user needs as a framework for library services." (New Library World)*

Technology Transfer: The Role of the Sci-Tech Librarian, edited by Cynthia Steinke, MS (Vol. 11, No. 2, 1991). *"Educates the reader about the role of information professionals in the multifaceted technology transfer process." (Journal of Chemical Information and Computer Sciences)*

Published by

The Haworth Information Press®, 10 Alice Street, Binghamton, NY 13904-1580 USA

The Haworth Information Press® is an imprint of The Haworth Press, Inc., 10 Alice Street, Binghamtom, NY 13904-1580 USA.

Recruiting, Training, and Retention of Science and Technology Librarians has been co-published simultaneously as *Science & Technology Libraries,* Volume 27, Numbers 1/2 2006.

© 2006 by The Haworth Press, Inc. All rights reserved. No part of this work may be reproduced or utilized in any form or by any means, electronic or mechanical, including photocopying, microfilm and recording, or by any information storage and retrieval system, without permission in writing from the publisher. Printed in the United States of America.

The development, preparation, and publication of this work has been undertaken with great care. However, the publisher, employees, editors, and agents of The Haworth Press and all imprints of The Haworth Press, Inc., including The Haworth Medical Press® and Pharmaceutical Products Press®, are not responsible for any errors contained herein or for consequences that may ensue from use of materials or information contained in this work. With regard to case studies, identities and circumstances of individuals discussed herein have been changed to protect confidentiality. Any resemblance to actual persons, living or dead, is entirely coincidental.

The Haworth Press is committed to the dissemination of ideas and information according to the highest standards of intellectual freedom and the free exchange of ideas. Statements made and opinions expressed in this publication do not necessarily reflect the views of the Publisher, Directors, management, or staff of The Haworth Press, Inc., or an endorsement by them.

Cover design by Marylouise E. Doyle.

Library of Congress Cataloging-in-Publication Data

Recruiting, training, and rentention of science and technology libraries /Patricia A. Kreitz, Joann DeVries, editors.
        p. cm.
    Includes bibliographical references and index
    "Co-published simultaneously as Science & technology libraries, Volume 27, numbers 1/2"
    ISBN 13: 978-0-7890-3555-4 (alk. paper)
    ISBN 10: 0-7890-3555-3 (pbk. : alk. paper)
    1. Science and technology librarians–Recruiting 2. Science and technology librarians–Training of. 3. Employee retention . I. Kreitz, Patricia A. II. DeVries, JoAnn. III. Science & technology libraries.
Z682.4.S35R43 2006
023′ .9–dc22   2006028643

Recruiting, Training, and Retention of Science and Technology Librarians

Patricia A. Kreitz
JoAnn DeVries
Editors

Recruiting, Training, and Retention of Science and Technology Librarians has been co-published simultaneously as *Science & Technology Libraries*, Volume 27, Numbers 1/2 2006.

The Haworth Information Press®
An Imprint of The Haworth Press, Inc.

New York • London • Victoria (AU)
www.HaworthPress.com

∞ ALL HAWORTH INFORMATION PRESS
BOOKS AND JOURNALS ARE PRINTED
ON CERTIFIED ACID-FREE PAPER

The HAWORTH PRESS Inc

Abstracting, Indexing & Outward Linking

PRINT and ELECTRONIC BOOKS & JOURNALS

This section provides you with a list of major indexing & abstracting services and other tools for bibliographic access. That is to say, each service began covering this periodical during the the year noted in the right column. Most Websites which are listed below have indicated that they will either post, disseminate, compile, archive, cite or alert their own Website users with research-based content from this work. (This list is as current as the copyright date of this publication.)

Abstracting, Website/Indexing Coverage . . . . Year When Coverage Began

- **AATA Online: Abstracts of International Conservation Literature (formerly Art & Archeology Technical Abstracts) <http://aata.getty.edu>** 2004

- **ABC POL SCI: A Bibliography of Contents: Political Science & Government, ABC-CLIO (Now called Worldwide Political Science & Government) <http://www.csa.com>** 2003

- **Abstracts/METADEX (Cambridge Scientific Abstracts) <http://www.csa.com>** 2003

- **AGRICOLA Database (AGRICultural OnLine Access): A bibliographic database of citations to the agricultural literature created by the National Agricultural Library and its cooperators <http://www.natl.usda.gov/ag98>** 1989

- **AGRIS <http://www.fao.org/agris/>** 1989

- **Aluminum Industry Abstracts <http://www.csa.com>** 2003

- **Biosciences Information Service of Biological Abstracts (BIOSIS) a centralized source of life science information <http://www.biosis.org>** 1982

- **BIOSIS Previews: online version of Biological Abstracts and Biological Abstracts/RRM (Reports, Reviews, Meetings); Covers approximately 6,500 life science journals and 2,000 worldwide meetings** 1982

- **Cambridge Scientific Abstracts is a leading publisher of scientific information in print journals, online databases, CD-ROM and via the Internet <http://www.csa.com>** 2003

- **Ceramic Abstracts <http://www.csa.com>** 2003

(continued)

(continued)

(continued)

Special Bibliographic Notes related to special journal issues
(separates) and indexing/abstracting:

- indexing/abstracting services in this list will also cover material in any "separate" that is co-published simultaneously with Haworth's special thematic journal issue or DocuSerial. Indexing/abstracting usually covers material at the article/chapter level.
- monographic co-editions are intended for either non-subscribers or libraries which intend to purchase a second copy for their circulating collections.
- monographic co-editions are reported to all jobbers/wholesalers/approval plans. The source journal is listed as the "series" to assist the prevention of duplicate purchasing in the same manner utilized for books-in-series.
- to facilitate user/access services all indexing/abstracting services are encouraged to utilize the co-indexing entry note indicated at the bottom of the first page of each article/chapter/contribution.
- this is intended to assist a library user of any reference tool (whether print, electronic, online, or CD-ROM) to locate the monographic version if the library has purchased this version but not a subscription to the source journal.
- individual articles/chapters in any Haworth publication are also available through the Haworth Document Delivery Service (HDDS).

As part of Haworth's continuing committment to better serve our library patrons, we are proud to be working with the following electronic services:

AGGREGATOR SERVICES

EBSCOhost

Ingenta

J-Gate

Minerva

OCLC FirstSearch

Oxmill

SwetsWise

LINK RESOLVER SERVICES

1Cate (Openly Informatics)

CrossRef

Gold Rush (Coalliance)

LinkOut (PubMed)

LINKplus (Atypon)

LinkSolver (Ovid)

LinkSource with A-to-Z (EBSCO)

Resource Linker (Ulrich)

SerialsSolutions (ProQuest)

SFX (Ex Libris)

Sirsi Resolver (SirsiDynix)

Tour (TDnet)

Vlink (Extensity, *formerly Geac*)

WebBridge (Innovative Interfaces)

Recruiting, Training, and Retention of Science and Technology Librarians

CONTENTS

ABOUT THE EDITORS

Patricia Kreitz, MLS, MS, is currently Director of Technical Information Services for the Stanford Linear Accelerator Center, a national laboratory of the Department of Energy managed and operated by Stanford University. She is responsible for a diverse set of information management and delivery services including Web services and architecture, Publications and Media Services, the Archives and History Office, and the Library and HEP databases–the primary suite of online research databases used by the worldwide particle physics community. She holds an M.L.S. from the University of California at Berkeley and an M.S. in medieval history from the University of California at Davis. Before becoming a director of a science library in Texas, she was head of General Reference Services in the Main (Graduate) Library at U.C. Berkeley and a collection development librarian in the social sciences. She has written on scientific information management and is active in the Association of College and Research Libraries (ACRL), a division of ALA. A list of her activities and publications can be found at: www.slac.stanford. edu/~pkreitz. Currently, she is studying for a Ph.D. in Managerial Leadership in the Information Professions, a new program at Simmons College created to train the next generation of library leaders.

JoAnn DeVries, MLS, (retired) was a science and technology librarian at Magrath Library, University of Minnesota when she co-edited this volume.

Introduction

Forty-five percent of librarians will reach age 65 starting in 2010. This represents the early wave of baby-boom librarians reaching traditional retirement age according to a January 2005 article in *American Libraries*. Many of those in the baby-boom generation are the managers and leaders of today's libraries. Normally, retirement is good news for those newer to the profession, presenting them with career opportunities. At the present rate of new librarians entering the profession, however, the field is not replacing itself and the nation's libraries will be dangerously de-populated.

In response, a 2002 Association of College and Research Libraries task force included recruiting and educating a new generation of librarians and library leaders as one of the top seven academic library issues facing the profession. Encouraging innovative solutions, the Institute of Museum and Library services began the *Librarians for the 21st Century Program*, a grant program to recruit, educate and retain librarians. In 2005, IMLS funded this initiative at nearly $21 million, supporting the recruitment programs of libraries, universities, and library organizations around the country.

This 'replacement gap' affects all areas of librarianship but it will hit science and technology libraries particularly hard. Many of the articles in this volume document an existing, decades-long difficulty recruiting and training science librarians just to stay abreast of standard turn-over rates. The difficulties will only be exacerbated as the baby-boom generation of science and technology librarians begins to retire.

[Haworth co-indexing entry note]: "Introduction." Co-published simultaneously in *Science & Technology Libraries* (The Haworth Information Press, an imprint of The Haworth Press, Inc.) Vol. 27, No. 1/2, 2006, pp. 1-4; and: *Recruiting, Training, and Retention of Science and Technology Librarians* (ed: Patricia A. Kreitz, and JoAnn DeVries) The Haworth Information Press, an imprint of The Haworth Press, Inc., 2006, pp. 1-4. Single or multiple copies of this article are available for a fee from The Haworth Document Delivery Service [1-800-HAWORTH, 9:00 a.m. - 5:00 p.m. (EST). E-mail address: docdelivery@haworthpress.com].

Available online at http://stl.haworthpress.com
© 2006 by The Haworth Press, Inc. All rights reserved.
Digital Object Identifier: 10.1300/J122v27n01_01

What are the particular challenges faced by science and technology librarians and administrators in recruiting and retaining the next generation of science-savvy librarians? Where does the search begin? Whom should be recruited and how should they be trained? The profession is struggling with these questions, as one can see from the articles in this issue. Yet there is passion and innovation as various authors seek solutions. One debate–that of recruiting specialists (those already trained in a scientific discipline) or generalists (those non-scientists with qualities of 'good' librarianship)–has passionate advocates. Both sides are eloquently represented in this publication. Do generalists or specialists give better service? Wherever one stands on this issue, all science and technology librarians would agree that the field needs to seriously attract and hire well-trained and effective professionals.

Every special issue provides the opportunity to identify what has not been addressed or highlighted in previous and current studies. Here are a few areas the editors recommend for further study.

- Promotion of science librarianship as a mid-life career choice–what are the most effective ways to do this? Does the individual's current career choice influence how attracted they are to librarianship– that is, are there some professions from which we draw more consistently?
- What would it take to establish and sustain a program like the Future Educators of America model for science librarianship in middle and secondary schools?
- Should we recruit scientists and then train them to be librarians or recruit generalist librarians and train them in the sciences they will be supporting? Does this answer change, as one author asserts, depending on the institution's degree-granting level? What are the data that could inform reasoned choices for administrators needing to hire new sci-tech librarians? How can we assess through measurable techniques the generalist vs. specialist service quality controversy?
- What should science and technology librarianship's standards for competence be? Who should develop them and at what level? How could library educators play a role in developing and teaching such standards?
- What is the future of sci-tech librarianship and how should that inform whom we recruit and how we train them?

Assembled here are the thoughts of both leaders in our field and new, fresh voices. Included also are the most recent surveys of science librarians as well as innovative, thought-provoking models to follow. We hope the articles below inspire both more research into the issues and more experimentation and activity in recruiting, educating, and retaining the next generation of science and technology librarians.

Anne K. Beaubien calls us to action, urging science and technology librarians to communicate with potential recruits about the variety and challenge of our jobs and to change the ingrained and somewhat unappealing cultural image of librarians.

Pali U. Kuruppus reviews the literature of previously published works on recruitment and retention of science and technology librarians. Pali provides a needed foundation for understanding the current research articles in this issue.

Professor Cecelia Brown challenges employers and search committees to cultivate candidates who show a dedication to service and a love of research and learning.

Lorraine J. Pellack provides realistic, concrete ways individual librarians can improve the visibility and attractiveness of science librarianship.

Donna M. Beck and Rachel Callison, Peter Fritzler and Sarah H. Jeong, in separate articles, identify what attracted them to the profession and what combination of skills, support and talents enabled their successes as science librarians.

Kawanna M. Bright et al. report on the recruitment phase of the "Science Links" program, an innovative project funded by a grant from the Institute of Library and Museum Services. The program will recruit and educate diverse students with strong backgrounds or interest in science and technology to become science librarians.

Linda Eells conducted an in-depth survey of practicing science and technology librarians to gather data on education, work, and personal histories in order to better understand how to recruit, educate and retain the next generation of science and technology librarians.

Innocent Awasom discusses science librarianship in Africa and gives insight into the complexities and challenges facing the field in such a diverse geographical and cultural area.

Professor Linda C. Smith boldly proposes a leadership role for library and information science educators in recruiting and retaining science and technology librarians.

Allison V. Level and Joanna Blair not only propose creative recruitment efforts but also identify ways libraries can help retain librarians and keep them fresh in their field. They assert that institutional support for professional development, for research, and for involvement in national professional organizations is critical for retention.

Jeanne R. Davidson and Cheryl A. Middleton analyze the extent of librarian involvement in professional activities and the role such involvement plays in professional growth and renewal.

Jodee L. Kawasaki suggests libraries could adapt aspects of first-year student retention programs as a model for library retention programs.

And finally, Sara R. Thompson's article concludes our issue, calling on the profession to develop measurable performance standards and goals for science and technology librarians. Competencies can be used to educate new librarians and retrain and renew practicing science and technology librarians.

The editors would like to thank all of the authors who contributed to this volume. It was a privilege and a pleasure to work with everyone. Additionally, we would like to thank past *Science and Technology Libraries* editor, Julie Hurd, whose enthusiasm and support was critical to this effort.

Patricia A. Kreitz
JoAnn DeVries

Recruiting Science Librarians: A Call to Action!

Anne K. Beaubien

SUMMARY. Sci-tech librarians who understand the unique culture and language of science, and who enjoy being part of an investigative team, are a gift to researchers. The ranks of science librarians can be increased by encouraging people with a solid science background to train as librarians. Strategies to recruit scientists include identifying science/engineering students who love their field but may not be particularly interested in laboratory work and science researchers employed in industry who may be looking for a different environment. We need to communicate with potential recruits about how varied and challenging our jobs are. The technological changes in libraries should make our profession attractive to Millennials and Generation Y. Managers should rewrite job descriptions for science librarians to emphasize technology, scholarly communication, digital transformation of key source material, and instructional collaboration. Each of us can contribute to changing the ingrained (and limited) cultural image of librarians. Innovative and exciting opportunities abound for those who combine solid scientific knowledge with an

Anne K. Beaubien, AMLS, is Director, Cooperative Access Services and Grants Officer, University Library, University of Michigan, Ann Arbor, MI 48109-1205 (E-mail: beaubien@umich.edu).

[Haworth co-indexing entry note]: "Recruiting Science Librarians: A Call to Action!" Beaubien, Anne K. Co-published simultaneously in *Science & Technology Libraries* (The Haworth Information Press, an imprint of The Haworth Press, Inc.) Vol. 27, No. 1/2, 2006, pp. 5-9; and: *Recruiting, Training, and Retention of Science and Technology Librarians* (ed: Patricia A. Kreitz, and JoAnn DeVries) The Haworth Information Press, an imprint of The Haworth Press, Inc., 2006, pp. 5-9. Single or multiple copies of this article are available for a fee from The Haworth Document Delivery Service [1-800-HAWORTH, 9:00 a.m. - 5:00 p.m. (EST). E-mail address: docdelivery@haworthpress.com].

Available online at http://stl.haworthpress.com
© 2006 by The Haworth Press, Inc. All rights reserved.
Digital Object Identifier: 10.1300/J122v27n01_02

eagerness to share and extend it in our dramatically changing information world. doi: 10.1300/J122v27n01_02 *[Article copies available for a fee
from The Haworth Document Delivery Service: 1-800-HAWORTH. E-mail address: <docdelivery@haworthpress.com> Website: <http://www.HaworthPress.
com> © 2006 by The Haworth Press, Inc. All rights reserved.]*

KEYWORDS. Recruitment, science librarians, millennials

INTRODUCTION

If we want to increase the ranks of science librarians, the two obvious
ways are to encourage people with a solid science background to train as
librarians, or to persuade experienced librarians to develop expertise in
the sciences. I believe the former is far easier (and hence more effective)
because it takes less time to learn the principles and practice of information science, whether via a traditional MLS degree program or some
form of mentored internship, than it does to take the many years needed
to master the subject matter and research methods of even one of the
physical or biological sciences, let alone several of them.

IDENTIFYING PROSPECTIVE SCI-TECH LIBRARIANS

So, where are we likely to find compelling candidates to recruit? If
we work at a college or university or in a research institution where
postdocs are employed, then the answer is literally *right in front of us.*
There are science and engineering students at all levels who love their
field but may not be particularly interested in laboratory or experimental work. They complete their degrees and training but do not necessarily see themselves "doing science" for a living. Often, I think, they are
just not aware of other career options. For instance, how many people
realize that science librarians do more than fetch facts for researchers?
That an intrinsic part of a librarian job is to teach scientists efficient
ways to identify published and unpublished papers? That librarians
select the best journals, databases, and reference tools to make research
possible? We should seek out students who are considering primary or
secondary school science teaching, or perhaps becoming a science
instructor at a community or liberal arts college, to let them know that

librarians also teach and to emphasize the public service aspects of our profession. Sharing search strategies and illustrating how to use information resources are gratifying activities that occur in a library rather than a laboratory. We should also tell potential recruits that there are opportunities to do research *about* the creation and transmission of new knowledge in the sciences. Furthermore, many science librarians are expected to collaborate with faculty or experimentalists in course design and support of primary research.

A second pool of potential recruits to science librarianship are scientists who have decided that employment in industry will not satisfy them for the rest of their lives. They may be looking for a different environment and are willing to retool, but still want their scientific background to be at the core of a new career. Perhaps these science researchers are working for a business that is downsizing, or their company has been purchased and their division dissolved or merged with another corporation. The trick is to find good people with science backgrounds who are looking for new options, and to persuade them that library work will allow them to keep up with the intellectual side of science while still contributing to their original field, just in different ways and settings.

APPEALING TO YOUNGER GENERATIONS

Most of today's undergraduate science majors were born in the 1980s and are considered "Millennials." They expect information to be instantly available and they interact with technology in a manner unique to their generation. We all know that technology is changing everything about how we function in libraries, but we do not always realize that those same changes are what should make our profession attractive to Millennials. We now offer chat reference, instant messaging, and technical advice on accessing an ever-wider range of materials in a variety of electronic formats. We communicate with our patrons through blogs and via e-mail. We are creating instruction "sound bites" that can be podcast so that information is available to users exactly when and where they need it. We routinely design web pages that are both intuitive and interactive. Millennials and members of the overlapping Generation Y already understand similarities between interfaces and keyword search logic. They have a curiosity and willingness, if not a compulsion, to innovate in their quest for information–particularly if they have spent any time gaming. Experience with gaming tends to increase risk taking in people; they are not afraid to try something with technology, because they have learned that they can start over with few or no consequences. As libraries embrace more digital initiatives and make the transition to having an increased portion of our collections available electronically it is critical that we have librarians with facility in navigating these resources comfortably. Given the characteristics of Millennials and Generation Y, and given the urgent need to attract tech-savvy recruits to librarianship, scientifically trained people from both of these younger groups should be our primary focus. Their interests and our needs are a perfect match.

TAKING THE INITIATIVE

Those of us who are managers should rewrite job descriptions for those who report to us now–without waiting until we have vacancies to fill–with input from both our colleagues and the scientist-patrons we serve. We should draft these statements carefully to accomplish several things: (1) emphasize the technological knowledge we need in future science librarians; (2) include the crucial role of the science librarian in scholarly communication, institutional repositories, and digital transformation of key source material; (3) incorporate work on scientific publishing, instructional collaboration, and emerging information technology; (4) highlight the subject expertise we need, and (5) relate the intellectual and decision-making aspects of each position to the scientific field(s) in question. Boilerplate descriptions will not do to attract the candidates we want.

In addition to articulating the nature and qualifications we seek in an ideal science librarian, each of us can contribute to changing the ingrained (and limited) cultural image of librarians as conservators of collections to a vision of the innovative work that we do. This will help recruit outstanding people to our field. Who better than we–who already love what we do–can encourage others to join and succeed us?

There are a number of strategies we can use in our day to day interactions to inform people who already have a science background about sci-tech librarianship. An easy place we can start is by chatting informally with individual science majors and graduate students whom we encounter in the library. They might be students who come to the reference desk, ask frequent questions via our chat or e-mail services, attend library research instruction classes, or work for us. A good way to broach the subject is to simply ask the students what they envision doing when they finish their degree. If they express uncertainty, suggest they consider combining their background with additional education in information science, leading to a possible career as an academic, research, or special librarian. Make sure to refer students who wish to learn more to people and Web sites that will answer their questions about science librarianship as a profession today and in the future.

Although sciences vary, chemistry is a field with an especially strong, and long, relationship with its literature. Hence chemists will likely have interacted with librarians in the course of their education and work. The American Chemical Society Web site, www.chemistry.org, has a two-page fact sheet on its Career Resources page titled "Chemical Information Specialists" that clearly portrays the variety of responsibilities a librarian in that field can choose from. Other discipline associations will have similar resources, such as offices or interest sections, on career opportunities.

Let's not overlook such traditional approaches to recruiting as participating in career fairs, speaking to science clubs and student organizations, or volunteering to mentor students as they consider various employment options in their field. Arranging for possible recruits to spend a day shadowing you and your colleagues can be a powerful means of stimulating interest and worth every minute spent.

CONCLUSION

Sci-tech librarians who can communicate with scientists easily, who understand the unique culture and language of science, and who enjoy being part of an investigative team, are a gift to researchers. It has long been clear to me that many bright, creative people do not consider librarianship as a profession simply because they do not have the faintest idea what we do or how varied and challenging our jobs are. But we can overcome this by showing people how information science complements and supports every other scientific endeavor. Innovative and exciting opportunities abound for those who combine solid scientific knowledge with an eagerness to share and extend it in our dramatically changing information world. That should be our message.

Recruitment of Science and Technology Librarians–A Review

Pali U. Kuruppu

SUMMARY. For science and technology (sci-tech) librarians to be effective, thorough knowledge of the relevant information resources of the discipline they serve is essential and expected. In addition, familiarity with the subject matter, as well as an understanding of the research philosophies, processes and trends of the respective disciplines, improves the quality of services that sci-tech librarians deliver to their user communities. The question of how to recruit sci-tech librarians with the strengths they need is being investigated and discussed in the library literature. This article examines the literature on subject knowledge of sci-tech librarians, the ongoing debate on recruiting science subject specialists versus generalists-in-training to the profession, obstacles associated with the recruitment of sci-tech librarians and strategies that can be used to improve recruitment, the changing nature of the profession, challenges faced by sci-tech librarians, and their continuing education needs. Continuous examination of these critical areas will no doubt contribute to the improvement of the profession of sci-tech librarianship. doi: 10.1300/J122v27n01_03 *[Article copies available for a fee from The Haworth Document Delivery Service: 1-800-HAWORTH. E-mail address: <docdelivery@*

Pali U. Kuruppu, MLIS, PhD (Plant Pathology), is Assistant Professor and Science & Technology Librarian, Iowa State University Library, Ames, IA 50011 (E-mail: pkuruppu@iastate.edu).

[Haworth co-indexing entry note]: "Recruitment of Science and Technology Librarians–A Review" Kuruppu, Pali U. Co-published simultaneously in *Science & Technology Libraries* (The Haworth Information Press, an imprint of The Haworth Press, Inc.) Vol. 27, No. 1/2, 2006, pp. 11-39; and: *Recruiting, Training, and Retention of Science and Technology Librarians* (ed: Patricia A. Kreitz, and JoAnn DeVries) The Haworth Information Press, an imprint of The Haworth Press, Inc., 2006, pp. 11-39. Single or multiple copies of this article are available for a fee from The Haworth Document Delivery Service [1-800-HAWORTH, 9:00 a.m. - 5:00 p.m. (EST). E-mail address: docdelivery@haworthpress.com].

Available online at http://stl.haworthpress.com
© 2006 by The Haworth Press, Inc. All rights reserved.
Digital Object Identifier: 10.1300/J122v27n01_03

haworthpress.com> Website: <http://www.HaworthPress.com> © 2006 by The Haworth Press, Inc. All rights reserved.]

KEYWORDS. Science and technology librarianship, educational backgrounds of science and technology librarians, recruitment of science and technology librarians, continuing-education needs of science and technology librarians

INTRODUCTION

The knowledge bases in science and technology fields are expanding at unprecedented rates. Emerging new subfields and specializations, increased interdisciplinary research among these subfields, and information technological advances increase the complexity of the information environment of science and technology fields. Science and technology (sci-tech) librarians can be considered the most important interface between today's complex science and technology information systems and scholars in these fields. To deal successfully with the challenges associated with this role, demand is intensifying for recruitment of capable sci-tech librarians to the profession. The question of how to recruit sci-tech librarians with the strengths demanded of them is being investigated and discussed in the library literature. This article examines the literature on (a) the educational backgrounds and subject knowledge of sci-tech librarians, (b) recruitment needs, obstacles, strategies, and responsibilities, (c) the changing nature of the profession of sci-tech librarianship, and (d) continuing education needs.

The 'Graying of the library profession' is a much-discussed topic in library communities. On the basis of 1990 census data, Lynch (1999) predicted that librarian retirements will peak between 2010 and 2014. However, on the basis of the 2000 census, Lynch et al. (2005) reported that although the prospect of a retirement surge in the near future is evident, retirements will apparently peak slightly later, between 2015 and 2019, rather than in 2010-2014 as predicted previously. According to the 2000 census, by 2010, 45% of today's librarians will have reached age 65, the traditional retirement age. If these demographics are similar to those of sci-tech librarians, we can assume that there are potentially many sci-tech librarian retirees. Wilder (2003) reported that in 2000, two-thirds of the librarians employed in the Association of Research Libraries (ACRL) affiliated libraries were over the age of 45, and only about 11% of librarians in the United States were 25-34 years old. Based on the number of years in the field reported by two-thirds of the physical science librarians responding to their survey, Ortega and Brown (2005) suggested that many physical science librarians may retire soon.

In addition to retirements, reduced recruitment to sci-tech librarianship, leading to a shortage in this important group, is a concern that has been raised by many authors (Mount 1985, Dewey 1986, Brown 1988, Vazakas and Wallin 1992, Stuart and Drake 1992, Storm and Wei 1994, Hallmark and Lembo 2003). According to placement service statistics of the American Library Association (ALA), from 1998 to 2002 the number of librarian job seekers was less than the number of available librarian vacancies. However, since 2002 the trend has reversed, so that the number of job seekers is now slightly higher than the number of available positions (ALA Office of Human Resources Development and Recruitment, 2005). We do not have trends specific to sci-tech librarian positions as the ALA placement service does not identify sci-tech positions or job seekers as a specific category they track. This lack of specificity confirms what, Matarazzo and Mika (2004) pointed out–we do not have accurate, up-to-date information about our profession. But it is clear that the time has come to think seriously about a major sci-tech librarian recruitment initiative. If we are going to start recruiting, whom should we recruit? What combination of education, training, personal qualities, skills, and abilities make the 'ideal' sci-tech librarian?

DO SCI-TECH LIBRARIANS NEED STRONG SCIENCE OR TECHNOLOGY SUBJECT BACKGROUNDS?

Educational Background

No examination of the literature debating what training sci-tech librarians *should* be fully understood without a clear picture of what education or training practicing sci-tech librarians now have. Over the past 20-30 years, several analyses of this topic have been done.

The educational backgrounds of sci-tech librarians vary considerably and have been a topic of discussion among concerned information professionals for years. Several surveys examined the educational backgrounds of sci-tech librarians. Based on a survey in 16 colleges and universities conducted in 1983, Mount reported that 51% of respondents had some college science or engineering training (no degree), 19% had a bachelor's degree and 13% had advanced degrees. Findings of a survey conducted in 1997 by the Student Relations Committee, Science-Technology Division of the Special Libraries Association (SLA) indicated that 67% of respondents had either an undergraduate degree or extensive course work in a field of science or technology, but that 33% had no such background (Sandy et al. 1998). Winston (2001), who conducted a survey in 1998 to examine the educational background of science and engineering academic librarians, reported that although 32.2% of respondents had undergraduate science degrees, the physical sciences were not well represented. Only 3.3% had majored in engineering; 4.4% had physics or chemistry as a minor; and 3.3% had science and math as a minor. In addition, a relatively small percentage (8.9%) had earned an additional masters degree in a science or engineering-related discipline; and an equally small percentage (8.9%) had earned doctorates, mostly in science-related disciplines.

Looking at a specialized sub-group, Hooper-Lane (1999) surveyed the academic backgrounds of chemistry librarians and reported that 94% of the respondents had at least some college-level coursework in the sciences with less than half of these at the graduate level. Nearly two-thirds (63%) of respondents had a degree in one of the science disciplines and a surprising 43% had a degree in chemistry. The Association of College and Research Libraries' (ACRL) Science and Technology Section's (STS) Continuing Education Committee reported that 54% of the respondents of their 2003 continuing education survey had undergraduate degrees in science and technology (Christianson 2004).

According to the findings of a study conducted by Hallmark and Lembo (2003), of information specialists who were practicing scientists and engineers with science or engineering degrees, 67% had BS or BA degrees, 25% held an MS or MA as their highest degree, and 8% had earned doctoral degrees. Ortega and Brown (2005) reported that 63% of the physical science information professionals they surveyed had majored in the sciences as undergraduates and 18% had earned a Masters degree in a science field. These findings indicate that more science and technology majors are joining the profession of librarianship. However, it appears that without a concerted, extraordinary effort to recruit more subject specialists into the profession of sci-tech librarianship, only slightly more than half of librarians will have science or technology education or training.

THE DEBATE: SCIENCE SUBJECT SPECIALISTS VERSUS GENERALISTS-IN-TRAINING

The Proponents of a Strong Science Background

Are science librarians with subject-specialized backgrounds more effective than those generalists who develop their scientific knowledge through on-the-job experience? Information professionals have been debating this question for more than a half-century, and many articles have been written discussing the advantages of employing librarians with strong subject knowledge. Some authors (Hunt 1946, Krupp 1984, Stuart and Drake 1992, Wiggins and Monnier 1994, Lucker 1998) stressed that librarians need a strong scientific background in order to provide effective library services to patrons. In 1946, writing about science librarianship, Hunt stated that science librarians "must have a high degree of intelligence, intellectual curiosity, and an excellent memory. In part, such qualities can be demonstrated by his scholastic record. He must have an advanced degree in either the physical or biological sciences, with emphasis on these subjects which have major representation in the collection under his supervision" (Hunt 1946). In general, authors who support a strong subject foundation argued that, because of the complexity of knowledge bases of science and technology fields and the unique nature of the information needs of these scholars, sci-tech librarians must have in-depth understanding of and familiarity with subject fields as well as the information seeking behavior of these scholars. Discussing the tightly knit organizational and communication structure of the scientific community, Dewey (1986) wondered if any librarian is a full member or a partner in the scientific community and questioned if librarians with non-science background would be "utilized to the fullest as information mediaries?" [sic]

Writing about information professionals in chemistry, Silverman (1993) argued that the complexity of the information environment has created a need for librarians who "not only retrieve and organize complex scientific data, but also understand its meaning and applications" (Silverman 1993). According to Hooper-Lane (1999), information professionals affiliated with the field of chemistry well understand the "importance of knowing the subject" because of the interconnectedness of laboratory research activities with "molecular modeling, computational chemistry, and molecular analysis, database searching, and general information retrieval." The need for informational professionals to understand the core terminology and principles of chemistry and keep up with current research has become a challenging task in the chemical information field. They also argued that for someone "without comprehensive specialized subject knowledge this is going to be challenging, if not formidable." Frank (1989) stated that, "In general, the librarian who is able to analyze the relevant variables in a particular situation and integrate the major elements into an intelligible whole will make realistic decisions on a consistent basis." Those advocates writing in support of subject specialized education for sci-tech librarians would argue that a librarian who does not have a strong subject understanding will not be able create that "intelligible whole."

As Preston (2004 p. 123) stated, "The most important defining characteristic of science as a field or body of knowledge is change. The constancy of change is the direct result of the nature and quantity of scientific research.... Researchers in science, different from research personnel in other disciplines, find homes in colleges and universities, corporate R&D [research and development] departments, government laboratories, and nonprofit think tanks. Therefore, the nature of the field and the extensive research activity within the field ensure that the body of knowledge that we term 'science' is evolving rapidly both in absolute terms and in relation to the knowledge in other fields." Librarians working in such dynamically evolving fields need to have strong subject knowledge in addition to other qualities of skilled librarians.

Mount (1975 p. 37), discussing supervisory and administrative positions in university science and engineering libraries, wrote that "a degree in science or engineering, plus library science, is the minimal educational requirement for such a position; several years of pertinent experience are also required." However, Mount did not place emphasis on the need for subject knowledge in the 2nd edition of his book. Similarly, although professional competencies for special librarians published in 1996 by SLA stated that, "[a] special librarian has specialized subject knowledge appropriate to the business of the organization," the revised 2003 version of competencies do not discuss the importance of subject knowledge in information professionals. At a time when science and technology fields are expanding and becoming increasingly complex, it is surprising to see the authors and information professional associations are not emphasizing the need for strong subject knowledge.

Does a lack of science education marginalize sci-tech librarians? Pinelli (1991) stated, "Engineers look for quick, intelligible answers which applies [sic] directly to research problems," and argued that "librarians tend to fall near the bottom of the list of preferred sources."

According to him, information services fall short because they do not take into account the research habits or information needs of specific patron-groups. Stuart and Drake (1992) agreed with Pinelli and stated that the research and information gathering behaviors of most scientists and engineers indicate that libraries and librarians are not the first choices of consultation when they search for information. They argued that "the quality and information services provided to scientists and engineers is less effective when the librarians serving them have little or no experience in these disciplines." According to Stuart and Drake (1992), "scientists and engineers often presume that if the librarian has no grounding in the discipline there is no personal knowledge base to aid the researcher and no common frame of reference. In short, reliance on librarians will not occur if there is no perceived benefit. The individual involved in research will acquire information from [other] proven sources." They warned that the "technology is making it possible for scientists and engineers to access information without libraries. The need for libraries may disappear unless librarians are viewed as contributors rather than obstacles to the information transfer process." Those who assert that sci-tech librarians should have strong subject knowledge in science argue that such librarians will have a greater understanding of the needs of science and technology scholars and will be able to communicate more effectively with them (Stuart and Drake 1992; Hallmark 1998).

The Proponents of Recruiting Generalists

On the opposite side of the debate, there are authors, who argue—some very passionately—that librarians without science backgrounds can learn to be successful if they possess certain important characteristics or skills and have the desire to learn (Haselbauer 1984, Frank 1989, Frank and Kollen 1989, Storm and Wei 1994, Morris-Knower 2001). Haselbauer (1984) argued that a well educated hardworking person with a high degree of intelligence, an excellent memory and intellectual curiosity, who has an appreciation for scholarship and its needs, can become a competent science librarian, "especially in the cross-disciplinary science and technology libraries often found in small or medium-sized undergraduate academic institutions." She rejected the idea that librarians with a science degree are better able to establish rapport with other scientists than librarians without a science degree. As rapport is quite a personal matter, she argued, an experienced public service librarian usually has no problem with rapport. Frank and Kollen (1989) also defended sci-tech librarians who lack a science background, arguing that the keys to effective reference service by such sci-tech librarians is effective communication with patrons, "ability to 'place' reference question within an appropriate 'field' or discipline of the reference questions," and a willingness to refer difficult questions whenever necessary. Storm and Wei (1994) expressed the opinion that, because of increased reliance of vendor approval plans, online databases and bibliographic utilities, as well as more faculty involvement, the work of science bibliographers may not benefit greatly from a science degree. They further argued that "relevant knowledge about science can be learned" but that it is more difficult "to teach a new librarian how to work on a team or get along with his or her peers."

Morris-Knower (2001) who described himself as a science librarian with a non-science educational background, used some anecdotal examples to discuss how he provides reference service to a community of scientists. His objective in writing the article was to assure librarians, "especially new and prospective science librarians without science backgrounds, that you can do a fine job without that degree." He argued that digital technology has made our patrons more self-sufficient and given librarians the ability to find information instantaneously even if they do not know the exact Dewey or LC subject headings. According to him, the skeptics' arguments about non-science librarians having "fear-inducing reference interactions" are becoming increasingly moot, because patrons increasingly use digital reference services to ask questions from librarians without coming to the library.

Some authors have criticized the advocates of subject background arguing that no one science major can prepare you adequately for the variety of scientific or technical fields one may need to support in a particular library. As Krupp (1984) argued, a librarian with strong subject knowledge in one scientific field may find it challenging to adjust to a different science or technology field. However, Haselbauer's (1984) argument was that a science degree "immediate implies specialization" and cannot possibly prepare one to be proficient in the various science disciplines that come under the academic science librarians' purview in a university with only a teaching mission. Therefore, she argued, a person with a science degree has to do more or less the same preparatory "homework" as the person with a general degree. Can these be reasonable arguments in rejecting the hypothesis that a general science degree may have no advantage over a non-science degree when it comes to providing more effective services?

It is true, as Hallmark and Lembo (2003) stated, there are highly successful science librarians who do not hold a formal degree in the sciences or engineering. These are individuals who have an appreciation for the literature and methodology of science and engineering and who have worked diligently over time to gain science knowledge and related skills and experiences.

Some authors acknowledge the strength of a subject background but recognize that finding librarians with those backgrounds might not always be possible or necessary. Stuart and Drake (1992) agreed that "given time, effective training, personal incentive, and nurturing peer relationships," new librarians may gain basic science and technology competence but argued that science and engineering libraries may compromise their effectiveness by hiring librarians without science or engineering degrees. They reasoned that, "without a knowledge of mathematical concepts, basic scientific principles, engineering applications and the communication channels used by scientists and engineers to acquire scientific and technical information, the non-science or engineering person begins with a disadvantage that is difficult to overcome."

Lucker (1998) believed that "for research libraries, whether academic, public, or corporate, we need to have individuals with strong undergraduate preparation if libraries are to provide the qualitative[sic] and depth of service required to support advanced educational and research programs especially in today's increasing[sic] complicated and highly structured information environment." As Lucker suggested, a strong undergraduate grounding in science and/or engineering would be the best preparation for sci-tech librarianship. However, it may not be realistic to insist on hiring librarians with these qualifications in every instance. For example, academic libraries serving mainly teaching institutions or libraries serving undergraduate student communities might adequately support those faculty and students by hiring non-science librarians who have the desire and enthusiasm to gain scientific knowledge. A Ph.D.–granting university might be better served with subject-trained sci-tech librarians to work more effectively with advanced researchers. Therefore, library administrators need to make informed and wise decisions based on the requirements of the communities they serve; if they hire librarians without a strong science background, they should take the responsibility of providing for the training of these new librarians under the supervision of experienced sci-tech librarians.

As this survey of the specialist vs. generalist debate shows, there are well-reasoned arguments on both sides. Proponents of hiring sci-tech librarians who have an educational background in a scientific field argue that the complexity of science fields, their methodologies and strategies, require a more thorough preparation in the field if a science librarian is going to be truly a research partner. On the other hand, all the arguments to hire specialists, however cogent, may be meaningless if there are, as some of the proponents of the generalist side of the debate argue, not enough trained science majors willing to go into the library profession. A number of authors have studied candidate pools and hiring practices. Their findings help inform the debate.

RECRUITING SCI-TECH LIBRARIANS

A Persistent Problem

Because it is hard to find qualified applicants with a strong science background for sci-tech librarian positions, some suggest that it would be helpful to be less restrictive in the wording of position announcements to increase the pool of candidates (Dewey 1986) and some employers according to Jones et al. (2002) "seem to be resigned to not finding candidates with [science and technology] degrees and therefore not insist on them." As we've seen, many authors have argued that hiring librarians for entry level science and technology positions without science and technology backgrounds can affect the quality of the profession. Although a skilled, experienced librarian with a non-science background who is familiar with science and technology information resources may become a good science librarian with time and hard work, it seems that hiring new librarians with a strong subject background is a valuable effort to make.

Although there is an encouraging trend of more people with strong science backgrounds becoming sci-tech librarians, concern is expressed by library professionals and library administrators about the poor quality of candidate pools for sci-tech librarian positions. Dewey (1986) reported the results of a study designed to determine whether "there exists a science librarian hiring crisis" and examined the qualifications of librarians actually hired as compared to the qualifications specified in the position announcements. She examined all job openings requiring or desiring science backgrounds received by the Indiana University School of Library and Information Science Placement Office during

January-June, 1985 and by the ALA Annual Conference Placement Center in 1985. This study revealed that, in general, libraries were able to hire persons who have either an academic background in science or science library experience. According to her findings 56% of positions required a science background, and although for 76% of all positions, experience could replace a science background, employers indicated that the academic science background was valued over science library experience.

Strangely, 15 years later, an analysis of science and technology position announcements by Jones et al. (2002), showed that science and technology specific qualifications were not even among the three most required qualifications for sci-tech librarian positions. For 15% of the positions, a Bachelor's degree was preferred and for 26% of positions, a Master's degree in a science/technology field was preferred. The authors examined advertisements published during June and December of 2000 period in a variety of library journals including *American Libraries*, *The Chronicle of Higher Education*, *College and Research Libraries News*, *Information Outlook* and listservs used by sci-tech librarians.

As far back as 20 years ago, administrators were experiencing problems with candidates' qualifications and the number of applicants. Dewey (1986) reported that employers were concerned about the size of the applicant pool (usually 5 to 20 applicants). Fifty-eight percent were not satisfied with the quality of the applicant pool; 10% had mixed feelings. Thus only 32% were satisfied with the applicant pool. Fifteen years later, according to the findings of Jones et al. (2002), half of the employing institutions reported a small applicant pool, (5 or fewer applicants), while the remainder were more fortunate, with pools averaging 14 applicants. However, one university reported that the pool was small and that most applicants did not meet the minimum requirements. Most often, science and technology background was the lacking required qualification. Although experience in a science and engineering library was the most commonly met preferred qualification, two-thirds of employers were not satisfied with the level of preferred qualifications among applicants.

Given the reported dissatisfaction with applicant pool size and qualifications, Dewey's further findings are interesting. Dewey's findings (1986), showed that only 21.5% of the positions were filled with applicants lacking an academic science background, and employers were pleased with the results of their hiring decision. In contrast, half of the employers in the Jones et al. study (2002) reported a poor outcome of the search, whereas the other half of the employers were satisfied, with two indicating extreme satisfaction.

Obstacles in Recruiting the Best and the Brightest

Salaries

Sci-tech librarians entering the profession now will shape the future of 21st century sci-tech librarianship. How can we entice young and energetic science majors, as well as experienced biologists, chemists, physicists, mathematicians, geologists and engineers, to join the profession? Understanding the main obstacles in attracting "the best and the brightest" to sci-tech librarianship is important in formulating successful recruitment efforts.

Low salaries offered for librarians can undoubtedly be considered the main or one of the main barriers to attracting candidates with subject expertise in sci-tech librarian positions. According to Osorio's (1999) findings the actual dollar value of the average minimum salaries of sci-tech librarians, when the Consumer Price Index is taken into consideration, have not increased in last three decades. It is no secret that high paying professional positions can be obtained in some scientific and technology disciplines with only an undergraduate degree. To compete, library administrators need to offer better salaries and attractive employment benefits to individuals with science subject expertise, and provide incentives for librarians with non-science backgrounds who are willing to take courses to improve their scientific and technical subject knowledge.

Stuart and Drake (1992) thought that librarians with science degrees may prefer to join special libraries because of the "expectation of job gratification, prestige and recognition of one's value to the research effort." Academic libraries may have difficulties in offering higher salaries because of established salary scales and budget constraints. Hooper-Lane (1999) showed how higher salaries of chemistry librarians in academia have attracted librarians with better-than-average qualifications; according to his findings, 64% of academic chemistry librarians had a science degree and 43% had a degree in chemistry. More studies like Hooper-Lane's are needed to give library administrators the data they need to argue for bringing sci-tech librarian salaries in line with the specialized qualifications demanded of them.

Salaries of science information professionals vary widely depending on the type of employer. These variations can be illustrated by figures reported by Silverman in 1993 obtained through a survey of chemistry information professionals (with or without LS or LIS Masters degree) conducted during 1991-92. The average salary for academic positions was $36,900, the average for government, $54,900 and the highest, $57,000, was in industry. According to Silverman, although industry offers higher salaries to information professionals, they do not pay librarians with scientific training at the same level that they pay researchers hired into scientific positions. The reason is that companies are reluctant to increase the salaries of information professionals because of continuing transfer of chemists from laboratory jobs into information jobs.

Professional Image

The image of the library profession poses an additional hurdle in attracting individuals with science subject expertise. According to one of the employers responding to a survey conducted by Dewey (1986), "Good applicants with a strong science background are harder and harder to find. Our impression is that science students do not find librarianship particularly attractive because of the usual reasons–low status and prestige, low pay. Even though our salaries are competitive, they do not appear to be a great enticement" Dewey (1986). According to David and Sherdin (1994) librarians are struggling to overcome their "occupational stereotype that has been created by society and further augmented by the mass media." Is it hard to overcome this occupational stereotype? Perhaps not. Librarians may just have to find different ways to sell themselves.

David and Sherdin (1994) described how 3,000 people requested career information from the American Library Association after a stimulating article appeared in the April 1994 issue of *Glamour* describing how technology has transformed the work of librarian and portrayed librarians as technology gurus. According to Mount (1985, p. 65), "librarians do not often think of their activities in terms of promotional work, or marketing.... However, promotion does have a positive, legitimate side which should be recognized by library professionals, including those responsible for sci-tech academic libraries." Echavarria (2001) suggested that an 'impersonal' ad campaign with sufficient follow up might seem like a good way to entice prospective librarians into the profession. Scientific and technological professional journals may be ideal places to advertise the 'intellectually stimulating careers' of sci-tech librarians.

It can be argued that a way to improve the relatively low status and prestige of the profession is to attract experts from other professions. Librarians with subject expertise undoubtedly enhance the status of librarianship as a profession. However, some librarians unfortunately do not welcome these experts because they assume that librarianship is not the first choice of individuals who come from other professions (Gilman 2005). If science students are familiarized with opportunities in the library field, they might make a career decision at the undergraduate level which would mean that librarianship would be a first choice, according to Hunt (1946) and "not a second or third choice made only after frustration." Does it matter if librarianship is someone's first or second choice? Bosseau and Martin argued that librarianship is "a profession populated overwhelmingly by people who discovered it while detouring from some other planned career." Hardesty (2002) stated, "many come to us in mid-life after examining and rejecting other opportunities." Why don't we think that these professionals/scholars who consider a career change are choosing librarianship because it is a 'challenging and intellectually stimulating profession'? Perhaps we do not respect our own profession sufficiently.

No Qualified Candidates–Recruit Scientists as Librarians

Preston (2004) reported that, according to the university data, more than a third of individuals who have invested extensive time and money in science education leave science because they find alternative careers more interesting and rewarding (Preston 2004, p.115). Ortega and Brown's study (2005) observed that nearly 18% of physical science information professionals hold an additional Master's degree in a science field. This percentage is higher than that observed 20 years ago, when 7% of respondents held a science master's degree (Mount 1985). Hallmark and Lembo (2003) examined why scientists and engineers choose to become librarian and information professionals. Three-fourths of those responding were drawn to the profession for the following reasons: their love of scientific and technical literature, cutting-edge technology, fascination with the information explosion, the prestige that arises from contributing to the organization's mission, and the satisfaction of working as a team member with faculty and other researchers. These findings indicate that scientists are attracted to science librarianship and find it interesting, challenging, and enjoyable (Hallmark and Lembo 2003).

There are some interesting experiments taking place that attempt to build on the fact that a third of trained scientists choose alternate career paths. As a solution to the problem of the shortage of librarians with strong subject knowledge, some library directors have decided to hire scientists to fill science librarian positions, a decision supported by some library professionals and educators. Stuart and Drake (1992) argued that the time has come to seriously consider "dropping the library degree as a requirement for science and engineering library positions." They proposed that libraries could focus their energy on developing recruitment programs to attract and recruit new science and engineering graduates directly into the ranks and train them to be effective librarians by providing training in information services. Linda Smith, Professor and Associate Dean of the School of Library and Information Science, University of Illinois, Urbana-Champagne argues that "just as there's a body of expertise in science, there's a body of expertise in library science, but it can be learned in a particular setting" Kreeger (2004).

Morris-Knower thought the idea of recruitment of science majors to librarian positions straight out of college is "provocative." Quoting Grogan, Haselbauer (1984) argued that a "librarian's particular strength ... lies in his grasp through systemic study of the underlying pattern discernible in the literature, and his familiarity with the variety in which it manifests itself ...," and scientists-drafted-as-librarians may not have this strength with the exception of the person who is keenly interested in the overall service that a skilled librarian provides. If this is a concern as Kreeger (2004) suggested in her article in Career Corner in *The Scientist*, there are opportunities to learn skills of librarianship in library settings and scientists can take advantage of online LIS degree programs to gain the expertise of librarianship.

There is a new initiative by the Council on Library and Information Resources to recruit humanities scholars for postdoctoral fellowships in research libraries, and about 15 top academic and research libraries are expected to participate (Berry, 2003). The objective of this program is to bring the expertise of humanities doctorates to libraries and give the postdoctoral fellows the background and values of those who work in research libraries. Although the postdoctoral system is not common in the humanities, it is common in the sciences; most new PhDs in the sciences work as postdoctoral fellows before they go into teaching or research positions. Therefore, this system might be easily adopted with advanced degrees in the sciences and may be worth experimenting with, especially by academic research libraries.

Recruiting Sci-tech Librarians: Whose Job Is It?

The Role of Academic Librarians

Librarians undoubtedly play an important role in recruiting new librarians. Based on a study conducted in 1997 by the Student Relations Committee of SLA's Science-Technology Division which examined how, as students, librarians gained awareness of, and developed an interest in sci-tech librarianship, Sandy et al. (1998) reported that slightly more than half of the respondents had worked in a science or technology library prior to or while attending library school. Bosseau and Martin (1995) calling upon librarians to do more to attract young talent to librarianship, were somewhat critical of academic librarians not doing enough even though they have opportunities to interact with college and university students. They wrote, "When students work in the library, they are given the dullest and most routine of jobs. Fifteen hours a week shelving or arguing with patrons about overdue books, are representative of the tasks that are likely to turn more people away from the profession than they attract." They suggested implementing a system that allows interested and bright student employees to assume more responsibility in the library and to acquire a better understanding of the opportunities available in the profession.

More than half a century ago, discussing strategies for recruiting science undergraduates to pursue a degree in library science (LS), authors such as Hunt (1946) suggested the need to familiarize science students with opportunities in the library and information field. Undergraduate students in science and technology disciplines often do not get exposed to traditional library research methods (Dewey 1986). Therefore, neither students nor faculty advisors often think about career possibilities in the LIS field. Bosseau and Martin suggested that academic librarians should educate students about today's and tomorrow's information environment in more meaningful ways through the use of institutional career days or newsletters and by including students on library advisory committees.

The Role of Library and Information Science Schools

Various LIS schools actively recruit students for their degree programs. Dewey (1986) suggested that these schools should maintain high visibility within their own academic institutions. In particular, they should find ways of educating the academic community about their graduate programs, their research, and the opportunities within the library and information science professions. Dougherty (1986) stressed the need for cooperation between practitioners and educators in preparing graduate students for academic librarianship. LIS schools might coordinate their recruitment programs with those practicing librarians who are considered to be effective recruiters. In return, librarians should communicate with library and information science schools regarding the professional competencies and skills expected of LIS graduates.

Some LIS schools offer dual/joint degree programs to encourage graduate students in science disciplines to become sci-tech librarians. For example, Indiana University's School of Library and Information Science offers a dual degree Master's program with the Department of History and Philosophy of Science and a joint degree program in chemical information specialization with the Chemistry Department (http://www.slis.indiana.edu/degrees/joint/). The University of Hawaii at Manoa offers a dual Master's degree program in Library and Information Science (MLISc) and Information and Computer Science (ICS)MS (http://www.hawaii.edu/slis/programs/ics.htm). The Simmons Graduate School of Library and Information Science currently has an innovative program to encourage undergraduate students in science disciplines to begin taking LIS courses. Students pursuing an undergraduate degree in a science discipline are able to take some graduate courses in LIS. After completion of the Bachelor's degree, they are required to earn the other credits in the Graduate School of Library and Information Science in order to obtain a Master's degree (http://www.simmons.edu/gslis/academics/programs/dual/).

The Training Role of Library and Information Science Schools

In addition, to Master's degree programs, some LIS schools provide post graduate training programs that allow recent graduates to obtain practical experience in their field of specialization. Frank (1989) proposed that directors of major science-engineering libraries need to work with graduate LIS school administrators in creating either internships or formal, rigorous orientation and training programs for new science and engineering librarians. He suggested that such programs are especially critical for librarians with humanities and social science academic backgrounds who are hired into sci-tech librarian positions. The "Research Library Residency Program" implemented by the University of Michigan provides opportunities for recent library school graduates to participate in intensive library activities within the library system, and students interested in science librarianship can gain experience in one of several sci-tech libraries. The educational component of the residency program includes professional discussions, workshops and seminars.

Even though LIS schools should actively recruit students in science and technology fields, the number of such recruits may not be sufficient to fill the need. Schools therefore need to accept recruits who lack science and technology backgrounds but wish to become sci-tech librarians. In formulating programs and course work for such students, educators need to give special consideration to the educational backgrounds of undergraduates without science backgrounds. According to Peterson and Kajiwara (1999), the U.S. K-12 is filled with required courses in English and Social Studies but has far fewer courses in the sciences. Moreover, discussing the results of a ten-year longitudinal study conducted at the Center for Education Statistics of the U.S. Department of Education on undergraduate education of LIS programs entrants, Brown (1988) pointed out that "there is far less preparation in the sciences for non-science majors than vice versa."

Frank (1989) advised library schools that "Practical and philosophical differences in the utilization of the literature of science and technology and the literature of humanities and social sciences should be recognized and examined in formal courses." Because almost all of the research in the humanities is carried out in the library, humanities scholars have considerable understanding and appreciation of the library (Hunt 1946). However, because scientific research is usually conducted in the laboratory or/and in the experimental fields, scientists may have less appreciation than humanities scholars have for the library. This difference in research methods of scientists compared with the methods of humanities and social science scholars should be included in LIS training.

Exposing LIS graduates who are interested in sci-tech librarianship to the scientific research environment may be one of the best ways to educate them about the scientific research process. In 1966, an innovative postgraduate training program funded by the National Library of Medicine was initiated for science librarians at the University of Tennessee Medical Unit in Memphis. Trainees with a degree in LS were assigned to laboratories of senior scientists and became integral parts of working research teams (Lasslo 1968), giving them an excellent opportunity to learn how scientists work and do research. Martin (1973) discussed the logistics of the program, the impact of the experience gained by trainees, what the advising scientists thought about the program and its influence upon their research, teaching, and service efforts. While trainees considered the program to be very effective, advisors also reacted positively, citing the contribution made by the trainees in keeping the advising scientists and their staff better informed about developments in their own fields and better informed about the library's services and facilities. Martin (1973) stated, "By participating as a team member, the trainee librarian learned to speak and understand the language of the scientist and to appreciate the origin of his information needs. The scientist, on the other hand, came to understand better the personality traits of a professional librarian."

Although most LIS schools offer courses in science and technology information resources, Stuart and Drake (1992) complained that "there is almost no attempt to relate these sources to the unique research habits, context of work or information gathering techniques employed by scientists and engineers." The importance of continuous evaluation and reformulation of LIS curricula to reflect the changes in the information environment and user-needs and the information-seeking behaviors specific to disciplines has been stressed by information professionals. In 1998, an entire issue of *Science and Technology Libraries* was devoted to the subject of how to better prepare LIS graduates for sci-tech library careers. Various articles discussed new directions needed in formal educational programs to educate students for careers in health sciences, geosciences, chemistry, and engineering.

Availability of financial support for graduate studies is another key factor for a successful recruitment program. Dewey (1989) suggested that LIS schools need to consider working with other departments of their institutions to create innovative financial aid packages. Hallmark and Lembo (2003) stated that recruitment of scientists into LIS programs was successful when federal or university funding was available.

In conclusions, not only LIS schools, but libraries as well, need to take the initiative in recruiting and training new science librarians. A collaborative project to recruit and train science graduates to become sci-tech librarians was launched during 2004-2005 by the libraries of Iowa State University, the University of Iowa, and the University of Nebraska, partnering with the School of Library and Information Science at the University of Iowa. Supported by assistantships, graduate students were assigned to one of three libraries to gain experience in various facets of library activities while they were earning Master's degrees in LIS (Pellack, 2006). This is an excellent example of how libraries and LIS schools can work together to recruit and train students with science and technology degrees into the profession.

THE CHANGING NATURE OF SCI-TECH LIBRARIANSHIP

The kinds of training discussed up to now have been to acquaint beginning librarians with the principles and practices of the scientific fields they will be serving or to teach scientists who wish to become librarians about the principles and practices of librarianship. However, the entire issue of training is broader–since it encompasses training of both beginning and continuing librarians. Studies have shown that training itself needs to be continually updated as job responsibilities, technology and the scientific fields served all grow more complex.

Reflecting on his personal experiences, Lucker (1998) described how sci-tech librarianship has changed over the last four decades of the 20th century. He identified the obvious major change; the impact of technology on almost every aspect and practice of sci-tech librarianship. He also listed the skills of the profession that had not changed over time; the familiarity with the organization and structure of science and technology literature, the nature of research and scientific 'work,' and the scientific method as a process of discovery and invention. According to Lucker, a thirst for knowledge, good listening and comprehending abilities, personal organizational skills, and managerial and administrative skills are the skills that have not changed over time. Youngman et al. (1998), discussed how the roles of sci-tech librarians had changed as reflected in the history of *Engineering Index* and concluded that "patron service today involves the use of broad complex information tools, coupled with the librarian's understanding of the literature, the research process and specific patron needs."

Osorio (1999) analyzed the position descriptions of sci-tech academic librarians in job advertisements that appeared during the years 1976, 1986 and 1998 in *American Libraries* and in *College and Research Libraries News*. According to the findings of this study, there was a consistent increase in required, preferred and desired qualifications for sci-tech librarian positions. It is interesting to note that the number of responsibilities listed in these job advertisements increased consistently as well.

Discussing the results of a survey conducted by the American Chemical Society's Division of Chemical Information, Silverman (1993) reported that chemistry librarian respondents from industry performed more diverse functions including computer research, database management, marketing, patent and legal research, and managing information centers. Many academic chemistry librarian respondents reported duties including cataloging, purchasing, and online or literature searching.

Based on a 1998 survey conducted by Winston (2001), frequently mentioned academic sci-tech librarian position responsibilities included collection development, bibliographic instructions and online searching in science and engineering disciplines, and faculty liaison activities, as well as general reference duties. Cataloging, digital projects, web site creation/management, and management/administration were the other responsibilities reported by a few respondents. Ortega and Brown (2005) reported that reference, bibliographic instruction, collection development for specified subjects, acting as liaison for academic departments and functioning as heads of units were the common duties of physical science librarians. Sci-tech librarians operating in a complex and dynamic information environment face greater challenges when entrusted with increasing job responsibilities.

CONTINUING EDUCATION OF SCI-TECH LIBRARIANS

In addition to the necessity of training librarians without science backgrounds through on-the-job training, the increasing complexity of sci-tech librarians' work makes access to continuing education essential. However, this training can rarely occur without the support of the institutions they work for. In 1998 Lucker wrote, "The effectiveness of individuals in scientific and technical library work is highly dependent upon an enlightened and supportive environment. It is especially important that librarians beginning their careers are provided with career guidance, continuing educational opportunities, and the potential for personal and professional advancement and growth." Do they get the needed guidance and continuing education support?

To understand the continuing education needs of sci-tech librarians, the Continuing Education Committee of ACRL's Science and Technology Section designs and conducts a biennial member survey. Based on results in 2001, respondents were most interested in information literacy/instruction issues, especially web-based instruction, and in electronic resources, including their selection and management (Desai 2002). The most important continuing education topic for science librarians in 2003 was to improve liaison relations with academic faculty, which had ranked seventh in the 2001 survey (Christianson 2004). Discussing the 2003 survey result, Christianson argued that the results "tell the story of science librarians eager to work with their patrons to survive in the current costly and fluid environment." She interpreted the science librarians' interest in improving relationships with faculty members as an eagerness to teach faculty members about the wealth of material available through their libraries and how to use it. Also, a good relationship with faculty members is important in developing information literacy programs, the second-ranked interest of sci-tech librarians in 2003 and the first ranked in 2001 (Christianson 2004). Surprisingly, skills in Web tool use (Java, CGI scripting, etc.) received no mention at all in the findings. According to Christianson, the lack of interest may be because librarians usually provide content information but do not become involved in university library Web site development activities. Sci-tech librarians demonstrated very little interest in traditional management skills in surveys in 2001 and 2003 (Desai 2002; Christianson 2004).

According to the 2003 STS Continuing Education Survey findings, in-person workshops and web-based instruction were the preferred mode of delivery of continuing education among sci-tech librarians. Teleconferences and e-mail tutorials attracted modest interest with lesser interest shown in for-credit distance-education courses and in mentors. The lowest rating was given to traditional credit courses.

Varlejs (1999) reported that nearly 77% of ALA members working in U.S. libraries were engaged in self-directed learning rather than in formal continuing education. As sci-tech librarians constitute a subset of this population, it may not be wrong to assume that sci-tech librarians spend a considerable time in self-directed learning. Contrary to expectations concerning the relationship between self-directed learning and professional achievement, her data suggested that these self-directed learners are not necessarily achievers. If this is so, should we emphasize formal and relatively structured continuing education rather than self-directed learning for sci-tech librarians?

Christianson (2004) commented that "the relatively small number of votes for credit courses place science librarians' interests in contradistinction to other professions' requirements." She pointed out that other professional groups (e.g., physicians, nurses) depend on continuing education credits to maintain their professional licensing requirements and/or to demonstrate their understanding of current professional practice. The Medical Library Association sponsors and accredits a formal continuing education program for the benefit of their members. SLA also has launched an online learning community for the benefit of its members based on a vision proposed by Lowery (2004), to have a certification program for SLA designed to allow members to demonstrate achievement of each of the core competencies. Sci-tech librarians may benefit from similar online learning programs.

At present, the knowledge bases of many science and technology fields are expanding at an unprecedented speed and new sub-disciplines of science and technology are emerging and converging. Given this rapid change, it will be difficult to stay abreast of developments in scientific fields even for people who have advanced degrees. Do science librarians spend enough time and effort on improving their scientific understanding both in general and specifically in the scientific area(s) they serve? Unfortunately, the STS Continuing Education Studies Committee did not examine the time spent and effort made by science librarians on improving their subject knowledge. Hooper-Lane (1999) examined the amount of time that chemistry librarians spent per week in keeping up with the field through both traditional sources (journals, personal contact, classes) and electronic sources (discussion lists, World Wide Web). He found that respondents spent on average nearly five hours per week keeping up with chemistry/science topics. The use of electronic discussion lists was ranked the top choice of chemistry information professionals to keep up with the field with browsing/reading science journals ranked second and using World Wide Web resources and taking classes ranked next. Nearly 37% of the respondents had attended at least one chemistry-related conference or workshop in 1998, and one-third of respondents had attended at least one chemistry/science database workshop (Hooper-Lane 1999).

Based on the findings of a survey conducted by Ortega and Brown (2005), 86% of the physical science librarians who responded spent five or fewer hours per week reading the research literature of librarianship while the remaining respondents spent six or more hours per week. Forty-three percent of the respondents claimed to find the research literature useful, especially for keeping current with development of the profession. However, Ortega and Brown's survey did not address the reading relevant to keeping up with the literature in specific subject areas.

Because the knowledge bases of many science disciplines are rapidly expanding, it can be expected that science librarians, especially those with a non-science background, would need to spend considerable time learning about the science fields they support. However, Peterson and Kajiwara (1999) pointed out that "there is little written on training non-science librarians in-house to provide a level of help for science fields for which they have no background." Haselbauer (1984), arguing that librarians with non-science backgrounds can evolve to become effective science librarians, suggested ways to arrive at a perception of a discipline's bibliographic structure, to acquaint oneself with the basic science reference sources and to develop science reference skills.

Haselbauer (1984), a strong supporter of sci-tech librarians without formal science backgrounds, wrote, "Acquainting oneself with the basic reference sources for the sciences is, of course, a useful method for developing reference skills, but combining this with citation research and production of research guide is even more rewarding in the sense of gaining a reliable grasp of a discipline's bibliographic structure." These methods may be useful for getting a basic grasp of a discipline but will not be enough for a good understanding of a scientific field or its research philosophies and research trends.

By reading widely in selected journals such as *Scientific American*, Science and *Nature*, librarians with non-science backgrounds can improve their current awareness of science in general. Attending lectures or seminars on scientific topics is another effective way to improve the familiarity of science subjects. Discussing how he improved his science subject understanding, Lucker (1998) wrote that an "excellent means of keeping abreast of new developments is attending graduate seminars, thesis defenses, and lectures by local and visiting faculty." He further wrote, "[I] was fortunate in being able to audit the first year Princeton graduate seminar that engendered in me a lifelong interest in this field.... I have long held the view that science and engineering subject specialists could find no better way to expand their knowledge of current research than by attending undergraduate and graduate lectures." Taking courses for credit or audit can be a very effective way to learn a new subject. Lucker suggested that librarians should be encouraged to take advantage of educational programs offered on local campuses. Attending scientific professional meetings is an effective way to learn about scientific research trends and current activities for sci-tech librarians, especially for librarians with non-science background.

Scientists hired for science librarian positions without the MLS or MLIS need to be encouraged to learn about the profession of librarianship and more importantly about its dedication to public service. Attending professional library meetings will provide them a broad understanding of the profession and allow them to learn about issues that librarians feel passionate about. Encouraging these scientists to obtain MLIS degrees, or at least to do extensive LIS course work, should be given serious consideration. As many SLIS schools are offering online MLIS programs, taking online courses or obtaining MLIS degrees has become much easier.

Regardless of academic background, sci-tech librarians need to continue their education, learning about the evolving profession of librarianship and about science and technology developments in general. They need to keep up with developments in the scientific and technological subject areas they work with, and learn about the research philosophies and research trends of the specific discipline(s) and about the information needs of the community they serve. Sci-tech librarians in the 21st century need to be active learners of anything and everything if they are to know how to be active information providers in their organizations.

CONCLUSION

For sci-tech librarians to be effective, it is essential and expected that they understand thoroughly the information resources relevant to their subject areas. In addition, a broader familiarity with the subject matter as well as an understanding of the research philosophies, processes, and trends of the respective disciplines improves the quality of services that sci-tech librarians deliver to their user communities. Together with other attributes of today's skilled librarian such as interpersonal communication skills and computer literacy, such knowledge will allow the sci-tech librarian to become an active provider of science and technology information services to the patron communities. Admittedly, however, it is difficult to find individuals with all of these qualifications and qualities.

While some stress the need to hire individuals with strong subject background, in other words, at least a bachelor's degree in a science or technology discipline, others argue that effective communication and interpersonal skills as well as experience and training in online searching are more important for sci-tech librarians than a science or technology degree. They argue that librarians without a science background will eventually learn about and become familiar with the information resources and the general structure of the literature 'on the job.'

The importance of technology skills (computer skills) was clearly understood by information professionals in order to survive the whirlwind of changes in the information environment, especially those that took place during the late '80s and '90s. Because of these changes, employers were inclined to consider computer technology skills more important qualifications for sci-tech librarianship than subject knowledge (Osorio 1999; Jones et al. 2002). However, continuing education interests of sci-tech librarians in 2003 indicated that sci-tech librarians are more interested in building liaison relationships with their subject departments and information literacy skills of students rather than thinking of improving technology and computer skills. For building relationships with faculty and improving the science information literacy of students, isn't the subject knowledge more important?

Instead of trying to minimize the importance of strong subject knowledge to the successful functioning of sci-tech librarians, we need to concentrate our energy on attracting individuals with science and technology backgrounds to this challenging profession. To attract these individuals, we need to promote and advertise the 'science and technology information profession' to science and technology communities in universities, research institutions and perhaps even in industries.

If, because of the lack of candidates with preferred qualifications, librarians without science and technology backgrounds are hired, library administrators need to take responsibility to make sure that these new employees become skilled sci-tech librarians by gaining knowledge in the subject areas they serve. Because this can be quite challenging, new employees should be given incentives and time free of other duties to acquire the knowledge and other skills needed for effective sci-tech librarianship. On the other hand, if library administrators decide to hire scientists to fill librarian positions, it is equally important to encourage these scientists to gain the expertise and skills of librarianship, including effective communication and interpersonal skills, and even to obtain a degree in LIS.

All the stakeholders of science and technology information services–science and technology information professionals, Library and Information Science services, Library and Information Science educators, and professional Library and Information Science organizations–are confronted with the challenge of recruiting the best candidates to the profession and preparing them, as well as those who are already in the profession, to face the challenges of today's dynamic science and technology information environment. Therefore, all of these stakeholders need to do their part to recruit the best and the brightest to this challenging profession.

REFERENCES

Berry, John N. 2003. But don't call'em librarians. *Library Journal*, 128(18): 34-36.

Bosseau, Don L., and Susan K. Martin. 1995. The accidental profession: seeking the best and brightest. *Journal of Academic Leadership*, 21(3):198-199.

Brown, Lorene B. 1988. Recruiting science librarians. In Moen, William E. and Kathleen M. Helm (eds), *Librarians for the new millennium*. Chicago: American Library Association, Office for Library Personnel Resources, p. 65-71.

Christianson, Marilyn. 2004. The 2003 STS Continuing Education Survey: Selected analyses of science librarians' Interests. *Issues in Science and Technology Librarianship*, 41. http://www.istl.org/04-fall/refereed.html.

David, Indra and Mary J. Scherdin. 1994. Librarians in transition: profiles on the strong interest inventory. In Mary Jane Scherdin (ed) *Discovering Librarians: Profiles of a Profession*. Chicago: Association of College and Research Libraries, American Library Association. p. 102-121.

Dougherty, Richard M. 1986. The underline rationale (of) the residency program at the University of Michigan Library. *Library Journal*, 111 (Feb. 15):118-120.

Desai, Christina M. Spring. 2002. Continuing education needs of science and technology librarians: Results of the 2001 STS continuing education committee survey. *Issues in Science and Technology Librarianship*, 34. http://www.istl.org/02-spring/article5.html.

Dewey, Barbara I. 1986. Science background required–others need not apply: a study of the science librarian hiring crisis. ASIS '86: Proceedings of the 49th ASIS Annual Meeting, Sept, 28- Oct.2, 1986. Chicago IL. 64-68.

Echavarria, Tami. 2001. Reach out to recruit new librarians. *ALKI*, 17(1). http://www.wla.org/publications/alki/2001iss1alki.pdf.

Frank, Donald G. 1989. Education for librarians in a major science-engineering library: Expectations and Reality. *Journal of Library Administration*, 11(3/4): 107-116.

Frank, Donald G, and Christine Kollen. 1989. Humanities and social sciences librarians in the science–engineering library: utilization and implications for effective collection development and reference services. *Science and Technology Libraries*, 9 (3): 63-71.

Gilman, Todd. 2005. Suspicious minds. *Chronicle of Higher Education*, March 3, 2005. http://chronicle.com/jobs/2005/03/2005030301c.htm.

Grogan, Denis. Science and technology: an introduction to the literature. 3rd ed. London; Clive Bingley; 1976: p. 7.

Hackenberg, Jill M. Sept 2000. Who chooses sci-tech librarianship? *College and Research Libraries*, 61(5): 441-450.

Hallmark, Julie. 1998. Education for the successful Geoscience information specialist. *Science & Technology Libraries*, 17(2): 81-91.

Hallmark, Julie and Mary F. Lembo. 2003. Leaving science for LIS: interviews and a survey of librarians with scientific and technical degrees. *Issues in Science and Technology Librarianship*, 37. http://www.istl.org/03-spring/refereed1.html.

Hardesty, Larry. 2002. Future of academic/research librarians: a period of transition–to what? *Portal: Libraries and the Academy*, 2(1): 79-97.

Haselbauer, Kathleen. 1984. The making of a science librarian. *Science & Technology Libraries*, 4(3/4):111-116.

Hill, Susan and Marcia Owings. November 1986. *Curricular Content of Bachelor's Degrees, OERI Bulletin,* (Washington, D.C.: Office of Education Research and Improvement, Center for Education Statistics, U. S. Department of Education) ED# 278-313.

Hooper-Lane, Christopher. 1999. Spotlight on the subject knowledge of chemistry librarians: results of a survey. *Issues in Science and Technology Librarianship*, 23. http://www.istl.org/99-summer/article1.html.

Hunt, Judith W. 1946. Science librarianship. *Science, New Series*, 104 (2695): 171-173.

Jones, Mary Lou B., Mary F. Lembo, James E. Manasco, and John H. Sandy. 2002. Recruiting entry-level sci-tech librarians: an analysis of job advertisements and outcome of searches. *Sci-Tech News*, 56(2):12-16.

Kreeger, Karen. 2004. Science librarians shout about their careers. *The Scientist*, 18(1): 52.

Lowery, John. 2004. The future of professional development: a vision and a roadmap. (Professional Development Update). *Information Outlook*, 8(2): 32-33.

Lucker, Jay K.1998. The changing nature of scientific and technical librarianship: a personal perspective over 40 years. *Science and Technology Libraries*, 17(2): 3-10.

Lynch, Mary Jo, Stephen Tordella, and Thomas Godfrey. 2005. Retirement and Recruitment: A Deeper Look *American Libraries*, 36(1): 28.

Martin, Jess A. 1973. University of Tennessee postgraduate training program for science librarians: a six-year review. *Bulletin of Medical Library Association*, 61(4):396-399.

Matarazzo, James M. and Joseph J. Mika. 2004. Workforce planning for library and information science. *Library and Information science Research*, 26(2): 115-120.

Morris-Knower, James. 2001. Phyllostachys Aurea–didn't he work with Socrates? Reference work in science libraries by librarians who are not scientists. *The Reference Librarian*, 72:155-169.

Mount, Ellis. 1975. Staffing and personnel management. In University and engineering libraries their operation, collections, and facilities. Westport, Conn: Greenwood press, p 36-49.

Mount, Ellis. 1985. Promoting and marketing the library. In University and engineering libraries. 2nd ed. Westport, Conn: Greenwood Press, p 65-71.

Neal, J.G., 2003. Forward. In: Wilder, S.J., (ed). *Demographic changes in academic librarianship*, Association of Research Libraries, Washington, DC, p. ix.

Osorio, Nestor L. 1999. An analysis of science–engineering academic library positions in the last three decades. *Issues in Science and Technology Librarianship*, 24. http://www.istl.org/99-fall/article2.html.

Ortega, Lina and Cecelia M. Brown. 2005. The face of 21st century physical science librarianship. *Science & Technology Libraries*, 26(2):71-90.

Pellack, Lorraine J., Head, Science and Technology Department, Iowa State University. Personal communication.

Pinelli, Thomas E. 1991. The information seeking habits and practices of engineers. *Science and Technology Libraries*, 11(3): 5-25.Preston, Anne E. 2004. Does the rapidly changing knowledge within science affect exit? In Leaving science, occupational exit from scientific careers. New York: Russell Sage Foundation, p123.

Sandy, John H., M.F. Lembo and J.E. Manasco. 1998. Preparation for sci-tech librarianship: results of a survey. Sci Tech News, 52(1):16-17.

Silverman, Edward. March 22, 1993. Chemical Information: A career alternative for chemists. *The Scientist*, 7(6): 21.

Special Libraries Association, Competencies for Special Librarians http://www.sla.org/content/SLA/professional/meaning/competency.cfm (Accessed on Jan. 2006) http://www.sla.org/content/learn/comp2003/index.cfm#appliedscenarios (Accessed on Jan. 2006).

Storm, Paula and Wei Wei. 1994. Issues Related to the Education and Recruitment of Science/Technology Librarians. *Science and Technology Libraries*, 14(3):35-42.

Stuart, Crit and Miriam A. Drake. 1992. Education and recruitment of science and engineering librarians, *Science and Technology Libraries*, 12(4):79-89.

Thomas, Joy. 1988. Bibliographic instructors in the sciences: a profile. *College and Research Libraries*, 49(3): 252-262.

Varlejs, Jana. April 1999. On their own: librarians' self-directed, work-related learning. *Library Quarterly*, 69(2):173-201.

Vazakas, Susan M. and Camille Clark Wallin, March 1992. Where are all the science librarians? *College and Research Libraries News*, 53(3):166-171.

Wiggins, G. 1998. New directions in the education of chemistry librarians and information specialists. *Science and Technology Libraries*, 17(2):45-58.

Wiggins, G. and Cynthia Monnier, 1994. Assessment of library science program specializing in chemical information. *Special Libraries*, 85(3):130-138.

Winston, Mark D. 2001. Academic science and engineering librarians: a research study of demographics, educational backgrounds, and professional activities. *Science and Technology Libraries*, 19(2): 3-24.

Youngmann, Daryl C. Spring 1998. Changing roles for science & technology librarians as reflected in the history of engineering index. *Issues in Science and Technology Librarianship*, 18. http://www.istl.org/98-spring/then-now.html.

doi: 10.1300/J122v27n01_03

Recruiting the Best

Cecelia Brown

SUMMARY. Analysis of position announcements appearing in the archives of the CHMINF-L and STS-L online discussion forums dated January 2005 through February 2006 indicates the persistence of the requirement for a background in science for success as a candidate for a position as a science and technology librarian. This paper challenges employers and search committees to look beyond this constraint and cultivate individuals who possess a dedication to service, a love of research and learning, and a Master's degree from an ALA accredited institution. Such individuals, regardless of background, when placed in a supportive and inclusive environment where continuing education is encouraged and competitive compensation is received, will prove to be not only successful, but exemplary, practitioners of science and technology librarianship. doi:10.1300/J122v27n01_04 *[Article copies available for a fee from The Haworth Document Delivery Service: 1-800-HAWORTH. E-mail address: <docdelivery@haworthpress.com> Website: <http://www.HaworthPress.com> © 2006 by The Haworth Press, Inc. All rights reserved.]*

KEYWORDS. Recruitment, science and technology librarianship, science education

Cecelia Brown, MLIS, PhD, is Associate Professor, School of Library and Information Studies, University of Oklahoma, Norman, OK 73019 (E-mail: cbrown@ou.edu).

The author would like to thank, Julie Kreft, graduate assistant in the School of Library and Information Studies at OU, for her able and swift analysis of the position announcements and survey of the ALA accredited Master's programs.

[Haworth co-indexing entry note]: "Recruiting the Best." Brown, Cecelia. Co-published simultaneously in *Science & Technology Libraries* (The Haworth Information Press, an imprint of The Haworth Press, Inc.) Vol. 27, No. 1/2, 2006, pp. 41-53; and: *Recruiting, Training, and Retention of Science and Technology Librarians* (ed: Patricia A. Kreitz, and JoAnn DeVries) The Haworth Information Press, an imprint of The Haworth Press, Inc., 2006, pp. 41-53. Single or multiple copies of this article are available for a fee from The Haworth Document Delivery Service [1-800-HAWORTH, 9:00 a.m. - 5:00 p.m. (EST). E-mail address: docdelivery@haworthpress.com].

Available online at http://stl.haworthpress.com
© 2006 by The Haworth Press, Inc. All rights reserved.
Digital Object Identifier:10.1300/J122v27n01_04

INTRODUCTION

The day after Halloween in 1996 I began my career as the head of the Chemistry-Mathematics library at the University of Oklahoma (OU). Despite the potential ominous nature of the season, the candy wrappers strewn about, totes of unbound journals spilling onto the floor, and the haphazard decorations festooning the staff office, I felt confident to face the day. After all I was armed with my newly minted MLIS, a year's worth of experience as a Graduate Assistant at the main library's general reference desk, 135 hours as an intern at a health sciences library, and, my ace in the hole, a doctorate in Nutritional Sciences. You might be thinking, "This woman has the ideal pedigree for a Physical Science librarian, especially that doctorate," right? Well, after about 10 long hours of rearranging the librarian's office (the staff office would have to wait), fumbling with the circulation system (did I mention my technician was taking a long overdue and well deserved vacation my first day?), as well as looking for trivial names (if they are trivial why are they important?) in something called *Beilstein*, and finding Raman data (noodles have data?) in a completely ominous set of misfiled Texas Engineering Experiment Station binders (my staff thought one simply stuck the updates in the least full binder!), I discovered that it was not the doctorate nor the hundreds of hours spent in the laboratory communing with radioactivity and rats, that helped me get through that first day. Rather, it was the invaluable combination of mentoring received and experience gained at the reference desks and in library school that gave me the courage and self-assurance (both tinged with anticipation), to come back the next day–if they would still have me!

Fortunately they did not change the locks and I subsequently spent the next five years contentedly working as a physical science librarian. In 2001 my career path took a turn back to academia when I became a faculty member in the School of Library and Information Studies (SLIS) at OU. Since then I have had the pleasure to see individuals from a wide variety of backgrounds find success in libraries and information centers in which they had never dreamed of working. Seeing the former lawyer become a school library media specialist and the English major find happiness as the technology services manger of a public library, further cemented my belief that success in librarianship has its roots in an American Library Association (ALA) accredited Masters' degree. My conviction has steadily deepened over the past ten years, so much so that I was surprised to find at this year's Science and Technology Section's (STS) Hot Topics Discussion Forum at the ALA Midwinter Meeting in San

Antonio, that it is not necessarily shared by my colleagues. For many of the attendees, a science background is essential for success as a science and technology (sci-tech) librarian. As a result, we find ourselves in the middle of the first decade of the new millennium in the same dilemma we have been in for the past 25 years. Employers can't find people with the qualifications they deem necessary to fill their sci-tech librarian positions.

This paper strives to convince the reader that the situation is not as dire as it seems, as a science background is not essential for success, and even excellence, in sci-tech librarianship. For those who hold fast to their ideals of recruiting individuals with the coveted background, the paper will also provide suggestions to help them reach their goal. The ideas and suggestions are presented in light of an analysis of 88 unique position announcements appearing on two online discussion lists of interest to sci-tech librarians, Chemical Information Sources Discussion List (CHMINF-L) (2006) (STS is explained in prior paragraph) and STS-L (2006), from January 2005 to February 2006 as well as a review of the current literature. It is hoped these analyses coupled with my rather unique perspective gained from life as a scientist, cum physical sciences librarian, cum professor of library and information studies, will serve as a catalyst for generating a pipeline of individuals well suited to careers as successful, productive, and happy sci-tech librarians.

THE CURRENT STATE OF THE SCIENCE AND TECHNOLOGY LIBRARIANSHIP

Over 20 years ago the often quoted Ellis Mount (1985) wrote that the "relatively small number of job-seekers at one time who have the exact subject background desired for a given university sci-tech library" complicates the recruitment for subject specific libraries. At that time, approximately 54% of sci-tech librarians lacked a scientific background. More recent studies suggest that the crisis in recruitment of sci-tech librarians with science backgrounds may be lessening. Lina Ortega and I invited members of five electronic sci-tech librarian discussion groups to participate in an online survey to elucidate the information behavior of physical sciences librarians (Ortega and Brown 2005). The demographic questions posed in the survey discovered that of the 72 respondents, most have an educational background in the sciences, with approximately two-thirds having majored in a science field as undergraduates and almost one-fifth having earned a master's degree in a scientific discipline. Ninety-six percent of the respondents also hold a Master's degree in library or information science (MLS or MLIS) with an impressive 29% holding an additional master's degree. Notable are the two out of the three individuals who do not have an MLIS yet have doctoral degrees in chemistry. The third respondent does not hold a graduate degree, but has a bachelor's degree in the history of science. Three additional respondents listed having attained a doctoral degree in chemistry in addition to the MLS or MLIS.

An earlier study conducted by Jill Hackenberg in 2000 surveyed a wider sample of eight sci-tech librarian online discussion lists via e-mail and discovered that almost 60% of the 311 respondents entered the field with some type of science background. Similarly, a study conducted in 1999 by Christopher Hooper-Lane using mailed questionnaires found 64% of 35 academic chemistry librarians respondents have a science degree, with 43% having a chemistry degree. In contrast, Mark Winston's 2001 mail survey of 103 members of STS was less encouraging, with only 20 and 12% of the respondents holding biology and physics or chemistry degrees respectively. It is not clear why an overwhelming majority of respondents in Winston's study were found not to have a scientific background while over 60% of respondents in the three other studies had studied science. The discrepancy may be due to differences in the methods of dissemination of the questionnaire. Perhaps online and e-mail surveys are more likely to be responded to by sci-tech librarians who have a science background than are printed surveys. However, Hooper-Lane's survey, like Winston's, was distributed by mail. Also, it is possible that Hopper-Lane specifically targeted population of chemistry librarians are simply high survey responders regardless of the delivery mode. The most likely scenario is that a more diverse audience, including chemistry librarians, was reached electronically and thereby enhanced the possibility of gaining responses from practitioners with science backgrounds. Although these recent studies suggest that there has been an increase in individuals with science training working as sci-tech librarians, approximately 40% of those currently practicing sci-tech librarianship do not have backgrounds in science. Who are these people and are they successful?

IS A SCIENCE BACKGROUND NECESSARY FOR SUCCESS?

A few voices rang out at the STS Hot Topics Forum to say that a background in science is not, in their experience, required for success in sci-tech librarianship. Haselbauer (1984), Frank and Kollen (1989), and Slutsky (1991) concur stating that librarians who lack a degree in science or engineering can provide effective collection development and reference services in a sci-tech library. Indeed these writers took their stance over 15 years ago and it is likely that the explosion of molecular biology, space science, and high energy physics information generated by large, high profile projects such as the Human Genome Project, the Hubble Space Telescope program, and at Fermilab has made it even more difficult for the librarian without a science background to master the complex vocabulary of science. However, Hackenberg and Chu's (2002) more recent report of their survey of 311 sci-tech practitioners found that even though 169 of the respondents believe their scientific background to be a valuable asset, the 29% who did not have any scientific background discovered that they were able to overcome this perceived lack with strong mentoring and a demonstrated commitment to providing exemplary service. As a physical science librarian, I also found this to be the case. Through the expression of a genuine interest in my patrons' work and information needs, I found faculty members would readily assume their professorial role and provide the necessary tutoring. These exchanges of information with the chemists, mathematicians, physicists, and astronomers who formed by patron base were the highlights of my job as a physical science librarian.

Although I am well educated in the sciences, my PhD and postdoctoral work focused very narrowly on two areas of Nutritional Sciences and one area of Endocrinology. As a result I understand physiology and biochemistry, but I am not as well versed in the terminology of the disciplines of physical chemistry, mathematics, physics, and astronomy, for which I was also responsible as a physical science librarian. Nonetheless, I believe I was able to meet the information needs of my diverse clientele through the development and maintenance of an up-to-date and relevant collection and the provision of conscientious and thorough reference services. In essence, being a really good librarian! This is echoed in James Morris-Knower's (2001) delightful account of how he, an English major, navigates as a science librarian. Most notably, Morris-Knower addresses the fear that science questions such as where can I find "good reverse-phase high-performance liquid chromatographic methods for analyzing complex mixtures of triglycerides in aged cheese" instill in librarians without a science background. Rather than panicking, a good librarian blithely and eruditely employs their reference negotiation skills to understand their patron's query and then uses the collection of resources they have developed to resolve their patron's information need. Confidence in one's ability gained through education and experience is key to providing service to any patron whether they are looking for equations to calculate hadronic β decay rates or for the first two lines to a Longfellow poem (the later being more intimidating than the former in my mind!).

EDUCATION IS THE KEY!

The expectation for one individual to be savvy in a wide array of science and engineering disciplines is terribly idealistic while demanding a thorough knowledge of the structure of the literature of science is not as unrealistic. Being cognizant of one's patrons' work and communication patterns and preferences is critical to the basic functioning of any library. Study of the scholarly communication patterns and information behavior of scientists is fundamental to the success as a sci-tech librarian. Jones and colleagues' (2002) analysis of 50 job advertisements for sci-tech librarians reveals that the most commonly required qualifications are an undergraduate degree in science and an understanding of the needs or research methods of scientists. In fact our analysis found that 23% of the 88 unique position announcements posted on CHMINF-L and STS-L from January 2005 to February 2006 require knowledge of the current scholarly communication patterns of scientists as well as the present state of the scientific literature. It is the role of schools of library and information science to provide both retrospective and cutting edge course content about the publication patterns and information behavior of scientists and engineers. This emphasis on a well-rounded education in librarianship is echoed by Frank (1989), Lucker (1998), and Hallmark (1998). Being currently aware and up-to-date is especially critical for a sci-tech librarian as the traditional mode of communication among scientists that was first described over 25 years ago by Garvey et al. (1979) is seeing a new and dynamic renaissance. As more and more information is shared freely and openly on the Internet the time honored tradition of peer-review is being challenged and new paradigm and patterns of scientific scholarly communication are rapidly developing.

Examination of the websites of the course offerings published on the websites of 52 ALA accredited and conditionally accredited schools in the United States and Canada indicates that such education is widely available to students and practitioners alike. Courses in scientific reference services are available at 60% of the schools in addition to 88% offering courses in general reference. Even those who do not live within reach of a university may have access to a science and technology sources and services course via online delivery such as that available at through the University of Illinois' Graduate School of Library and Information Science LEAP program (Graduate School of Library and Information Science, the University of Illinois 2006). Additionally, online continuing education opportunities are available to practitioners in industry, government, and academia interested in chemical informatics via Indiana University's School of Informatics Graduate Certificate in Chemical Informatics (Wiggins 2006). Indiana University's chemoinformatics program, funded by the National Institutes of Health, requires four courses which students can complete on sight or by using tele- and web-conferencing technology. Also, members of SLA (formerly Special Library Association) have access to Click University which holds great promise and potential for the continuing education of sci-tech librarians through the provision of online learning opportunities (SLA 2006). Armed with strong course content in sci-tech as well as general reference training plus continuing one's education and actively participating in organizations such as STS, the Science and Technology Information Special Interest Group of the American Society for Information Science and Technology, and SLA, will provide any librarian with the knowledge and confidence to provide the highest caliber service regardless of their background.

Although the traditional channels of formal and continuing education are the foundations of librarianship, another invaluable educational resource lies within reach of all librarians–the users of their library. It is clear that our users want our collections to be comprised of all the databases, journals, and books available in their field and to be housed in a facility that is open around the clock. But we must also strive to understand how our users really use the information gleaned from the resources and which of the panoply of sources they prefer and why? I would like to challenge readers to look up from their daily routines of reading book and databases reviews, attending collection development meetings, honing their search skills, and creating staff schedules, and engage their patrons in an ongoing dialog about their information wants and needs. Only then will a sci-tech librarian's education become well rounded and approach a level of completeness necessary to provide the level of service our users deserve.

WHOM TO HIRE?

Our survey of the position announcements posted on CHMINF-L and STS-L between January 2005 and February 2006 indicates that the preference for sci-tech librarians with a science background remains the coin of the realm for employers. Of the 88 unique job announcements analyzed, 59% require or prefer the candidate to posses a science background in the form of an undergraduate degree or graduate degree in the sciences or at least one year's worth of experience working in a science library. Of the 59%, 29 announcements call for both an MLIS or MLS from an ALA accredited program and a science background, while 14 advertisements desire, rather than require, a sci-tech background in addition to the requisite Master's degree. The remainder of the position announcements indicate that the successful candidate will have either an MLIS or a degree in science.

I would like to propose another challenge, to remove the scientific background from the catalog of required qualifications entirely from sci-tech position announcements or at least to move it to the list of desired qualifications. Having done that, the quest for the best librarian can begin! What qualifications go into the recipe for the finest librarian? The Master's degree in Library and Information Studies from an ALA accredited program, good communication skills, and a degree of facility with computers and technology. This inventory of qualifications will not effectively serve to narrow your applicant pool as all graduates of ALA accredited library schools are educated in order to possess these skills, yet it will provide an entrée for individuals who may not have a science background yet have the flexibility, service orientation, and willingness to learn–in essence, the qualities we all look for in our colleagues.

Careful wording of the job announcement to highlight an eagerness to participate in continuing education, to conduct outreach to the user community, as well as a knowledge of research and scholarship will entice the individuals you want to hire to respond your position announcement. Although these are thought to be given qualities of all librarians, a survey conducted by Gordon and Nesbeitt in 1998 of 391 job seeking librarians discovered that just two-thirds of the respondents enjoy working with people and doing research and just slightly more than half love learning. Through careful scrutiny of applicants' cover letters and letters of reference, it is possible to identify the standouts in the crowd to interview. When on campus, those interviewees who possess a desire to learn and natural curiosity will readily shine, if you are willing to set aside expectations for an extensive command of several fields of science. Once recruited and brought to campus, the new colleague will require moral support and mentoring by senior librarians, intensive orientation to faculty patrons, as well as encouragement for participation in continuing education. The time and effort invested will be well spent as the new librarian will feel comfortable, supported, and valued and therefore in turn strive to develop an exemplary collection and to provide the very best service for their users for a long time to come.

Still Want to Hire a Scientist?

Hallmark and Lembo (2003) learned through interviews and an online survey that one of the major factors for scientists' and engineers' shift into careers as sci-tech librarians was personal recruitment by practitioners. The sci-tech practitioners interviewed by Hallmark and Lembo suggest attending the career fairs at their colleges and universities. The attendees at the STS Hot Topics concur with this suggestion. Another excellent tactic proposed by Stuart and Drake (1992) and seconded more recently by Stoss (2005) is to use the personal touch by growing one's own sci-tech librarian workforce from the promising students currently enrolled in science and engineering who frequent your library or are part of your student staff. I experienced such success during my time as a physical science librarian when two students, one a psychology major and another a mathematics major, enrolled in library school. Recruitment of science majors and scientists to the field was once successful through the funding provided by Higher Education Authority Title IIB Fellowships. I was a lucky recipient of one of these generous fellowships, the source of which now has, unfortunately, run dry. However, the Institute for and Library Services' Laura Bush 21st Century Librarian Program supports efforts to recruit and educate the next generation of librarians (Institute for Museum and Library Services 2006). Although the program is not specifically aimed at enhancing the sci-tech librarianship workforce it does supports projects for recruitment of future librarians, especially those designed to attract promising junior high, high school, and college students to consider careers in librarianship. Creation of partnerships between employers of sci-tech librarians and schools of library and information studies to develop a proposal for competition in this program is highly recommended and may prove to be very fruitful.

In addition to forging partnerships between practitioners and library and information studies faculty, it may be productive to enlist the assistance of the science and engineering faculty in the recruitment of individuals with a sci-tech background. Faculty members have direct access to students and are often intimately involved in their course selection and career planning. By working with the faculty, practitioners can develop an understanding of the field of sci-tech librarianship which is much more than a second tier choice. Instead, sci-tech librarianship should be cast in its true light as an exciting and stimulating career for those who love research and discovery yet are disinterested in pursuing a career in bench or field research. An interesting possibility is to suggest to faculty members to invite librarians to participate in their projects including the preparation and execution of grant proposals as well as daily laboratory life. A scientist may be more attracted to the field of librarianship if he or she had been an integral and active participant in a collaborative team of scientists, students, and information professionals. A perfect match is made as the librarian carries out the primary role of mining the literature for the relevant papers and related information to support the research, teaching, and creative activities of the research group while the scientists are liberated to do to what they do best–science!

One of the main problems of recruiting science and engineering majors and enticing scientists and engineers to the field is the discrepancy in salaries between the two careers paths. Although Hackenberg and Chu (2002) found that the salary of sci-tech librarians is perceived to be higher than that of librarians specializing in other disciplines, our analysis of the 88 unique position announcements posted on CHMINF-L and STS-L between January 2005 and February 2006 indicates the average minimum salary for sci-tech librarians is less than the $44,500 median salary garnered by inexperienced chemistry master's degree recipients who graduated between July 2003 and June 2004 (Heylin 2005). The average minimum salary of $38,640 is up slightly from that of $34,000 which was advertised in the position announcements scrutinized by Osorio in 1998, yet the salaries of sci-tech librarians remains depressed compared to those with a master's degree and working as scientists. As only 34 off the 88 announcements scrutinized chose to post minimum salaries, it would be interesting to survey first year sci-tech librarians to gain a more complete sense of the starting salaries and how they compare to similarly educated scientists and engineers. Nonetheless, in order to be competitive, and if a sci-tech background remains the ideal, employers must educate their administration about why it is critical to the mission and goals of their institution to hire and retain individuals with a scientific or engineering background and that these individuals demand a salary more comparable to that they would garner as a scientist or engineer.

CONCLUSION

The pipeline of sci-tech librarians is primed and ready to be tapped. For recruitment of the best, the tasks ahead for search committees and employers are clear. First, look beyond the coin of the realm and mine the field for individuals who exhibit promise through a positive service commitment, a passion for research and learning, and a solid foundation gained from an ALA accredited program of study. Second, offer a competitive compensation package as well as a supportive and stimulating work environment in which the candidate can grow and thrive. The diamonds in the rough thus revealed will flourish and thrive as the next generation of sci-tech librarians.

REFERENCES

CHMINF-L: Chemical Information Sources Discussion List. (2006). Available online at: https://listserv.indiana.edu/cgi-bin/waiub.exe. Accessed 3/19/06.

Frank, Donald G. 1989. Education for Librarians in a Major Science-Engineering Library: Expectations and Reality. *Journal of Library Administration* 11(3/4): 107-116.

Frank, Donald G. and Kollen, Christine. 1989. Humanities and Social Sciences Librarians in the Science-Engineering Library: Utilization and Implications for Effective Collection Development and Reference Services. *Science & Technology Libraries* 9 (Spring): 63-71.

Garvey, W.D., Lin, N., & Tomita, K. 1979. Research Studies in Patterns of Scientific Communication; III, Information-Exchange Processes Associated with the Production of Journal Articles. In *Communication: The Essence of Science. Facilitating Information Exchange Among Librarians, Scientists, Engineers and Students.* Edited by William D. Garvey. New York: Pergamon, pp. 202-224.

Gordon, Rachel Singer and Sarah Nesbeitt. 1999. Who We Are, Where We're Going: A Report from the Front. *Library Journal* 124 (May 15, 1999): 36-39.

Graduate School of Library and Information Science, the University of Illinois. (2006). *Course Detail.* Available online at: http://www.lis.uiuc.edu/oc/courses/course-detail.html?id=LIS522LE&year=2006&semester=SP. Accessed 3/5/06.

Hackenberg, Jill M. 2000. Who Chooses Sci-tech Librarianship? *College & Research Libraries* 61(5): 441-450.

Hackenberg, Jill M. and Barbara Chu. 2002. Why Does One Choose Sci-Tech Librarianship? Findings of a Survey. *Science & Technology Libraries* 23(1):3-16.

Hallmark, Julie and Mary Frances Lembo. 2003. Leaving science for LIS: Interviews and a survey of librarians with scientific and technical degrees. *Issues in Science and Technology Librarianship* Spring 2003, http://www.istl.org/03-spring/refereed1.html.

Hallmark, Julie. 1998. Education for the Successful Geoscience Information Specialist. *Science & Technology Libraries* 17(2): 81-91.

Haselbauer, Kathleen. 1984. The Making of a Science Librarian. *Science & Technology Libraries* 4(3/4): 111-116.

Heylin, Michael. 2005. Class of 2004 Starting Salaries: Constant-Dollar Pay of New Chemists Remains Depressed; Little Change in Soft Job Situation. *Chemical & Engineering News*, 83(16): 51-55.

Hooper-Lane, Christopher. 1999. Spotlight on the Subject Knowledge of Chemistry Librarians: Results of a Survey. *Issues in Science and Technology Librarianship* 23 (Summer) http://www.istl.org/99-summer/article1.html.

Institute of Museum and Library Services. 2005. Grant Applications. Available online at: http://www.imls.gov/applicants/grants/21centuryLibrarian.shtm. Accessed 3/5/06.

Jones, Mary Lou Baker, Mary Frances Lembo, James E. Manasco, and John H. Sandy. 2002. Recruiting Entry-Level Sci-Tech Librarians: An Analysis of Job Advertisements and Outcome of Searches. *Sci-Tech News* 56(2): 12-16.

Lucker, Jay K. 1998. The Changing Nature of Scientific and Technical Librarianship: A Personal Perspective Over 40 Years. *Science & Technology Libraries* 17(2): 3-10.

Morris-Knower, James. 2001. *Phyllostachys Aurea*–Didn't He work with Socrates? Reference Work in Science Libraries by Librarians Who are Not Scientists. *The Reference Librarian* 72: 155-169.

Mount, Ellis. 1985. *University Science and Engineering Libraries, 2nd edition.* Westport, CT: Green wood Press, p. 38.

Ortega, Lina and Brown, Cecelia M. 2005. "The Face of 21st Century Physical Science Librarianship" *Science and Technology Libraries 26(2): 71-90.*

Osorio, Nestor L. 1999. An Analysis of Science-Engineering Academic Library Positions in the Last Three Decades. *Issues in Science and Technology Librarianship* Fall 1999 http://www.istl.org/99-fall/article2.html.

SLA. 2006. Click U Live. Available online at: http://www.sla.org/content/learn/learnmore/distance/2006cul/index.cfm. Accessed 3/5/06.

Slutsky, Bruce. 1991. How to Avoid Science Anxiety Among Science Librarians. *Science & Technology Libraries* 12(1): 11-19.

Stoss, Fred. 2005. Recruiting Scientists Into Our Profession. *STS Signal* 20(2): 6.

STS-L: ACRL Science & Technology Section Discussion List. (2006). Available online at: http://lists.ala.org/wws/arc/sts-I. Accessed 3/19/06.

Stuart, Crit and Miriam A. Drake. 1992. Education and Recruitment of Science and Engineering Librarians. In *Sci-tech Libraries of the Future*, ed. Cynthia A. Steinke, Binghamton, NY: The Haworth Press, Inc. pp. 77-87.

Wiggins, Gary. 2006. Graduate Certificate in Chemical Informatics Item #029133. *Archives of CHMINF-L@LISTSERV.INDIANA.EDU: The Chemical Information Sources Discussion List*. Available online at: https://listserv.indiana.edu/cgi-bin/wa-iub.exe?A2=ind0603&L=CHMINF-L&P=R9938&I=–3. Accessed 3/19/05.

Winston, Mark D. 2001. Academic Science and Engineering Librarians: A Research Study of Demographics, Educational Backgrounds, and Professional Activities. *Science & Technology Libraries* 19(2): 3-23.

doi:10.1300/J122v27n01_04

Uncle Albert Needs You!
Individual Recruiting Efforts
Are a Necessity and an Obligation

Lorraine J. Pellack

SUMMARY. The terms "recruiting" or "recruitment" are regularly used in two very different connotations: hiring (and retention) practices and also recruiting into the profession itself. This article will focus exclusively on recruiting to the profession. There has been a shortage of science librarians since the 1950s, or earlier, and yet the problem has still not been adequately resolved. While there is a general acknowledgement that something needs to be done, in many cases, practicing librarians seem to feel they only have impact in one particular area–encouraging library student assistants to pursue a library science degree. There are many other ways individual librarians can participate in recruiting, even on a very small scale. Recruiting need not be a daunting, time-consuming task. This article provides some radical ideas to get people thinking and acting in ways to improve the visibility and attractiveness of science librarianship as a profession . . . and not just by serving as a good role model for student assistants they may (or may not) supervise. doi:10.1300/J122v27n01_05 *[Article copies available for a fee from The Haworth Document Delivery Service: 1-800-HAWORTH. E-mail address:*

Lorraine J. Pellack is Head, Science & Technology Department, 152 Parks Library, Iowa State University, Ames, IA 50011-2140 (E-mail: pellack@iastate.edu).

[Haworth co-indexing entry note]: "Uncle Albert Needs You! Individual Recruiting Efforts Are a Necessity and an Obligation." Pellack, Lorraine J. Co-published simultaneously in *Science & Technology Libraries* (The Haworth Information Press, an imprint of The Haworth Press, Inc.) Vol. 27, No. 1/2, 2006, pp. 55-70; and: *Recruiting, Training, and Retention of Science and Technology Librarians* (ed: Patricia A. Kreitz, and JoAnn DeVries) The Haworth Information Press, an imprint of The Haworth Press, Inc., 2006, pp. 55-70. Single or multiple copies of this article are available for a fee from The Haworth Document Delivery Service [1-800-HAWORTH, 9:00 a.m. - 5:00 p.m. (EST). E-mail address: docdelivery@haworthpress.com].

Available online at http://stl.haworthpress.com
© 2006 by The Haworth Press, Inc. All rights reserved.
Digital Object Identifier:10.1300/J122v27n01_05

<docdelivery@haworthpress.com> Website: <http://www.HaworthPress.com>
© 2006 by The Haworth Press, Inc. All rights reserved.]

KEYWORDS. Recruiting, Each One Reach One, vocational guidance, science librarians, engineering librarians, academic librarians

INTRODUCTION

Librarianship is clearly experiencing a graying of the profession. The American Library Association has done a great job in recent years of publicizing this to attract more students into library schools, and a number of initiatives are going on at the national level to encourage more individuals to pursue librarianship as a profession. The shortage of science[2] librarians, however, is not a new phenomenon. There has been a shortage since the 1950s, or earlier, and yet the problem has still not been adequately resolved (Brown 1953, Brown 1988, Dewey 1985).

Science librarians are at a loss as to how to deal with recruiting beyond what library schools already do. There seems to be a "catch-22" where librarians are unwilling to step on the toes of library educators by suggesting that there might be a need for alternative recruiting methods when, in fact, most practicing librarians do not have a clue as to what recruiting methods are currently being employed. While there is a general acknowledgement that something needs to be done, in many cases, practicing librarians seem to feel they only have impact in one particular area–encouraging their student assistants to pursue a library science degree (Stoss 2005).

Contrary to popular opinion, student supervisors are *not* the only individuals in a position to recruit new blood into the profession. Every person who has a positive interaction with a librarian is a potential recruit and a walking advertisement for the profession. The late Lawrence Clark Powell (Chief Librarian at UCLA from 1944-1966 and founder of the UCLA School of Library Service) was a very passionate bibliophile and librarian who repeatedly went on the record espousing that every library staff member had an obligation to interest students in librarianship as a career:

> There are riches to be found beneath the minimum wage; there are refreshments not served at the coffee break; there are rewards unseen by Recordak [brand name of a microfilm reader]. We who

have found them in library work must tell young people about them . . . (Powell 1958, p. 168-169)

In the good old days, it used to be much easier to recruit students if there was a nearby library school and individuals could commute or take courses part-time. Many of the students were working full-time and librarianship was not their first career choice. Library schools, such as the one at UCLA, could attract a sufficient number of students by just recruiting locally (and many still can). With the advent of distance education and, more recently, web-based courses, this has geographically widened the net of possible students; however, it still requires that prospective students know about career possibilities and become interested in pursuing the degree.

WHO ARE WE?

Demographics are always fun to analyze and can be extremely useful. Newly-minted librarians, on the whole, are choosing librarianship as a second or third career in increasing numbers. In 1989, Heim and Moen (p. 44) reported that 30.2% of students surveyed chose to pursue their LIS degree after working in a non-library field. By 2005, Maatta (p. 30) found that 53% of recent library school graduates went to library school as a second or third career.

Science librarians, on the other hand, appear to have made up their minds about librarianship a lot earlier in life. Hackenberg & Chu (2002) surveyed sci-tech librarians and reported that 57% replied that they intended to become sci-tech librarians from the start, and 60% of the responding librarians had some type of science background before becoming sci-tech librarians. Winston (2001) surveyed sci-tech librarians in academic and research university libraries in the United States. He reported that only one-third of the librarians he surveyed had held professional or paraprofessional positions in the sciences or engineering prior to entering librarianship. Undergraduate majors for this group varied, but most often included biology, physics or chemistry. Only 8.9% had an additional master's degree in a science or engineering-related discipline.

WHAT MAKES THE PROFESSION ATTRACTIVE?

Librarians have speculated on this question for some time. The prevailing thought appears to be that the way to answer this question is to

poll various groups of current librarians to see why they chose the profession. Berry (2003b) reported results from an e-query of recent library
school students asking, among other things, why they chose the profession. The findings were quite varied but contained a number of themes.
Those who worked in libraries as support staff members loved the work
and chose to pursue the professional degree as a form of job advancement. Others loved books and reading, had the desire to help people find
information they need, or desired a career that serves the needs of both
individuals and society. Hallmark and Lembo (2003) surveyed science
librarians to find out why they switched from science to LIS.
One-fourth of the respondents had become disillusioned or dissatisfied
with their science career due to reasons such as industry layoffs, limited
career opportunities in sciences without a PhD, wanted more regular
hours, etc. The other three-fourths were drawn to LIS due to "their love
of the scientific and technical literature as well as the fun and challenge
of information research." What a powerful concept!

Sheehy (2000) is one of the few to focus almost exclusively on the
unseen benefits of library work as an essential tool in recruiting. She
was not targeting her comments specifically to any particular segment
of the library profession, but at librarianship in general. She very eloquently describes the intangible plusses of library work as: cooperation
and congeniality, opportunity to make a difference, intellectual stimula-
tion and life-long learning, variety, and job security. The very fact that
she feels these benefits are "unseen" and "intangible" is interesting in
and of itself. Clearly, these are benefits that need to be promoted more.

Why someone chooses a profession is not necessarily the same thing
as what makes the profession attractive. Given the variety of job duties
in a particular library it may be difficult to generalize about what makes
the profession attractive (e.g., what may be attractive to a cataloger
might not be attractive to a reference librarian and vice versa); however,
job attractiveness is a key element in recruiting and something that each
of us needs to think about prior to talking to a potential recruit. If you cannot describe the profession, or at least your own job, in a way that makes
someone eager to jump on board, then they are not likely to do so.

RECENT RECRUITING ACTIVITIES

There have been a number of recent articles in library science journals addressing a predicted librarian shortage in the United States. (See
St. Lifer 2000 for a general overview and Wilder 2000 for research

libraries.) This, in turn, has sparked a number of recruiting initiatives at the national level. In 2001, the American Library Association began a multi-year public education program called "@ your library, The Campaign for America's Libraries." During 2003, this program featured the "Academic and Research Library Campaign"–an element of which was to showcase academic and research librarianship as a "desirable career opportunity." In 2003, the Institute of Museum and Library Services (IMLS) began a new grant program, *Recruiting and Educating Librarians for the 21st Century*, designed specifically at bringing more individuals into librarianship. The vast majority of the individual IMLS grants in this program have been aimed at recruiting ethnic minorities, but there are also a couple of other unique groups being targeted such as rural librarians and science librarians. Unfortunately, none of these programs to date have published information on any sort of unique process they went through to recruit a specific target group. Chemistry librarians have been very active in promoting science librarianship (Barnett 2005, Silverman 1993). There have also been association efforts to promote academic and science librarianship (Association of College & Research Libraries 2003, Association of Research Libraries 2004) as well as a few individual, lower-visibility efforts (See Kreeger 2004, Pellack 2004, Stoss 2005).

In reading through the literature and talking to colleagues on listservs, it is difficult to tell exactly what recruiting methods are being employed by individual library schools. Clearly the higher-ranking library schools don't need to do *any* recruiting to fill their incoming classes; however, very few of them appear to be going on record as to exactly how much, or what sort of, recruitment is being done. Garoogian (1981), of the Pratt Institute, in discussing the historical recruitment efforts by library schools said "[a]s a matter of fact, the schools have played a very small role in seeking and tempting excellent candidates, those with special qualities, into the profession." She goes on to suggest library schools take a more active role in marketing and advertising. Dewey (1985), then Director of Admissions and Placement at Indiana University SLIS, made several suggestions for changes in recruitment strategies for library schools. Most of the suggestions focused on keeping librarians up-to-date on things to tell potential recruits. "Library schools can help to correct erroneous perceptions about their activities by sending pertinent materials to librarians about current programs and trends and by attending professional meetings to discuss issues concerning current library education topics." Berry (2003b) reported information he gathered in talks with several library school deans and directors about their recruiting efforts and actually mentions a number of them specifically. Unfortunately, the majority of comments focused on the impact of their website as their main recruiting tool, with only a few "targeted efforts" beyond their website. They are, quite correctly, presuming that once individuals become interested in librarianship they will visit a particular website in order to find more details; however, few efforts appear to be aimed at catching the attention of those who have not yet discovered an interest in librarianship.

RECRUITING UNTAPPED STUDENTS

A number of librarians highly recommend starting to recruit at a much earlier age. For example, Robles (1998) recommends regular contact at elementary and secondary grade levels since many minority students may not graduate from high school otherwise. Hauge (1997) also lists things school librarians can do to help recruit future librarians. While this will clearly be difficult for science librarians to carry out at the school library level, it speaks to the need for getting to know nearby school librarians and informing them of career options that they can in turn pass along to their students. Recruiting at the undergraduate level has also been emphasized quite a bit. Lucker (1998) recommends recruiting among high school and undergraduate students. Vazakas and Wallin (1992) considered undergraduate students to be a largely untapped group and a good target for recruiting science librarians as did Stuart and Drake (1992). Berry (2003b) also chimed in validating undergraduate students as "the best place" for recruiting librarians. Other, more controversial, suggestions have included: hiring people with subject specific PhDs instead of an MLS (Berry 2003a) and interesting librarians with non-science backgrounds to switch and learn science areas (see Hackenberg and Chu 2002; Morris-Knower 2001; Stuart and Drake 1991). Regardless of which opinions you have about "best recruits" there are clearly a number of possibilities to draw from.

One of the most common themes coming out of the library literature is that the single most effective way to recruit library school students is by serving as a role model for students you supervise. This has been particularly successful for student assistants on campuses with a library school. Unfortunately, this is only a *small percentage* of the available pool of student assistants! There are many more colleges and universities without a library school that hire student assistants to work in their libraries, who may be science majors. Consider the other students at these same colleges and universities who may not choose to work in the library but might consider librarianship as a profession if they had a little encouragement. Or, science majors who discover close to graduation that job duties in their discipline are not what they expected. Or, the scientific corporations who may have researchers that are unhappy with their lack of job security, are tired of spending their entire day in a lab, or dislike the intense competitiveness of their field. Or, teachers who are burned out by classroom stress and might want another career that allows them to help students succeed. There appears to be a wealth of untapped prospective library school students.

EACH ONE REACH ONE

In July 1988, the ALA Office of Library Personnel Resources sponsored a preconference entitled *Each One Reach One: Recruiting for the Profession* at the ALA conference in New Orleans. The title was intended to stress the importance of individual librarian efforts. The objectives were: "to convey the library profession as an interesting, dynamic career choice, provide recruitment strategies, and develop a national recruitment plan" (Matarazzo 1989). A handbook was distributed to participants at the preconference. Additions were made to the handbook based on comments from the preconference and it was reissued in 1989 *as Each One Reach One: Recruiting for the Profession Action Handbook*. The intent of the publication was to give librarians some practical tips on recruitment, and the organizers put together a phenomenal collection of ideas ranging from small individual efforts to much larger projects and publicity campaigns. James Matarazzo, who attended the preconference and relayed the information to Special Libraries Association members in the form of an article in *Special Libraries*, reported that the preconference was attended by more than 200 people and the meeting "resembled a rally convened to convince those who teach, those who practice, and those who manage professional associations there is a need to bring more students into the interesting and dynamic library profession. It was difficult to determine whether those at the preconference actually had the necessary zeal to recruit more students" (Matarazzo 1989). He concludes by saying " [t]he result is likely to be little action and little by way of acknowledging the problems of a much-needed national recruitment effort." Nowhere in his report does he emphasize the concept of individual librarian efforts even though that appears to have been the intent of the preconference. As with many similar campaigns, it can be difficult to gauge the effectiveness or impact on either individuals or the profession; however, the "Each One Reach One" concept could become extremely powerful if *individual* librarians put forth even a small amount of effort by initiating some of the suggestions mentioned in the handbook. "Each one of us can reach at least one other person ... we can do this in a personal manner that is respectful of our own personality preferences and demonstrates an interest in others. We are our own best recruiters" (Eschavarria 2001, p. 20).

IDEAS FOR RECRUITING SCIENCE LIBRARIANS

There are two noteworthy journal articles that do a very good job of providing ideas for recruiting science librarians. Vazakas and Wallin (1992) unfortunately appear to have slipped into the literature without much notice. Even though their article appeared in a prominent publication, and contains a number of useful suggestions, they have rarely been cited. They were among the first to advocate that individual science librarians could help combat shortages in the profession. In addition, they recommended reaching out to find potential recruits working outside the library field, an idea that very few others have even attempted to address. Hallmark and Lembo (2003) also present a number of talking points for successfully recruiting science and engineering students into library science. The following suggestions are not meant to be comprehensive, but rather to stimulate additional thoughts. The list contains ideas taken from a variety of sources, as noted, as well as a few new ones:

- Have bookmarks about library careers available at the Circulation Desk (Each One Reach One 1989).
- Use library instruction sessions to tout librarianship as a career (Bosseau and Martin 1995; Stuart and Drake 1992; Each One Reach One 1989).
- Sponsor a seminar specifically on Careers in Information Science– inviting the entire campus community (Lauer 1984). This could easily be modified to be a seminar for science and engineering careers that includes librarianship as an option.
- Educate undergraduate advisers and career counselors in colleges of science and engineering to convince them to include LIS as an option for their graduates (Hallmark and Lembo 2003).

- Become student advisors–a logical part of advising would be to encourage interested students to consider librarianship (Studdard 2000).
- Participate in career days events at nearby high schools, colleges and universities (Bosseau and Martin 1995; Each One Reach One 1989).
- Volunteer to be a speaker for student clubs (Bosseau and Martin 1995; Each One Reach One 1989). This could be to talk about information careers or to feature cool new things in local library-land while slipping information on careers into the talk.
- Distribute a flyer or brochure about library careers in campus student mailboxes (Each One Reach One 1989) or wherever you work. Suggest that you can combine any college major with librarianship.
- Publicize distance education opportunities to allow getting a degree while working. Ideal for those seeking a second career.
- Branch out from traditional settings to capture the attention of potential library school students (Perry 2004). For science librarians, it means finding ways to alert scientists in commerce and industry to alternative careers–particularly in glutted fields–e.g., physics was glutted in the 1980s.
- Create an eye-catching career poster to put up in labs or staff/student lounges. There are also some posters and brochures available from professional associations such as SLA or ACRL–visit their websites or contact them to find out what they currently have available for promoting sci-tech library careers.
- Target areas that are known to have scientists leaving the field (see Preston 2004, introduction and pp. 111-138 for recent information on fields and reasons scientists are leaving).
- Jazz up the information and target specific groups. E.g., Engineers–tired of projects as lone ranger? Chemistry, Physics & Microbiology–get out of the isolation lab and into research? Physical Therapists–if arthritic thumbs are a problem, bring your hands and knowledge to the library profession. Tired of being isolated in a lab breathing noxious fumes? Put a breath of fresh air into your job by joining the library profession.
- Add Science and Engineering Librarianship to the *Occupational Outlook Handbook* or find ways to alert career counselors in high schools and colleges to careers in science librarianship–in both academic and special libraries–at local, state or national levels.
- Encourage students enrolled in MLS/MLIS programs to consider academic librarianship (Hewitt, Moran and Marsh 2003) or science

librarianship. This works best on campuses with a library school, but also works to advantage with personal acquaintances, student assistants or library patrons, who are attending library school via distance education programs. Few incoming library science students actually know what kind of library they want to work in post-graduation.

- Volunteer to be a guest speaker for science reference courses taught through distance education programs and use the opportunity to encourage LIS students to become science librarians. Many library science programs such as SUNY-Buffalo offer opportunities for their students to chat online with a practicing librarian as a guest speaker for course units.
- Hire LIS students with science and engineering backgrounds as graduate assistants to help fund their library school, and give them nifty science-related projects to work on (Hallmark and Lembo 2003). You could offer through a particular library school nearby or through distance education. Make contact with potential library school programs and find out the possibilities. This may be difficult to budget but it really gives back to the profession.
- Investigate the possibility of providing an internship for academic credit. These can be paid or unpaid, full-time or part-time, work experiences for students considering a particular career. The work experience does not necessarily need to be on the campus of that particular college or university–it could occur in *any* library. This sort of program is usually offered through the career center at colleges and universities and options vary at each educational institution.

VOCATIONAL GUIDANCE

In 1956, Nesbitt said library schools had failed in two ways: "We have not produced the kind of recruiting literature that will appeal to young people, and we have not given vocational guidance counselors an adequate picture of the library profession." Is this still true today? Stop and think about how you, personally, found out about what it takes to be a librarian–not how you found out about the *career*, but where you learned about what degree it takes, what schools offer the program, future job market, etc. Did you look it up in the *Occupational Outlook Handbook (OOH)*? Or, did you find out about it by talking to a high school career counselor, college career counselor, teacher, library supervisor, personal acquaintance who was in library school, library school brochures/website, or newspaper article? Chances are fairly good that even if you looked up the facts on a website or the *OOH*, you probably still talked to an enthusiastic individual about it somewhere along the way. I recently polled 50 academic librarians (including a wide mixture of science, social sciences, cataloging, reference, geographic locations in the U.S., and years in the profession) very informally by e-mail and asked this question. Of the forty who responded, thirty-seven of them had talked with an influential individual. Four of those individuals were guidance counselors but the other thirty-three were librarians. Seven of them had started with a guidance counselor and then talked with a librarian or two to get more details about the profession. There were no correlations between the number of years in the profession and where they received their information. Those who had talked with a guidance counselor or took a career test ranged from newly-minted librarians to those who had been in the profession for 20-30 years. Even though fewer came into the profession by solely talking with a guidance counselor, clearly it still pays to ensure they are knowledgeable about options for those who might be interested in librarianship as a profession. Go visit with vocational guidance counselors at nearby high schools and colleges–don't just call or send an e-mail–actually take the time to go meet them and become acquainted with their methods and tools. Take along some career brochures from professional associations and URLs for relevant websites that you can leave with the counselors. Take time to get to know nearby high school and public librarians. Give them your contact information in case they have questions or a prospective student wants to chat about science librarianship.

Recruiting requires up-to-date knowledge of library schools, admission requirements, etc., or knowledge of where recruits should look for that information. Garoogian (1981) noted that many library schools were changing their programs from a one-year degree program to a two-year program. Anyone who graduated from library school prior to this time may be unaware of this change and could be giving potentially incorrect information to interested enquirers. Giving out old information will not help the recruiting effort. Practicing librarians need to make it a point to keep abreast of changes in these areas in order to give accurate vocational guidance.

Holt and Strock (2005) also caution that it only takes a couple of years to turn out numerous, fresh MLS holders but it may be several years before the profession begins to see large numbers of those anticipated retirements. When recruiting, we need to be careful to alert prospective students to the cyclical nature of job openings and suggest that they may need to take a general library position and watch for science librarian openings. (Not to mention that it's good experience to learn interdisciplinary areas.)

ENTHUSIASM AND TIME

There are many ways that individual practicing librarians can become active in recruiting, but it first requires a belief or interest in doing something and, secondly, it requires a genuine enthusiasm for the job. "The most important thing we can share with others is our own enthusiasm for our profession" (Eschavarria 2001, p. 19). Few people outside the profession have any idea what a librarian does all day besides read books. The job is considerably more intellectually stimulating than outsiders suppose and we need to find ways to inform recruits of the fallacies inherent in the stereotypic librarian as personified by the media. "Self-confident librarians who are enthusiastic about their work make others not only curious but perhaps a little covetous" (Allen 1956, p. 10). What happens when you encounter individuals *outside* of the workplace that ask what you do for a living? How animatedly do you answer this question? Do you just say you work for *x* university or company? Or, do you say you're a librarian and you get to do things you love doing all day? "When someone asks what you do, be prepared to describe something interesting about your work" (Each One Reach One, 1989, p. 2).

Enthusiasm can be invigorated (or reinvigorated) by reading inspiring books or revisiting success stories. Try reading texts such as Powell's *A Passion for Books*, Gorman's *Our Singular Strengths*, or very passionate articles such as one by Steven J. Bell (2003). Visit some websites that outline library impacts on patrons such as those from ALIA's *Library Stories*, the *Feel-Good Librarian* or *Science Librarian Success Stories* (Pellack 2006). All serve as excellent reminders, to both librarians and prospective students, of the value of libraries and librarians.

Time is a precious commodity that always seems to be in short supply but we always manage to find time for things that are important to us. Recruiting for the profession does not require taking time aside from other activities unless you choose to do so. True, I sit writing this on a Saturday afternoon in the middle of a winter snowstorm, choosing to spend time on writing while ignoring the dirty laundry piles–but it illustrates the point nicely. Recruiting can be done as part of everyday tasks, whether at work, at home, or socially. It does not matter whether it's a little or a lot, but it does require a conscious decision to do something, anything.

CONCLUSION

Lucile Allen (1956, p. 9) was one of the first to suggest that "personal contact, whether on a social or professional basis, is one of the best ways of building recruitment programs." This still remains true today. Practicing librarians are, individually and collectively, the best advertisement for the profession. "Make more people aware of your existence and you provide a choice for those who would not have been aware of the field as a potential source of a career" (Garoogian 1981, p. 88). Librarians who work in public areas have the opportunity to interact with numerous potential librarians every time they answer a query. Librarians who work in non-public areas may not think they have as much contact with potential recruits but they still interact with a variety of people and have many of the other opportunities, mentioned above, to influence prospective students. With apologies to Powell, who was very book-centric, I have taken the liberty of broadening out and modernizing his original comments (1958, p. 184) by replacing his use of the word "books" with "information":

> Human values and human judgments are inseparable from good librarianship . . . salaries and certification, the classification of jobs, and the co-ordination of [library school] curricula, are all important, and must be dealt with, but beneath these complexities lie the great simplicities of humane librarianship–that information is basic, that people are good, and that bringing the two together, so that information is made more useful and people more fruitful, is one of the most exciting and rewarding experiences on earth. It is called librarianship.

It makes my emotions soar and reaffirms my professional being every time I think about it. You too can experience the satisfaction of having an impact–not just on library patrons–but also on the profession. Each of us should ask ourselves the question: What have I done recently to ensure science librarians do not become an extinct species?

NOTES

1. Uncle Albert is a popular nickname among scientists for Albert Einstein. He was a very outspoken pacifist and political activist well-known for his radical ideas.

2. The term "science" is used throughout the article for the sake of simplicity, but it could easily be swapped with a number of other words describing specific types of librarians–engineering, medical, academic, etc.

REFERENCES

ALIA. *Library Stories*, http://www.alia.org.au/advocacy/stories/ (accessed January 8, 2006).

Allen, Lucile. 1956. Recruiting the undergraduate. IN *Recruiting library personnel*. ACRL Monographs no.17. Chicago: Association of College & Research Libraries, pp. 9-14.

Association of College & Research Libraries. [2003.] *Your major + academic librarianship = A great career!* http://www.ala.org/ala/acrl/acrlissues/acrlrecruiting/recruiting.pdf (accessed November 21, 2005).

Association of Research Libraries. 2004. *ARL Academy: careers in academic & research libraries* (An IMLS-funded program), http://www.arl.org/olms/arlacademy/ (accessed November 5, 2005).

Barnett, Philip. 2005. *Some resources on careers in chemical information.* http://mail.sci.ccny.cuny.edu/~phibarn/careers.html (accessed November 21, 2005).

Bell, Steven J. 2003. A passion for academic librarianship: find it, keep it, sustain it–a reflective inquiry. *portal: Libraries and the Academy*, 3(4): 633-642.

Berry, John N. 2003a. But don't call 'em librarians. *Library Journal*, 128(18): 34-36.

———. 2003b. LIS recruiting: does it make the grade? *Library Journal*, 128(8): 38-40.

Bosseau, Don L., and Susan K. Martin. 1995. The accidental profession. *Journal of Academic Librarianship*, 21(3): 198-199.

Brown, Charles Harvey. 1953. Librarianship and the sciences. IN Shores, Louis (ed.), *Challenges to librarianship*, Dubuque, IA: Wm. C. Brown, pp. 69-91.

Brown, Lorene B. 1988. Recruiting science librarians. IN Moen, William E., and Kathleen M. Heim (eds.), *Librarians for the new millennium*. Chicago: American Library Association, Office for Library Personnel Resources, p. 65-71.

Dewey, Barbara I. 1985. Selection of librarianship as a career: implications for recruitment. *Journal of Education for Library and Information Science*, 26(1): 16-24.

Each one reach one: recruiting for the profession action handbook. 1989. Chicago: American Library Association, Office for Library Personnel Resources.

Echavarria, Tami. 2001. Reach out to recruit new librarians. *ALKI*, 17(1): 18-20, 24, http://www.wla.org/publications/alki/2001iss1alki.pdf (last visited November 4, 2005).

Feel-good librarian, http://feelgoodlibrarian.typepad.com/feelgood_librarian/(accessed January 8, 2006).

Garoogian, Rhoda. 1981. The changing role of library schools in recruitment and selection: implications for the profession. *Drexel Library Quarterly*, 17(3): 75-93.

Gorman, Michael. 1998. *Our singular strengths: meditations for librarians.* Chicago: American Library Association.

Hackenberg, Jill M., and Barbara Chu. 2002. Why does one choose sci-tech librarianship? Findings of a survey. *Science & Technology Libraries*, 23(1): 3-16.

Hallmark, Julie, and Mary Frances Lembo. 2003. Leaving science for LIS: interviews and a survey of librarians with scientific and technical degrees. *Issues in Science and Technology Librarianship*, no. 37, http://www.istl.org/03-spring/refereed1.html (accessed November 21, 2005).

Hauge, Mary. 1997. Recruit for the profession. *Book Report*, 15(4): 19.

Heim, Kathleen M., and William E. Moen. 1989. *Occupational entry: library and information science students' attitudes, demographics and aspirations survey.* Chicago: ALA Office for Library Personnel Resources.

Hewitt, Joe A., Barbara B. Moran, and Mari E. Marsh. 2003. Finding our replacements: one institution's approach to recruiting academic librarians. *portal: Libraries and the Academy*, 3(2): 179-189.

Holt, Rachel, and Adrienne L. Strock. 2005. The entry level gap. *Library Journal*, 130(8): 36-38.

Institute of Museum and Library Services. 2003 *Recruiting and educating librarians for the 21st century–grant application and guidelines*, http://www.imls.gov/grants/library/pdf/2003Guide21.pdf (accessed November 5, 2005).

Kreeger, Karen. 2004. Science librarians shout about their careers. *The Scientist*, 18(1): 52.

Lauer, Jonathan D. 1984. Recruiting for the profession. *College & Research Libraries News*, 45(8): 388- 390.

Lucker, Jay K. 1998. The changing nature of scientific and technical librarianship: a personal perspective over 40 years. *Science & Technology Libraries*, 17(2): 3-10.

Maatta, Stephanie. 2005. Closing the gap. *Library Journal*, 130(17): 26-33.

Matarazzo, James. 1989. Recruiting for the profession: a special report on a preconference meeting. *Special Libraries*, 80 (Spring): 132-134.

McCook, Kathleen de la Peña. See Heim, Kathleen M.

Morris-Knower, James. 2001. *Phyllostachys aurea*–didn't he work with Socrates? Reference work in science libraries by librarians who are not scientists. *The Reference Librarian*, no. 72: 155-169.

Nesbitt, Elizabeth. 1956. Recruitment as seen by the library schools. In *Recruiting library personnel.* ACRL Monographs no.17. Chicago: Association of College & Research Libraries, pp. 22-24.

Pellack, Lorraine J. 2004. *Careers in academic & science librarianship*, http://www.public.iastate.edu/~pellack/AcadSciCareers.htm (accessed November 21, 2005).

————. 2006. *Science librarian success stories*, http://www.public.iastate.edu/~pellack/SuccessStories.htm (accessed January 29, 2006).

Powell, Lawrence Clark. 1958. *A passion for books.* Cleveland: World Publishing Co.

Preston, Anne E. 2004. *Leaving science: occupational exit from scientific careers.* New York: Russell Sage Foundation, introduction and pp. 111-138.

Robles, Patricia. 1998. Recruiting the minority librarian: the secret to increasing the numbers. *College & Research Libraries News*, 59(10): 779-780.

Sheehy, Carolyn A. 2000. Who says it's always greener on the other side? Unseen benefits may be useful in libraries' recruiting efforts. *American Libraries*, 31(8): 52-54.

Silverman, Edward R. 1993. Chemical information: a career alternative for chemists. *The Scientist*, 7(6): 21.

St. Lifer, Evan. 2000. The boomer brain drain: the last of a generation? *Library Journal*, 125(8): 38-42.

Stoss, Frederick W. 2005. *Recruiting science students into academic library careers* [Discussion]. STS-L listserv discussion February 18-February 28. http://lists ala.org/wws/arc/sts-l/2005-02/msg00041.html (accessed December 29, 2005).

Stuart, Crit and Miriam A. Drake. 1992. Education and recruitment of science and engineering librarians. *Science & Technology Libraries*, 12(4): 79-89.

Studdard, Paul. 2000. Academic librarians as advisors: working with students to plan their futures. *College & Research Libraries News*, 61(9): 781-782, 792.

Vazakas, Susan M. and Camille Clark Wallin. 1992. Where are all the science librarians? *College & Research Libraries News* 53(3):166-171.

Wilder, Stanley. 2000. The changing profile of research library professional staff. *ARL Bimonthly Report*, no. 208/209, http://www.arl.org/newsltr/208_209/chgprofile.html (accessed November 21, 2005).

Winston, Mark D. 2001. Academic science and engineering librarians: a research study of demographics, educational backgrounds, and professional activities. *Science & Technology Libraries*, 19(2): 3-24.

doi:10.1300/J122v27n01_05

Becoming a Science Librarian: Accident, Serendipity, or Purposeful Plan?

Donna M. Beck
Rachel Callison

SUMMARY. Increasing concern has been expressed in the literature regarding the recruitment and retention of qualified librarians within the profession. Science and Technology Libraries share equally in considering the consequences of this trend. Two Science Librarians, neither possessing a degree in the sciences, will discuss the skills, competencies, and experiences that enable them to thrive in a challenging and dynamic work environment. Descriptive statistics from a survey of other newly hired science librarians, regardless of their science background, will also be incorporated. In addition to exploring perceived strengths, this paper will address the possible disadvantages that the lack of a science "background" may present. Science background will be discussed in terms of having previously obtained a degree in the sciences. The approach to the topic is from the perspective of the new hire (not necessarily a "new" librarian), rather than that of the hiring institution; however, strategies and methods that are useful to

Donna M. Beck, MLIS, is Engineering Librarian, Engineering and Science Library, Carnegie Mellon University Libraries, Pittsburgh, PA (E-mail: donnab@andrew.cmu.edu), and Rachel Callison, MLS, is Reference Librarian, Software Engineering Institute, Carnegie Mellon University, Pittsburgh, PA (E-mail: callison@sei.cmu.edu).

[Haworth co-indexing entry note]: "Becoming a Science Librarian: Accident, Serendipity or Purposeful Plan?" Beck, Donna M., and Rachel Callison. Co-published simultaneously in *Science & Technology Libraries* (The Haworth Information Press, an imprint of The Haworth Press, Inc.) Vol. 27, No. 1/2, 2006, pp. 71-98; and: *Recruiting, Training, and Retention of Science and Technology Librarians* (ed: Patricia A. Kreitz, and JoAnn DeVries) The Haworth Information Press, an imprint of The Haworth Press, Inc., 2006, pp. 71-98. Single or multiple copies of this article are available for a fee from The Haworth Document Delivery Service [1-800-HAWORTH, 9:00 a.m. - 5:00 p.m. (EST). E-mail address: docdelivery@haworthpress.com].

Available online at http://stl.haworthpress.com
© 2006 by The Haworth Press, Inc. All rights reserved.
Digital Object Identifier: 10.1300/J122v27n01_06

both groups will be offered. doi: 10.1300/J122v27n01_06 *[Article copies available for a fee from The Haworth Document Delivery Service: 1-800-HAWORTH. E-mail address: <docdelivery@haworthpress.com> Website: <http://www.HaworthPress. com> © 2006 by The Haworth Press, Inc. All rights reserved.]*

KEYWORDS. Science librarians–education, surveys–science librarians, librarians–careers, college and university librarians–status, recruitment and retention of science librarians

INTRODUCTION

The notion that individuals are "accidental" librarians because their original intent was not necessarily to become a librarian is difficult to measure. To take this proposition a step further would be to ask if an individual's intention at the start of their graduate program was to become a certain subject librarian. However, this too is difficult to measure. Is there really such a thing as an "accidental" librarian? Specifically, this paper will explore the question: Do individuals "accidentally" become science librarians? Or, do the librarians hired into academic science positions bring a certain mixture of skills, interests, experiences, and backgrounds (both formal and non-formal) that place them into more of a "serendipitous" category?

Horace Walpole is credited with creating the word "serendipity" in a 1754 letter to an English agent. In explaining his "derivation" of serendipity; rather than give a mere definition, Walpole shares the story of the *Three Princes of Serendi(b)p:* sons of a philosopher-king of Serendi(b)p, who utilize their deductive powers in various adventures. Walpole not only linked his newly coined word to the "act of 'accidental' discovery" by relating this tale but, more sagely and apropos to the use of the word in this paper, he connected serendipity to the concept of "sagacity"; i.e., "acute mental discernment, keenness and soundness of judgement, an aptitude for investigation, and adaptation of means to ends" (OED online; Britannica online; and Friedel, 2001). Other disciplines, including the sciences, have considered the role serendipity may play in various events and situations. A 1998 research study of prominent female faculty in counseling psychology, for example, explored their perceptions of serendipity with regard to their own career choices. This study wanted to see if they could determine "when people were ready to take advantage of chance events" in order to "help predict the effects of chance on career choices" (Williams, 1998).

We wanted to explore, and compare with our own experiences, the path one takes in becoming a science librarian. We prefer to illustrate how we arrived at our positions by describing the process as "serendipitous" rather than merely "accidental." When members of our own esteemed institution were considering us as candidates for reference librarian positions within our science libraries, they may have had serious deliberations over the fact that neither of us have an undergraduate or graduate degree in the sciences. In accepting our positions, we realized that many of the colleagues in our own profession might look upon us as "unqualified" based solely on this lack of degree. The authors contend that whereas we were fortunate to discover the field of science librarianship, we did not arrive to our positions because our employer felt resigned that we were the best available amongst a weak pool of candidates. Rather, we do not view ourselves as "accidents." Our combined backgrounds tell a tale of varied interests in many subjects and unique service within the library field. We believe that it is this range of experiences and intellectual curiosity that led us to find a niche in science librarianship.

How have others "discovered" that specializing in science librarianship would be a good career path? We designed a survey to identify the people who are being hired for academic science library positions and to find out whether or not they have a formal science background, i.e., a science degree. Are they seeking out professional librarian opportunities with a certain level of intent and "purposefulness," no matter what kind of educational background that they may have? The authors feel that any experience or learning about the sciences is an asset to success as a science librarian, but that understanding and utilizing the underlying principles and core competencies of the library profession, especially that of the concept of life long learning is what will ultimately serve them best as LIBRARIANS.

MATCHING LIBRARIANS TO SCIENCE LIBRARIAN POSITIONS

Job seekers scanning job postings for academic librarian positions are accustomed to noting that the standard requirement for any position is a Master's degree (MLS, MLIS, or equivalent) from an American Library Association (ALA) accredited library science program. For clarity, this degree will be abbreviated throughout this article as MLIS. In addition to the MLIS requirement, science library positions will often include a statement for a preferred qualification of a background in the sciences. Academic science librarians are already armed with a professional foundation, the MLIS. This article will examine other qualifications that science librarians possess, and it will address the questions: Is an "interest" in sciences enough? What about developing an interest in the sciences as a result of working as a science librarian–after being hired into a position? Or, is the additional degree in a science subject a prerequisite for success as a science librarian? Reasons that may have prompted them to apply for their current position and whether or not the possession of a science degree affected either their desire to apply or effectiveness in their position will also be discussed.

Matching people to positions is the biggest challenge of the hiring process and one of the most important decisions made by an employer. Numerous studies have attempted to benchmark how professionals compete and compare within their respective workforce spheres. Perspectives on the recruitment and retention issues of librarians from different library environments, including academic, have also been explored and discussed in the literature. Over the last 30 years, starting with Ellis Mount's initial findings published in *University Science and Engineering Libraries* in 1975 and including the follow-up in 1983, several surveys have sought to identify and address the specific recruiting and retention concerns of academic science libraries and science librarians.

The majority of studies about academic science librarians have presented the obvious conclusion that having a science background is an asset. Many of the same findings have also indicated that the possession of a degree is not necessarily the deciding factor for professional success and, quite possibly, not the greatest of the professional assets. Exclusively recruiting individuals with a science background may not always meet the expectations of an institution or the profession as a whole. Slutsky, writing in *Science & Technology Libraries*, agrees that a candidate "with a science/technology subject degree and an MLIS may not always be suited for a specific job situation" (Slutsky, 1991).

Hackenburg & Chu's 2002 *Science & Technology Libraries* article points out that a solid foundation in library science coupled with the competencies gained from experience, regardless of degree, is often a strong indicator of career success. Those without a science and technology background have found "that a good basis in librarianship could overcome a lack of science knowledge" (Hackenberg, 2002). An additional view that experience counts, and is not exclusive to the experience of having a science undergraduate degree, is Winston's article titled, "Academic Science and Engineering Librarians: A Research Study of Demographics, Educational Backgrounds, and Professional Activities." Winston points out that, "Recruitment of science and engineering librarians should not focus solely on those individuals with science backgrounds, but on experienced librarians as well" (Winston, 2001). A 2005 article by Mayer and Terrill presents the views of academic librarians on the topic of advanced degrees. Their survey responders indicated that an advanced degree "helped most by opening doors early in their careers, but later it was their experience that counted most" (Mayer, 2005). Several compelling reasons for possessing an advanced degree were presented; including statements that having a degree "assists with gaining tenure and promotion, gives librarians better credibility on campus, . . . can provide increased opportunities for scholarly projects, immerses one in academic culture, and exemplifies a commitment to the importance of life-long learning" (Mayer, 2005).

The authors' observations are that this debate will continue, but that real life data will serve to define future discussions. How can anyone define what "success" as a science librarian means? Even strong proponents of a science degree requirement are not truly able to state as a fact that those without a science degree are less successful. Having a formal background in the sciences has been the foremost issue to the debate. This may be an appropriate time to look beyond this factor alone. We propose to no longer separate the issue into black and white, but to find and discuss those "gray" factors within librarians' backgrounds that can benefit academic science libraries and the profession. While our stance may be that we do not feel an undergraduate science degree should be the main predictor for success, we also do not mean to claim that a belief in life-long learning or anything else is the sole factor either. Armed with confidence from our graduate training in library science, we were willing to take the risk to put ourselves in with the group of other non-scientifically trained science librarians.

SURVEY METHODOLOGY

We conducted a survey of newly hired science librarians to determine if any commonalities of experience exist among them, regardless of their backgrounds. A target group was identified by a search of job advertisements for science librarian positions that covered the 2003 through 2005 time period. Issues of *The Chronicle of Higher Education, College & Research Libraries News*, and *Sci-Tech News* were reviewed for ads that fit the description for science librarian positions in academic institutions. Medical librarians working in a library affiliated with a school of medicine within an academic setting were excluded from the targeted group. A subsequent search for the library websites of the institutions was made in order to obtain contact information for the person currently holding the position. Survey questions were reviewed and approved by Carnegie Mellon University's Institutional Review Board (IRB) and posted using SurveyMonkey software (SurveyMonkey.com). E-mail was sent to 90 librarians identified as the target group asking them to complete a survey consisting of 22 questions. A total of 35 responses were received, accounting for a 38.9% response. Female responses were almost double the male responses. To assure that the only responses received were from librarians working at libraries in educational institutions, this question was asked, "What is the name of the institution where you are currently employed?" It is interesting to note that although all respondents were recent hires, many were not new to the profession. Those working in the library field in a position requiring an MLIS were represented as follows: 2 years or less = 14, 3-6 years = 7, 7-10 years = 5, and 10 plus years = 9. These years do not necessarily represent only the time in their current positions or time in positions at other science libraries. The majority–63.9%–of those hired for science librarian positions posted between 2003-2005 held prior positions that required a MLIS degree with about half (33.3%) of those prior positions being within another science and technology library. Although the initial scope of this survey was not to measure if people both new to the profession and new to an academic science library job differed significantly in their answers from more experienced librarians, a few of these differences will be presented in this article.

The majority of the survey questions were designed to garner information about the educational background, work experiences, and interests of the new hires. New graduates of library science programs were not specifically included or excluded in the target group and, as stated earlier, respondents were broadly represented in terms of years of experience. The main objective was to obtain an overall perspective on the candidates recently hired into academic science librarian positions, i.e., What kinds and years of experiences do they possess? Do they consider themselves as having any unique qualifications that set them aside as a match for the position other than having a MLIS and/or a background in the sciences? What possibly made them an attractive hire beyond a science degree?

INTEREST IN LIBRARY SCIENCE

Professional librarian positions still require the minimum of a Master's degree in Library Science. Since all of our survey respondents acknowledged that a MLIS was a requirement of their current academic science library position; a look at who is initially attracted to enter a graduate program in library science is relevant in order to give a general picture of those applying to MLIS programs and what their career goals might be. A reasonable assumption regarding those that apply is that they have a general interest in and orientation to the library profession. Are there certain demographics that guide or hinder a library graduate student's decision to pursue specific area of librarianship; both type and subject discipline?

One could surmise that an 'ideal' pool of candidates for academic science library positions would be individuals with an undergraduate and/or advanced science degree and an MLIS. However, due to several factors, this is a consistently small group of individuals which does not appear to be increasing in a significant manner in the immediate future.

Not only have men historically dominated the science fields, they continue to do so. A 2004 United States General Accounting Office (GAO) report states that, "Although women's participation in the sciences has improved steadily over the last three decades, men still outnumber women in nearly every field in the sciences," and that, "In 1960 women constituted less than 1 percent of engineers, 8 percent of scientists, and 26 percent of mathematicians. By 2003, women made up 14 percent of engineers, 37 percent of scientists and 33 percent of mathematicians" (GAO, 2004). In contrast, the majority of entrants into the library profession are still women. Census data from 2000 (Table 1) shows that women are still dominant in the profession, making up 82% of all librarians. Although women dominant the profession overall, proportionately they are not the majority within academic settings. The 2004 *LJ (Library Journal)* Placements and Salary Survey indicates that there is a "disproportionately higher ratio of men working in (academic libraries) than within the library profession as a whole" (Maata, 2005). Recognizing these facts, it is clear that the largest pool of candidates entering library science degree programs (i.e., women) are also not likely to possess an undergraduate degree in the sciences. Survey results obtained for this article (Table 1, "2005 Science Librarian Survey"–Beck and Callison) showing a greater ratio of men to women within the science librarian specialty is not surprising.

TABLE 1. Gender Factors

	2000 Census data Librarian profession as a whole.[a]	2005 Science Librarian Survey (Beck & Callison)
Men	18%	33.3%
Women	82%	66.7%

[a] Lynch, Mary Jo; Tordella, Stephen and Godfrey, Thomas. 2005. Retirement and Recruitment: A Deeper Look. *American Libraries*, (January): 36(1). http://www.ala.org/ala/ors/reports/recruitretire/recruitretire-adeeperlook.pdf.

The intention of the authors is not to argue that a science degree is harder for women to attain than for men, or that the library field is not equally attractive to both men and women, including those who possess a science degree; but to provide some context on possible gender-related circumstances that may impact the overall pool of candidates available for or interested in academic science library positions. Librarians want to have a sense of credibility amongst their colleagues and their campus communities. Along with the thought that science librarians with a science degree have better credibility, the authors sense a perception by some to see the higher ratio of men as science librarians equated to an image that male science librarians are more credible. As female science librarians, without a formal science degree background, we strive to overcome these two credibility issues by arguing that our prior educational preparations and accomplishments serve to qualify us well.

The 2004 *LJ* Placements and Salary Survey asked MLIS graduates to discuss their backgrounds and 53% indicated that (by pursuing an MLIS degree) they were seeking a second or third career (Maatta, 2005). Regardless of where they were in their careers, at the point of deciding to pursue an MLIS, many entrants to library science graduate schools are likely not to have a science degree. Individuals represented in Winston's survey indicate that as a whole, "the (library) profession is dominated by English and history majors,"and that even within the majority of science librarians who do possess a science background, "there are very few reported engineering majors" (Winston, 2001). One could further illustrate this by observing that although a librarian has an undergraduate degree in the sciences, for instance in biology, they may actually be working in an engineering library. The authors (one with a Bachelor of Fine Arts and one with a Bachelor of Arts in Sociology) agree that the primary reason for their obtaining the MLIS was to work as a professional librarian. At the start of our graduate programs, we may not have envisioned ourselves in positions within science libraries. However, the pursuit of the library degree was one of the core influences that ultimately placed us on a course that we characterize as one of "positive serendipity" in the process of becoming science librarians.

REASONS FOR APPLYING FOR SCIENCE LIBRARIAN POSITIONS

Another survey question, "What influenced your decision to APPLY for your current position?" was posed in an effort to gauge why the respondents applied for positions as science librarians instead of another area of librarianship. Position titles of the respondents ranged from the general "Science Librarian" to the more specific "Biological Sciences Librarian and Coordinator for Digital Initiatives in the Sciences." Rather than rating what may have been the most influential factor(s) in becoming science librarians, the question was worded to give the librarians several choices. Instructions on the survey asked the librarians to check off all that they felt applied (Table 2).

As already noted, academic science librarian position descriptions state that the MLIS is required. When asked if a science background was described as a "required" qualification for their position, 27.8% of the respondents from the survey indicated it was; 55.6% responded that it was not; and 16.7% were unsure. Whereas 67.6% of the respondents stated that it was a "preferred" qualification in the job descriptions; 17.6% said that it was not; and 14.7% were unsure. These results are in line with the trend discussed in a 2002 article appearing in *Sci-Tech News* titled, "Recruiting Entry-Level Sci-Tech Librarians: An Analysis of Job Advertisements and Outcome of Searches." The authors of this article, in their review of 2000 and 2001 job ads, observed that recruiters appear to be adding more general types of qualifications as requirements in lieu of the science degree in the hopes of gaining a larger pool of candidates. The article states that, "Administrators, when recruiting candidates for science/technology positions, value communication and computing skills so highly that they do not want to consider candidates without them. It also appears that, even though they would very much like to get candidates who have science degrees, they seem to be resigned to not finding candidates with those degrees and therefore do not insist on them" (Jones, 2002). In light of the fact that candidates responding to most of the recent job advertisements are not required to have a science degree, although it is often still listed as a preference, looking at other

TABLE 2. Factors Influencing Decision to Apply to Current Position

Factors influencing decision	Percent Responding
Desired work as librarian in science affiliated subject area	69.4%
Felt qualified for the position based on the job advertisement	66.7%
Previously worked in a librarian position at a science/technology library	33.3%
Other (please specify)	33.3%
Wanted to work at a particular institution in any kind of librarian position	22.2%
Previously worked in a non-librarian position at a science/technology library	13.9%
Believed salary would be higher than for other non-science librarian positions	11.1%
Felt that the pool of candidates (competition) would be smaller for science librarian positions than other librarian positions	11.1%

reasons that influence their applying would be relevant. For example, a candidate might be attracted to a position for reasons other than the science aspect; such as supervisory responsibilities, helping to lead digital initiatives, instructional duties, or budgeting for acquisitions of science databases. One of our respondents states that their, "position involves (the) supervisory/management duties which I was seeking." These skills, which are not exclusive to those with formal science degrees, may also be extremely significant to the institutions' and departments' needs. Respondents also indicated that they were influenced to apply because they either felt qualified for the position based on the job advertisement or because they had previous experience related to science libraries. One author felt compelled to apply for a librarian position at the university where she had previously worked for 5 years since she had established collegial relationships. She felt prepared to take a leap into a lesser know subject area in order to gain further skill at providing subject specific reference support. The previous work that she had done placing orders for science materials also served to inform her of what kinds of collections the science library was building and where the interests of the researchers were leading. The challenge of working in her current position appealed to her and the knowledge that her role as a science reference librarian would reflect directly upon the science library's contributions to the research needs of the university was a strong motivator for her to apply; as was the desire for her to succeed.

Explanations as to what influenced our respondents to apply to their current science librarian positions, as listed in the "Other" category of Table 2, could be categorized under four general headings:

- Personal or family reasons, e.g., they were moving to a new area.
- Left industry for private or academic sector, e.g., they were downsized.
- Desired to work somewhere else, e.g., they wanted room for growth, to escape difficulties in a previous workplace, or to supervise.
- Admitted to having luck, e.g., they were in the right place at the right time.

These reasons are fairly universal and, in and of themselves, are not specific to the desire to work as a "science" librarian. However, they do factor into the equation of why these individuals may have ended up applying for their current positions.

How do salary expectations make an impact on the type of positions librarians are applying for? If academic science librarians have higher salaries than other academic librarians, candidates could conceivably be attracted to this specialty as opposed to other library specialties. *LJ's* 2004 Annual Placement and Salary Survey reported that "colleges and universities (have the) greatest difficulty in hiring librarians due to lower pay, even though there was an increase in academic salaries of 7.28% in 2004" (Maatta, 2005). As a baseline, one must first look at average salaries for all librarians in academic libraries. According to the 2006-2007 *Occupational Outlook Handbook*, the median salary for all academic librarians in 2004 was nearly $47,830 (Bureau of Labor Statistics, 2006-2007). More than five years earlier, the average salary reported in Winston's 1998 survey of academic science librarians was already between $45,000 and $50,000 (Winston, 2001).

Additional evidence can be found showing that differences in salary based on subject discipline do exist. For example, in the August 2005 issue of *The Chronicle of Higher Education*, two positions at the same university were in the same advertisement. Other than mentioning the different departments that the librarians would serve as in their respective liaison roles, the requested qualifications were identically described for both positions using the same sentences. The end of the ad stated that the English Librarian was to be given a minimum salary of $38,000 and the Science Librarian a minimum salary of $42,000. Our survey results (Table 2) present an interesting contradiction to salary concerns being discussed within various library spheres, i.e., low salaries are making it harder to recruit individuals into the field. The low survey results (11.1%) indicate that a higher salary was not considered to be a factor that greatly influenced the respondents to apply for their current science librarian positions. Whereas it cannot be denied that livelihood is important, salary in and of itself may not be ranked as one of the top or deciding motivations for pursuing an academic library position due to the nature of what draws people to the library profession in general. Ho, in an essay titled, "Rationalizing Anxiety," argues that perhaps a "passion for scholarly work" makes those in academia more "willing to sacrifice financial rewards ... (because) ... Academics value the status of an institutional affiliation more than the money that goes with it" (Ho, 2006).

Looking at other survey results regarding reasons that they applied, an inference could be made that those hired into science librarian positions from 2003-2005 had a previous desire for this type of work. Of the choices influencing the respondents' decisions to apply, the highest percentage (69.4%) confirmed that they desired work as a librarian in a science-related subject area. This interest could have been established before starting a search for jobs. While in library school, for example, the thought that they might someday work in a science subject area would have been a motivating factor to take coursework supporting this possibility. Both authors attended library programs that offered a science technology resources course; one took the course and one did not; although she had considered it, but at the time it did not fit her schedule. She has recently considered auditing the course and has also been provided access to the courseware of a colleague teaching a science resources online MLIS course at another university.

Out of the 77.1% of respondents who confirmed that their library schools offered a course specific to science/technology resources (Table 3), 70.4% of the survey respondents indicated that they took the course. In regards to their reason for taking the course, only one person indicated "elective" as an answer. The others, even those who stated that the course was an elective, further explained that they wanted to know more about science resources and/or they wanted to become a science

TABLE 3. Years Experience: Science Resources Course Offered at Library School

Years in MLIS position	Took a MLIS Science Resources Course	Did not take MLIS Science Resources Course	MLIS Science Resources Course NOT offered	**Totals**
Less Than 1 year	3	1	3	**7**
1-2 years	3	1	3	**7**
3-4 years	3	2	0	**3**
5-6 years	3	0	0	**3**
7-8 years	3	3	0	**4**
9-10 years	3	0	0	**1**
10+ years	7	1	2	**10**
Totals	**19**	**8**	**8**	**35**

librarian. The authors find it intriguing to note that librarians who attended a library school not offering a science resources course tended to have 2 or fewer years of professional experience.

BACKGROUND IN THE SCIENCES

In addition to taking a science resources course in library school, prior interest in the sciences is reflected in both the librarians' formal (a degree) and informal backgrounds. Our findings parallel earlier studies. In Hackenberg and Chu's 1999 survey, "61% had a background in the sciences and 39% indicated that whereas they had no background in the sciences they did have an interest in the sciences" (Hackenberg and Chu, 2004). Their results compare to our survey results with undergraduate degrees in the sciences held by 66.6% of our respondents in areas of study ranging from computer science to animal science. The other 33.3% completed undergraduate degrees in such non-science fields as history and linguistics. When our respondents were asked if they agreed that having a formal degree in the sciences is important to their work as a science librarian, the following results were seen (Table 4).

In an expected result, most who disagreed with the statement that a science background is needed to perform their work as science librarians

TABLE 4. Importance of Science Degree

	Strongly Disagree	Disagree	Neither Agree nor Disagree	Agree	Strongly Agree
Science degree is important to my work as a science librarian	0%	17%	14%	42%	28%

did not have an educational background in the sciences. Their degrees were: Education, English Literature, International Relations, General Studies in Mathematics, English & Marine Science, and History. Conversely, those with an undergraduate degree in the sciences strongly agreed with the statement, but were also represented in the categories of "Agree" and "Neither Agree nor Disagree." When attempting to find possible differences in opinion between those new (working with MLIS in field for 2 or less years) and those established (working with MLIS in field for 10 or more years), no significant differences, at least in the strongly agree category, were seen. The new librarians' results were that 14.29% disagreed, 50% agreed, and 35.71% strongly agreed on whether a science degree was important. Of the respondents representing those in the field for the longest time, 22.2% disagreed, 22.22 agreed, and 44.44% strongly agreed with the statement. As previously mentioned, many individuals obtain their MLIS after obtaining other Master's levels degrees or after several years of work experience. Three of our survey respondents in the age range of 31-54 had less than 1 year experience in a position requiring a MLIS, yet one also had an additional Master's in Genetics, one a Ph.D. in Pharmacology, and one had two BS degrees. Obviously, then, a new librarian does not necessarily mean a person who is young in age and/or experience. Many factors that relate to having prior life and career experiences are important and should be considered. One of the authors had been working in the library field without a MLIS for 20 years. The learning opportunities from positions held at academic libraries, a medical library, and other special libraries during these years were invaluable to her in establishing her new role as an Engineering Librarian. The other author has been working in positions requiring an MLIS for over 10 years, 7 years within academic science libraries, but had no library experience prior to obtaining her MLIS. Both authors are close in age and fall near the middle of the 31-54 year range. Our education and experiences are different; however we have in common the MLIS.

To further explore opportunities for and attitudes toward additional educational and learning methods besides a formal science degree, all respondents were asked to "share any comments that you may have on the need for a science subject-specific background for your current position." Here are some of the points they make:

- "The willingness to help/provide service is more important than any kind of formal degree."
- "A will to learn about the sciences is necessary no matter what kind of educational background the librarian possesses."
- "Work experience in a non-academic, corporate environment provides perspective on how information is being used in the real world."
- "The academic environment is becoming increasingly complex and interdisciplinary; therefore, the science librarian has to adapt to various subjects since typical liaison responsibilities include more than one academic department."
- "Science blogs are one means of staying informed of relevant developments."
- "Having previous non-professional work experience or an internship in a science library is very useful for learning about science librarianship."

Several librarians, including those with and those without a science degree, mentioned the critical qualities that a science librarian must possess in order to maintain a high quality of professionalism. These include:

- Understanding the terminology/language of the relevant scientific fields.
- Understanding the flow of scientific literature (i.e., scholarly communication process).
- Having credibility with faculty.

Both groups expressed positive comments about the usefulness of a science education. Even if they felt that the degree was not a requirement, they implied that their work is or would be easier and more fulfilling to them with this kind of formal background. One respondent stated, "... it's certainly not an absolute requirement ... I'm grateful for it, though." Another respondent with degrees in Geography and Urban

Planning said, "At times I wish I had more subject knowledge especially in chemistry—but I find that willingness to help is the primary requirement for this job."

ADDDRESSING THE DEBATE

The debate becomes one of opinion, with those who believe that a science degree is a requirement for their work or position and others who feel that relevant and sufficient experience can be gained without the science degree. These contrasting viewpoints are also reflected in the "debate" literature. Not only do some believe that the science degree is a requirement, but, taking it a step further, they also believe that the science degree is more important than the MLIS for employment in an academic science library. Stuart (BA History) and Drake (BS Economic Analysis) neither a formal science undergraduate degree, writing an article in 1992 titled, "Sci-Tech Libraries of the Future," are vehement about the importance of the science degree. They argued, "The quality of information services provided to scientists and engineers is less effective when the librarians serving them have little or no experience in these disciplines … Perhaps the time has come to seriously consider dropping the library degree as a requirement for science and engineering library positions. Libraries could focus their energy on developing recruitment programs which identify and attract freshly minted scientists and engineers directly into the ranks" (Stuart and Drake, 1992).

To some extent, their proposal to drop the MLIS as a requirement has come true in the present day academic library. Wilder's analysis of the 1998 Association of Research Libraries (ARL) survey discovered that between 1990-1998, there was a definite 'rise' (72% of all hires during that time period) in "Functional Specialist" positions within academic libraries (defined as specialists who do not necessarily possess an MLIS degree), which "accounted for nearly one-quarter of all hiring in 1998" with "about 55% (having) MLIS degrees" (Wilder, 1998). Neal writes in his article, "Raised by Wolves" that, "Academic libraries now hire an increasing number of individuals to fill professional librarian positions who do not have the master's degree in library science . . . they hire staff to fill librarian positions who hold a variety of qualifications, such as advanced degrees in subject disciplines, specialized language skills, teaching experience, or technology expertise" (Neal, 2006). Neal does not imply that this is necessarily a negative trend; rather, he advises those of us in the library profession to carefully track this development.

Some people possessing a science degree, or even an advanced degree in another subject area, may view the MLIS as an unnecessary "hoop to jump through" to qualify them for an academic science librarian position, thereby causing a possible alienation, to use Neal's words, within the "culture of the profession." In fact, a respondent in the survey for this article went so far as to say, "I feel that my library science degree is of minimal importance to my job. In contrast, my background in the science is quite valuable to my job." The reasons why someone decides to pursue a career in library science may affect their overall perspective on the profession. Neal makes the observation that ideally, the pursuit of obtaining the MLIS is "a positive orientation to a new professional adventure" due to a "profound interest in and commitment to the service goals of librarianship" but that the pursuit could just as easily be "a reflection of a personal disappointment and compromise"; i.e., not able to secure a position in their original profession due to "limited opportunities" or "a problematic fit between previous job [non-library] and personal aspirations" (Neal, 2006).

DEVELOPING CORE COMPETENCIES AND EXPERIENCE

Responses to the question, "Rate your agreement as to the importance of the following resources to your continuing knowledge in your role as a Science librarian," indicate a high regard for mentoring, collegial collaboration and relationships in the science librarian's career. This question was asked in order to ascertain the degree of importance placed on the types of activities and resources being utilized for obtaining ongoing, professional knowledge.

Survey responses (Table 5) indicate that collaboration with colleagues via mentoring, conferences, and professional groups are ranked as the two strongest contributors to knowledge development activities. "Mentor and Colleague Collaborations" received a slightly lower percent of combined Agree/Strongly Agrees (80%) than the combined 88% of "Professional Organizations and Conferences"; however, "Mentor and Colleague Collaborations" received the highest percentage of Strongly Agrees than any of the other categories. Librarians' work activities have been continuously redefined due in large part to rapid changes in technology. The creation of seamless information environments and the increasing use of collaborative technologies;

TABLE 5. Rank of Resources Contributing to Continuing Knowledge

Contributing Resource and/or Activity	Percent of 'Strongly Agree' & 'Agree' Combined
Professional Organizations & Conferences	88%
Mentor and colleague collaboration	80%* *highest "strongly agree" response
Current Awareness Literature	82%
Listservs/Blogs/Websites	77%
Instructional Activities	77%
Independent Study	75%
Professional Development Workshops	66%
Continuing Education Courses	66%
Committee Work	40%

one-to-one, one-to-many and many-to-many exchanges are greatly impacting the day-to-day work of librarians. As such, there has been an increased awareness and a push for pursuing opportunities that allow for more cross-disciplinary collaborations. Neal points out that academic librarians have come to recognize the need to take a more active role in "broad collaborations both on campus and externally by expanding their teaching activities, innovatively implementing and using technology, and getting more involved with research teams" (Neal, 2006). Although our survey did not ask respondents to elaborate on the colleagues with whom they were collaborating, one natural group for academic (including science) librarians to forge relationships with are the teaching faculties within their institutions. It has been the experience of the authors that collaboration with departmental faculty can build and enhance working relationships within their academic institutions, thus increasing opportunities for "faculty to discover the extent of what the library and librarians have to offer (them and) their students" (Callison, Thomes and Budny, 2005). Including and involving librarians into the projects and programs that impact students demonstrates that we are perceived to possess "credibility" with our teaching faculty. Collaboration with fellow science librarian colleagues has likewise allowed for valuable professional development. Importantly, these interactions have been both with science librarian colleagues who do not possess a science degree and those that do. An emphasis on the will to learn what a librarian can about an unfamiliar subject is really essential and was brought to light by a few of our respondents. One said, "Although I don't think it is necessary that science librarians have a background in the sciences, it is necessary for them to have the will to want to learn about the sciences, if they don't have the background. Taking classes in departments or just sitting in on departmental seminars has added to my knowledge and expertise with my departments. For though I have a background in the sciences, my departments concentrate on areas other than those I specialized in during my undergraduate experience." Shortly after beginning her position and supporting the Materials Science and Engineering department as part of her new role, one of the author's colleagues promptly suggested that she read the 1998 ASM-American Society for Metals title by Harry Chandler, *Metallurgy for the Non-Metallurgist*. These types of popular works in the sciences provide another means for those lacking a science degree to learn more of the terminology of the subject in question.

In addition to collaborating with teaching faculty, formal mentoring programs and informal mentoring relationships with other library professionals can also play a powerful role in the work experience of new hires; even if the new hires are "seasoned" professionals. Mentors provide essential encouragement and support to their colleagues via these mentoring relationships. The value of mentoring is reflected in some of the survey responders' comments, such as "more learning is done through mentors than through formal education programs" and "a lot of learning really takes place through on the job training and other experiences on the job." Professionals in related science and technology fields, such as IT, also view mentoring as means for success. Margaret Hilton's 2001 research summary for the *Monthly Labor Review* states that, "Those IT (information technology) professionals who were able to build communications ties with experienced workers in their field had the most successful job performance" (Hilton, 2001). Both of the authors consider themselves fortunate to have had several excellent mentors establish supportive relationships with us in the beginning of our careers. As we have progressed within the profession, these collegial interactions have continued to evolve and expand and have allowed us to mentor in kind. Mentoring can also take on a greater significance in certain institutional environments, because science librarians may not be within the same building as other librarian colleagues. For instance, the survey also asked for a description of the physical space in which they work. Work locations ranged from a department, separate from the main library (37.1%) and a science collection incorporated within the main library (28.6%). Depending upon their respective physical work spaces, either limited or ample opportunities will exist for frequent interactions with faculty, students, and colleagues. Mentoring relationships, in this instance, can help strengthen professional relationships by increasing opportunities for communication.

Of the three categories involving more "traditional" or formal means of knowledge obtainment (Independent Study, Continuing Education, and Professional Development); "Independent Study" received the highest percentage (75%) of Agree/Strongly Agrees. Whereas 66% of the respondents Agreed/Strongly Agreed that "Continuing Education" and "Professional Development Workshops" were contributors, they also received the highest percent, 35% combined of Strongly Disagree/Disagree and Neutral responses.

"Committee Work" was also considered to be a lesser contributor to learning activities with only 40% Agree/Strongly Agree (combined) and 23% Strongly Disagree/Disagree (combined); yet a large percent (97.1%) responded that "Committee Work" was required in their current position. The majority (more than 90%) indicate that "Reference," "Instruction," and "Collection Development" are also part of their current responsibilities. As revealed in another survey question asking them to, "Estimate the percentage of total time spent at all job-related duties that involve knowledge of science resources," 42.9% of the respondents calculated that 26-50% of their duties involve the knowledge of science resources; an equal percent (42.9%) reported a much higher percentage, calculating 51-75% of their time is spent on activities requiring a knowledge of science resources. Naturally, the responsibilities and duties that any particular science librarian will have at his or her place of employment will vary and may reflect how they perceive themselves as learning and developing within their positions.

In the article, "Leaving Science for LIS: Interview and a Survey of Librarians with Scientific and Technical Degrees," Hallmark and Lembo point out that, "The challenge of producing qualified science librarians can be addressed either by attracting scientists and engineers to schools of LIS or by educating LIS students and graduates in science-technology disciplines" (Hallmark and Lembo, 2003). How much of being "qualified" can be reached through relying on these other resources and activities (Table 5) by the science librarian without a science degree–and who further did not have exposure to science subject specialty training as part of the MLIS program–continues to be an issue for discussion and further research. One survey respondent mentions the value she place on her science degree but also praises a colleague who does not have a formal science degree but had previous work experience in a science library. She says, "My general life long interest in science certainly helps inform my approach to working with students and others. While I do not have in depth knowledge related to many of the questions or issues I work on, the vocabulary is familiar and my background gives me a basis to begin my librarian science related tasks. While I feel that my science degree and additional comp sci [computer science] courses helps me in my position, I can say with certainty that the chemistry librarian here does an excellent job and does not have a science degree, but did have a fellowship in a science library."

JOB SATISFACTION

Job satisfaction can naturally be seen as one indicator of continuation within a position or career. Interestingly, when asked if they are planning to continue working as a science librarian, none of the survey respondents for this article responded "very unlikely" or "somewhat unlikely," and only 8.6% were uncertain. The majority replied that they do plan to continue working as a science librarian; with 22.9% saying it was "somewhat likely" and 68.6% saying it was "very likely." A 1998 survey of librarians' job satisfaction, by van Reenen, found that librarians who planned to be working in the same library five years hence were "significantly more satisfied than persons with other plans," and that "experienced employees were more satisfied than those with less experience." The factor that consistently scored the highest ratings in job satisfaction was "working directly with customers" (van Reenen, 1998). Whether or not science librarians we surveyed find satisfaction in their direct dealings with patrons was not measured. However, the majority do appear to be interacting directly with patrons via their reference and instruction duties (Table 5). The largest response (82.4%) for the question asking respondents to "Describe your non-formal background in science" was that they discuss science related information needs with their patrons (Table 6). Collection development duties were also ranked high (97%) in answer to the question regarding responsibilities of their positions. Although the survey does not rank how the science librarians enjoy these duties or even how they rate their importance, the fact that they are involved in decisions on the types of materials their institutions are collecting is relevant to their need to learn what areas their researchers are involved in. As far as satisfaction, Hallmark and Lembo also report that "scientists-turned-librarians had no idea that the library profession was so interesting, challenging and enjoyable . . ." and that since the ". . . general public (still) continues to

TABLE 6: Non-Formal Background in Science

Discuss with patrons their science related information needs	82.4%
View/listen to popular science pieces on television, radio, and/or Internet	79.4%
Read science section of newspapers	70.6%
Read popular science publications	61.8%
Participate or have participated in science related activities, such as non-credit courses or science fairs	58.8%
Read parts of textbooks and/or reference books	55.9%
Have family members that work in science-related field	50%
Have science-related hobbies	50%

(view) librarians" in a stereotypical fashion . . ." it is up to the individuals within the profession to locate, recruit (and retain) the likely candidates who can play a critical role in our field" (Hallmark and Lembo, 2003).

At least 50% or more of the respondents replied positively to the other categories (Table 6), indicating a broad range of ways that they stay abreast of scientific developments. Respondents provided additional information regarding "other" non-formal science interests. Several mentioned volunteer work. For example, one respondent volunteered as an interpretive nature leader and another volunteers as a museum docent. Others are active with community groups, including one librarian who served as a board member for a state flora survey. Another person simply stated, "I have always had an interest or curiosity to learn 'how things work.'" Over half (50%) of the respondents have hobbies or family members that revolve around the sciences. One of the author's family is comprised entirely of 'scientists': medical professionals and engineers–including her husband (computer scientist); thus she was surrounded, and continues to be immersed, in science topics and methods on a daily basis.

ROLE OF THE HIRING INSTITUTION

Questioning academic institutions on the reasons why they hired librarians without a science background should be a subject for more study. It is doubtful that academic libraries would reply that they had zero applicants with science backgrounds; but that for overriding reasons, the candidate without the science degree was a better match for their particular situation. Institutions must be considering these "other" qualifications, rather than just educational backgrounds, if for no other reason than that their job announcements consistently list an increasing number of expectations. Osorio studied this in a 1999 article, "An Analysis of Science-Engineering Academic Library Positions in the Last Three Decades." He looked at the years, 1976, 1986, and 1998 to evaluate the text of job ads. He concluded that ". . . a remarkable increase in required, preferred, desired qualifications and job responsibilities has occurred in the last three decades" (Osorio, 1999). Hiring institutions could also recognize that all of a candidates' experiences, rather than just a certain degree alone, are what is needed to make a good employee. Hilton's analysis of reports to the National Academies of Sciences substantiates that "Recruiters and employers recognize the power of learning through experience. In job advertisements and in IT workforce committee testimony, employers often stressed that demonstrated ability and experience were the most important hiring factors–college degrees and ranking were secondary factors" (Salzman, 1999).

The need to attract graduates to work as science librarians appears urgent when coupled with broader workforce concerns as they relate to professional education, cultural perceptions, aging workforce, and retirement. These issues should neither be underestimated nor viewed with apprehension; however, they should be monitored. Although this article has briefly touched upon some of these trends and how they may impact the available pool of candidate for science library positions, those trends are complex in nature and deserve additional, in-depth study.

SERENDIPITUOUS SCIENCE LIBRARIANS: MAKING THE ACCIDENTAL PURPOSEFUL

Emphasis has been placed on the perspectives regarding the educational background of academic science librarians. However, science librarians should possess traits that one would want in any employee; dedication, reliability, flexibility, and honesty. Modern librarians, including science librarians, are analogous to detectives; they need to have strong interviewing and listening skills, the ability to present the facts and verify citations, the know-how to conduct research using the appropriate resources, and the willingness to spend the time needed in seeking answers. These investigative librarians will detect that the student needing a document entitled CAMP is really referring to Current Advances in Materials and Processes, and not Computer Architecture for Machine Perception. Science librarians could be seen as explorers; possessing a mix of the competencies, skills and experiences needed to navigate their information seekers through the information labyrinth in order to discover the wealth of resources available to address their information needs. In this role, librarians are not just experts dispensing information, but guides who can recognize and create opportunities for enhancing the library experience of their patrons. In addition, science librarians, like other librarians, are called upon to have teaching skills to direct users to the particularities of various modern databases and their interfaces and to recommend which databases would be most relevant to the needs of their particular institution's users. Librarians need to recognize the various learning styles and cultures of their users in order to best direct them towards becoming more self-sufficient in their research.

Often heard in informal collegial discussions are the statements, "I didn't start out to be a librarian, it sort of happened by "accident" or "I didn't plan on becoming a____librarian." It is more likely that cultivated approaches, rather than "accidents," are occurring; and that these methods result in professional and career success. We agree with Friedel that, "Serendipity . . . does not simply refer to "happy accidents." Insight is every bit as important as the accident. Simply to stumble upon something of value . . . requires a mental capacity that goes beyond the obvious" (Friedel, 2001). A philosophical stance would be to say that preparedness meets opportunity, thus striving to be prepared creates a self-fulfilling prophecy or as Louis Pasteur stated, "In the field of observation, chance favors only the prepared mind." As a collective group, librarians tend to actively support and engage in the continuous learning process, as it is deeply entrenched in the library profession. The authors collectively agree that our profession motivates us–if a problem is becoming persistent within our profession, we want to help resolve it. We allow our MLIS to act as our authority.

Science librarians who may be perceived to lack subject authority by the communities they work with, because they do not have a science degree or that they entered the field serendipitously, in actuality bring a unique perspective and other strengths to their position. These librarians can confer, collaborate, and contribute in a myriad of ways. Many of the survey participants, regardless of their educational background, feel that the desire and motivation to learn about the sciences is a crucial quality to successfully perform their duties as a science librarian. One could speculate that science librarians feeling unsure in a work situation will make the conscientious effort that is needed in order to explore and understand an unknown science subject area. The library profession serves us well in this effort, as it is designed to equip us with the types of research competencies that are needed to both teach others as well as to build upon own knowledge base. Possessing knowledge of information resources and retrieval skills, reference librarians help to find information for their users on any number of topics and subjects. As subject specialists, whether in the humanities, sciences, social sciences, law, medicine, business, etc., librarians strive to know about the prominent journals and researchers in the field. Librarians trained in understanding how documents are organized and classified are proficient at retrieving information, and can advise researchers on the appropriate subject terms and keywords to use in searching both controlled language databases and web search engines. Librarians also become adept at recognizing what a researcher needs; and that when a researcher asks, "Do you have the Journal of Thermology?" what she really wants is the journal titled Thermology. Experienced librarians knows that a library user's concept of "one stop shopping" should really mean "first stop shopping," and that true customer service hinges on our ability to reveal obscure links and resources.

Even though they might not be an "expert" in any one field, librarians can gain much from their interactions with their users. Reference transactions will spark an interest in the librarian, prompting the desire to learn more on the topic; leading to an opportunity to follow-up with the user. The process of developing relationships with users is what will establish librarians as approachable authority figures.

To be seen as a legitimate profession, Neal describes the need for "cultural authority" that he contends may be or may be not achieved in library science programs alone. If librarians are obtaining their "socialization into the profession," Neal suggests that other professionals coming to work in academic libraries, the "untamed librarians" will also need to be provided many opportunities by library administration in order for all "employees to 'pack' together more routinely." Subject librarians need to keep abreast of their own specialty, but being aware of other fields and subject resources is necessary and valuable in this ever interconnected and interdisciplinary world. The key for science librarians, as with many other library specialties, is to acknowledge that the field necessitates a commitment to ongoing training and professional development.

As the library profession continues to evolve and adapt to new needs, the goal for academic libraries will be to hire science librarians who are able to cultivate their skill sets, backgrounds, and experiences in order to benefit the organization. Evidence continues to support the importance of the role of mentors, a foundation in the field of librarianship, and opportunities to study subject specialty resources.

What has been gleaned from studying the survey results for this article does not really resolve the debate on whether or not a science degree is a necessary ingredient for an academic science librarian. Points have been made to redirect and focus the discussion on the host of factors and skills sets that science librarians should possess, foremost being a strong interest in both the sciences and the research needs of our scientists.

REFERENCES

Bureau of Labor Statistics. 2006-2007. *Occupational Outlook Handbook.* http://www.bls.gov/oco/ocos068.htm (accessed March 23, 2006).

Callison, Rachel, Kate Thomes, and Dan Budny. 2005. Library research project for first year engineering students: results from collaboration by teaching and library faculty. *The Reference Librarian* 43(89/90): 93-106.

Friedel, Robert. Serendipity is no accident. *The Kenyon Review.* Spring 2001. 23(2): 36

GAO-04-069. 2004. Gender issues: women's participation in the sciences has increased but agencies need to do more to ensure compliance with Title IX. July 2004, http://www.gao.gov/new.items/ d04639.pdf (accessed March 23, 2006).

Hackenberg, Jill M. and Barbara Chu. 2002. Why does one choose sci-tech librarianship? Findings of a survey. *Science & Technology Libraries* 23(1): 3-16.

Hallmark, Julie and Mary Frances Lembo. 2003. Leaving Science for LIS: Interviews and a survey of librarians with scientific and technical degrees. *Issues in Science and Technology Librarianship* Spring 2003, http://www.istl.org/03-spring/refereed1.html (accessed March 23, 2006).

Hilton, Margaret. 2001. Information Technology workers in the new economy. *Monthly Labor Review* June 2001, http://www.bls.gov/opub/mlr/2001/06/ressum2.htm (accessed March 23, 2006).

Ho, B. 2006. Rationalizing Anxiety. *Chronicle of Higher Education* Wednesday, February 22, 2006, http://chronicle.com/jobs/news/2006/02/2006022201c/careers.html (accessed March 23, 2006).

Jones, Mary Lou Baker, Mary Frances Lembo, James E. Monasco, and John H. Sandy. 2002. Recruiting entry-level sci-tech librarians: An analysis of job advertisements and outcome searches. *Sci-Tech News* May 2002: 12-16.

Lynch, Mary Jo, Stephen Tordella, and Thomas Godfrey. 2005. Retirement and Recruitment: A deeper look. *American Libraries* January 2005, http://www.ala.org/ala/ors/reports/recruitretire/recruitretire-adeeperlook.pdf (accessed March 23, 2006).

Maatta, Stephanie. 2005. Closing the gap: placements and salaries 2004." *Library Journal* October 15, 2005, http://www.libraryjournal.com/article/CA6269428.html (accessed March 23, 2006).

Mayer, Jennifer and Lori Terrill. 2005. Academic librarians' attitudes about advanced-subject degrees." *College & Research Libraries* January 2005, http://www.ala.org/ala/acrl/acrlpubs/crljournal/backissues2005a/crljan05/mayer.pdf (accessed March 23, 2006).

Neal, James G. 2006. Raised by wolves. *Library Journal* February 15, 2006, http://www.libraryjournal.com/article/CA6304405.html (accessed March 23, 2006).

Osorio, Nestor L. 1999. An analysis of science-engineering academic library positions in the last three decades. *Issues in Science and Technology Librarianship* Fall 1999, http://www.library.ucsb.edu/istl/99-fall/article2.html (accessed March 23, 2006).

"Sagacity." *Oxford English Dictionary* from Oxford English Dictionary Online. http://dictionary.oed.com/ (accessed March 23, 2006).

Salzman, Hal. 1999. Information Technology Labor Markets: Preliminary report to the NAS Committee on workforces needs in information technology, December 8 1999. In Hilton, Margaret. 2001. Information Technology workers in the new economy. *Monthly Labor Review*, http://www.bls.gov/opub/mlr/2001/06/ressum2.htm (accessed March 23, 2006).

"Serendib." *Encyclopædia Britannica* from Encyclopædia Britannica Online. http://search.eb.com/eb/article-9066828 (accessed March 23, 2006).

Slutsky, Bruce. 1991. How to avoid science anxiety among science librarians. *Science & Technology Libraries* 12(1): 11-19.

Stuart, Crit and Miriam A. Drake. 1992. Education and recruitment of science and engineering librarians. *Science & Technology Libraries* 12(4): 79-89.

van Reenen, Johann. 1998. Librarians at work; Are we as satisfied as other American workers. *Information Outlook* 2(7): 23-28.

Wilder, Stanley. 1998. The changing profile of research library professional staff, http://www.arl.org/newsltr/208_209/chgprofile.html (accessed March 23, 2006).

Williams, Elizabeth Nut et al. 1998. Perceptions of Serendipity: Career Paths of Prominent Academic Women in Counseling Psychology. *Journal of Counseling Psychology* 45(4): 379-389.

Winston, Mark. D. 2001. Academic science and engineering librarians: A research study of demographics, educational backgrounds, and professional activities. *Science & Technology Libraries* 19(2): 3-24.

doi: 10.1300/J122v27n01_06

APPENDIX

TEXT OF THE E-MAIL SENT WITH QUESTIONNAIRE:
We are targeting academic science librarians who have been hired to their current positions during the time period 2003 to the present. Are we describing you? If so, would you consider taking a few minutes to complete this survey? Or, if we are not describing you, would you kindly consider forwarding this e-mail to an eligible colleague?

Our goal is to gain insight into your background–what kind of formal education do you possess and how has this been an influence in your daily duties as a science librarian?

The questionnaire should take no more than 15 minutes to answer. These responses are confidential. Survey results will be presented in an article on the topic that will be appearing in a special issue of Science and Technology Libraries.

For questions or comments please contact:
Donna Beck
Rachel Callison

Made from Scratch:
The Creation and Development
of a Sciences Librarian

Peter Fritzler

SUMMARY. Science librarianship is a distinct occupation within the larger library profession. Drawing on my own experiences this article will discuss how librarians without scientific backgrounds at small institutions can position themselves to attain basic knowledge in the sciences–thus, increasing the effectiveness of library service and aligning themselves to fill the impending gap in science librarianship. doi: 10.1300/J122v27n01_07 *[Article copies available for a fee from The Haworth Document Delivery Service: 1-800-HAWORTH. E-mail address: <docdelivery@ haworthpress.com> Website: <http://www.HaworthPress.com> © 2006 by The Haworth Press, Inc. All rights reserved.]*

KEYWORDS. Non-formally trained science librarians, continuing education, professional development, information technology, RSS, library-faculty interactions

---

Peter Fritzler is Sciences Librarian, University of North Carolina Wilmington (E-mail: fritzlerp@uncw.edu).

[Haworth co-indexing entry note]: "Made from Scratch: The Creation and Development of a Sciences Librarian." Fritzler, Peter. Co-published simultaneously in *Science & Technology Libraries* (The Haworth Information Press, an imprint of The Haworth Press, Inc.) Vol. 27, No. 1/2, 2006, pp. 99-111; and: *Recruiting, Training, and Retention of Science and Technology Librarians* (ed: Patricia A. Kreitz, and JoAnn DeVries) The Haworth Information Press, an imprint of The Haworth Press, Inc., 2006, pp. 99-111. Single or multiple copies of this article are available for a fee from The Haworth Document Delivery Service [1-800-HAWORTH, 9:00 a.m. - 5:00 p.m. (EST). E-mail address: docdelivery@haworthpress.com].

Available online at http://stl.haworthpress.com
© 2006 by The Haworth Press, Inc. All rights reserved.
Digital Object Identifier: 10.1300/J122v27n01_07

Knowledge is of two kinds. We know a subject ourselves, or we know where we can find information upon it.

–Samuel Johnson

INTRODUCTION

Science librarianship is a distinct occupation within the larger library profession. Given the complexities and unique characteristics of the sciences, there has been significant discussion regarding the need for librarians to have scientific backgrounds when working in those fields. With increasing specialization in scientific research and transformations in information technology, some librarians have questioned the usefulness of the science degree as a prerequisite and have instead emphasized the librarian's role in preparing students to be information literate and lifelong learners. And with the impending retirement of many science librarians some have questioned how the profession will attract new recruits. Drawing on my own experiences this article will discuss how librarians without scientific backgrounds at smaller institutions can position themselves to attain basic knowledge in the sciences–thus, increasing the effectiveness of library service and aligning themselves to fill the retirement gap in science librarianship.

LITERATURE REVIEW

Debates regarding the need for undergraduate or graduate training in the sciences as a prerequisite for science librarianship have abounded for over forty years (Krupp 1984, Haselbauer 1984; Frank 1989; Frank and Kollen 1989; Stuart and Drake 1992; Gibbs 1993; Liu and Allen 2001; Liu and Wei 1993; Storm and Wei 1994; Lucker 1998; Hackenberg 2000; Morris-Knower 2001). Multiple studies have gauged the number of science librarians with and without formal training in the sciences while also discussing perceptions regarding the usefulness of such a degree in their positions (Mount 1985; Dewey 1986; Liu and Wei 1995; Mosley 1995; Sandy et al., 1998; Hooper-Lane 1999; Hackenberg 2000; Winston 2001; Watson 2005). Discussions regarding the recruitment of students with science backgrounds to library school have appeared in the literature (Frank 1989; Stankus 1990; Storm and Wei 1994; Wiggins 1998; Hallmark and Trembo 2003). A few articles have also addressed methods for non-science librarians and science librarians alike to acquire and sustain scientific literacy for work in such a specialized field (Storm and Wei 1994; Peterson and Kajiwara 1999, Morris-Knower 2001). Recently, Ortega and Brown (2005) found that many physical science librarians are in the latter stages of their careers and that librarians who have non-science backgrounds may fill these vacancies.

Recruitment of science librarians is of significant concern, especially at smaller institutions. While some of these smaller schools may have prolific research programs, they may be hindered by the inability to recruit subject specialists without the competitive salaries and benefits that a larger school may offer. How can these libraries deploy their personnel resources to minimize both the severity of the knowledge gap and the lack of competitiveness in their compensation practices? Peterson and Kajiwara (1999) offer some advice and Morris-Knower (2001) discusses several methodologies that can be used as well. However, these discussions address training issues from a larger institutional perspective where subject specialists are providing training to non-science librarians or non-subject specialists are supported by specialists who can be consulted when necessary. What can one do when serving as a new sciences librarian without colleagues who can provide training or assistance relating to science librarianship? What does one do when the position of a sciences librarian is entirely new?

Given the difficulties in recruiting librarians with formal training in the sciences, I will draw on my own experiences to complement arguments for and against having a formal degree in the sciences as a prerequisite for science librarianship. Generally having fewer resources available to me for travel-related training and development, my experiences may provide methods that administrators at similar and smaller-sized institutions can use to develop their own subject specialists who lack undergraduate or advanced training in the sciences. This article may also be of use to libraries at smaller institutions looking to create a sciences position where one has not previously existed or at a smaller institution that may find it difficult to compete with larger institutions to fill its recruitment needs. Current and future librarians may also find these strategies useful in preparing themselves for positions in science and technology librarianship given the impending retirement of many sci-tech librarians.

EXPERIENCES

In the fall 2004, I assumed the position of Sciences Librarian at the University of North Carolina Wilmington (UNCW), a comprehensive level one university located on the southeastern coast of North Carolina. Previously, I had served as an outreach and public services librarian at UNCW and it had been my primary responsibility to investigate and develop opportunities for the library to partner with and/or support faculty teaching and research efforts; many of my activities involved marketing and promotion of library services to areas in the sciences. Based on these experiences the position of Sciences Librarian was created in response to the growing research and teaching efforts in the life and natural sciences on the campus, particularly in the marine sciences.

UNCW's scholarly activity in the sciences is both highly regarded and expanding. Consistently ranked nationally in the top five for undergraduate programs in marine biology, UNCW also offers graduate-level programs in biology, chemistry, geology, marine biology, and marine science, along with a newly created minor in oceanography. Following several decades of commitment to research in the marine sciences, UNCW opened the Center for Marine Science, a 75,000 square-foot facility dedicated to facilitating interdisciplinary research in the marine sciences and biotechnology. Additionally, the facility supports an office for the National Undersea Research Center; an office of the North Carolina National Estuarine Research Reserve; an office for North Carolina Sea Grant; and also operates the Aquarius underwater laboratory located off the Florida Keys. Solidifying its commitment to research in the marine environment, UNCW established a doctoral program in marine biology in the fall 2002.

With my outreach initiatives to these areas, I was asked to transition into the newly created sciences librarian position, a position that did not have a prior history at UNCW. While excited by the opportunity to work in a distinct, specialized area of librarianship, I did have some reservations about the position. Having no formal education or significant training in the sciences, how was I going to become scientifically literate? Not only would I need to learn about the sciences in general, but also in the context of research and teaching within my institution. Fortunately, I had, over the few years prior to assuming the role of sciences librarian, become increasingly interested in the sciences–particularly in coastal and marine research. Perhaps it goes without saying, but nonetheless it should be noted that for anyone to have a remote chance of being successful in a job or task, the individual should be interested in it.

Gibbs (1993) bolsters this argument stating that, "a librarian must have liveliness, enthusiasm, and the desire to keep learning."

Aside from a few undergraduate courses in biology, astronomy, and environmental studies, and a graduate course in science and technology resources during library school, I felt wholly unprepared for the position. Images of the faculty member wanting chemical information or obscure information on peptides haunted me. These fears, whether perceived or real, have been acknowledged by others in the literature and have been a central point in the debate over science degrees as a prerequisite in science librarianship. Storm and Wei (1994) found in their survey of science and technology librarians that "all [librarians] mentioned that a science librarian needed to understand the methods, culture, and language of science; knowledge they believed would be difficult to obtain without a background in science." Morris-Knower (2001) reinforced this idea when recounting a recurring nightmare of his that a "bearded grad student in Birkenstocks and a frayed Fisherman's sweater will come to the reference desk and say, 'Hi. Can you tell me what the refractive index increments of proteins like thryroglobulin and ovalbumin are?'" He then added, "These kinds of questions–about thryroglobulin or mhd–generate fear because I honestly don't know what they are referring to or if they're even in English."

The Value of Continuing Education

Continuing education can help mitigate these fears. As an important aspect of work in many professions, continuing education is especially important in librarianship as librarians need to stay abreast of the latest advances in technology and changes in education and learning styles. Lucker (1998) reinforces this by stating, "Librarians should be encouraged to take advantage of educational programs both on the local campus and externally. I have long held the view that science and engineering subject specialists could find no better way to expand their knowledge of current research than by attending undergraduate and graduate course lectures."

With support and encouragement from library administration, I have been able to take courses that have increased my knowledge of the sciences. Taking one class per semester in the sciences, I have begun to develop knowledge that has not only enhanced me personally, but also professionally. With further awareness and insight into the technical language, culture, and ethos gained through coursework, I have been able to utilize that knowledge when providing library instruction sessions and interacting with students in one-on-one and group research consultations. With a developing appreciation for scientific foundations, methods, and terminologies I have been able to better demonstrate searches in advanced databases such as *Zoological Record* and *Aquatic Sciences and Fisheries Abstracts* while being able to communicate more effectively with students about their research problems as well. It has also assisted me in collection development duties along with the selection and management of electronic resources, particularly when making decisions about resources that were not easily identifiable as being relevant to the curriculum. The point is emphasized by Herbubel (1991) who states, "An informed appreciation of a discipline's mission and growth is especially critical to collection development that supports an institution's or a department's research and instructional vision. Subject expertise can only enhance a librarian's ability to interpret the collections to students and scholars."

Aside from enriching my own perspectives on science generally, there are several ancillary observations that support arguments for continuing education regardless of formal training. By taking a class that includes a weekly laboratory, I have found occasions to work with students and teaching assistants in their environment, as well as answer questions regarding electronic access to library resources. By actively participating in the curriculum and assignments, I am able to engage students and faculty more effectively and listen for opportunities to promote library services and resources when a potential need arises. Taking classes also provides more serendipitous opportunities to interact with faculty. With many faculty and librarians bemoaning the all too familiar malaise of information overload, I have found that I can communicate with faculty more effectively when passing them in the hall or by simply poking my head in their offices. This cuts down on e-mail communication while enhancing my visibility and presence hopefully resulting in greater satisfaction among faculty that the library is truly concerned with providing adequate support. Continuing education opportunities serve to advantageously position the library by providing librarians and administrators with more information regarding student and faculty perceptions of the library. This finger on the pulse will enable libraries to serve their university communities. With these reasons in mind, library administrators should consider as many opportunities as possible to equip librarians in new positions with continuing education support in order to facilitate the greatest return for the library.

Utilizing What You Already Know

Besides coursework, there are many other resources for non-science educated librarians to begin developing literacy in the sciences. As Morris-Knower (2001) emphasizes, by being "a good reference librarian" and utilizing one's skills as a librarian, one potentially has access to a world of information through the library's catalog, online databases, Internet, and collections that will enable one to learn more about not only the sciences, but the nature of science librarianship. Given the focus on coastal and marine sciences at UNCW, I have found various encyclopedias, handbooks, and dictionaries to aid in familiarization of various topics and themes. Such resources include but are not limited to the *Encyclopedia of Coastal Science* (2005), the *Encyclopedia of Ocean Sciences* (2001), the *Handbook of Marine Science* (1997), *Encyclopedia of Marine Mammals* (2002), the *Kirk-Othmer Encyclopedia of Chemical Technology* (1997), and the *Encyclopedia of Geology* (2005). When meeting with students who are new to a topic I often utilize these materials to help them formulate their research question. These materials provide excellent summaries on the status of research and what is known about an issue or topic while also identifying individuals, studies, and other resources that have made critical contributions to the question being studied. Heeding my own advice, I often examine these resources to boost my knowledge in areas that I am lacking.

Supplementing these resources, I have several other favorites that should certainly become classics in science librarianship. These include *Using the Biological Literature: a Practical Guide* (2002), *Guide to Reference and Information Sources in Plant Biology* (2006), *How to Find Chemical Information* (1998), *Guide to Information Sources in the Physical Sciences* (2000), and the *Guide to Reference and Information Sources in the Zoological Sciences* (2003). Each of these titles is a comprehensive annotated directory identifying core resources in their respective area of study. These include indexes and abstracts, bibliographies, biographies, encyclopedias, textbooks, classification schemes, journals, handbooks, guides, and associations. Each has excellent summarizations regarding the history of study along with characteristics of the literature in that respective area of study. These are particularly useful for the librarian without formal training in the sciences who needs a crash course in that discipline. For example, the *Guide to Reference and Information Sources in the Zoological Sciences* also addresses current issues in taxonomic identification, the impact of the Internet, and various efforts underway to provide centralized access to taxonomic information.

Get Connected: Harnessing Listservs, Blogs, RSS, and Mailing Lists

Recognizing the value of one's print collection is but one tool in the aspiring librarian's toolkit. Other, more non-traditional instruments, particularly those available via the Web, also provide me with occasions to learn not only about science librarianship, but about current research, funding opportunities, and issues being discussed among scientists. These include listservs, blogs, RSS feeds, and mailing lists. One example I use regularly is *MyNSF*, a weekly e-mail digest from the National Science Foundation (NSF) detailing new scientific discoveries along with news, funding, and employment opportunities. The *MyNSF* service allows me to learn about the current state of research and issues that are affecting NSF, one of the leading funding sources for basic research in the United States. Another resource is the *FishNews* automated e-mail-based newsletter from the National Marine Fisheries Service that includes news about regulatory information, polices and programs, research opportunities, and fisheries stocks. One other valuable resource is the *Science in the News* daily digest from Sigma Xi, The Scientific Research Society, which identifies top news stories in science. This tool has been particularly helpful in staying abreast of developments occurring across the broad spectrum of scientific inquiry.

One of my favorite technologies for keeping up with the latest in scientific research is RSS. While there is some discussion about what RSS represents, "Really Simple Syndication" has been a popular translation. RSS is a particularly attractive tool as it allows the user to find out about the newest information on selected websites without having to troll through individual sites. By using an aggregator, or reader, the user can select websites from which to receive feeds in a centralized location. When new content is added the user will receive it through the aggregator service, which also helps to minimize feelings of information anxiety. Using the aggregator service, the user can centralize all feeds into one account and can check it as frequently as he or she wishes without having to worrying about checking multiple websites for recently added content. One popular aggregator is Bloglines.com, which I utilize for receiving RSS feeds. Several examples of feeds that I receive include *Environmental Health Perspectives-in-Press* (*EHP-in-Press*), news from the *National Academies*,

Chemical and Engineering News from the American Chemical Society, news from Chemical Abstracts Service, and *EurekaAlert!-Oceanography*, a feed from the American Association for the Advancement of Science containing the latest information in oceanographic research. The application of tools like RSS and weekly email newsletters has helped me immerse myself more efficiently in news about current research, debates, and discussion in the scientific community. In some cases, when I receive news via a RSS feed that is relevant to a faculty member at UNCW, I send that information to the interested party. Hopefully, this helps to make connections and further develop rapport with faculty.

Table-of-Contents Services

Periodic reviews of the primary literature are also helpful for increasing one's knowledge of the sciences. Not only does this help me to identify and learn about scientific nomenclature, but it also gives me insights into how research is conducted and shared with members of the scientific community, along with an awareness of the issues affecting scientific research. Utilizing Ingenta, I subscribe to alerts from general science journals (e.g., *Nature, Science*) along with more specialized journals in areas relevant to faculty research at UNCW. These include *Marine Biology, Estuaries, Limnology and Oceanography, Journal of Coastal Research*, and *Estuarine, Coastal and Shelf Science*. My library also maintains a faculty scholarship collection in its archives. When I see an article published in a journal that has been authored by a faculty member at UNCW, I contact the scientist to inquire about obtaining a reprint for the collection while taking time to ask questions about the research presented in the article. In some cases, I read the articles and follow up with the researcher to discuss the research further. In other cases I might ask the researcher for an opinion regarding classic papers in the field which I then read and attempt to digest. Not always, but sometimes this leads to discussions about library services and resources–and in some cases opportunities for me to provide library instruction to the faculty member's class(es).

Learn from the Best

Aside from using the Web to monitor current developments in science, I also use it to learn about what other libraries and librarians are doing as a way of learning "how it's done"–what better way to learn about science librarianship than from those that make up the profession itself? Particularly advantageous resources for doing this are listservs. While some may complain that they feel bombarded by the e-mails generated by listserv discussions, I have generally found them to be a valuable tool for asking questions, mentoring, comparing resources, resource sharing, and other issues relevant to librarianship. Several of these listservs include STS-L, a moderated discussion list sponsored by the Science and Technology Section of the Association of College and Research Libraries (ACRL); the Chemical Information Sources Discussion List (CHMINF-L), which serves as a forum for exchanging information among librarians and other practitioners in the field of chemistry; and a discussion list hosted by the International Association of Aquatic and Marine Science Libraries and Information Centers (IAMSLIC), which focuses on information issues associated with the aquatic and marine sciences. Additionally, I also regularly use the Internet to examine subject and resource guides that have been developed by science librarians at other institutions. In many cases, the sources identified in the guides have annotations indicating their usefulness and importance to the topic being studied. For example, regarding my aforementioned fear of chemistry, one of the guides that I have used often to learn about core resources in chemical research is a guide developed and maintained by Teri Vogel at the University of California, San Diego (see: http://scilib.ucsd.edu/about/people/vogel.html).

Getting Involved

Besides these strategies for self-development, one must also be active and visible to faculty and students in order to create opportunities for building and growing relationships between the library and the community it serves. In effect, the library should consider meeting its users at their level. Drawing on my experiences at UNCW, there are several methods for accomplishing this task. Regular walkthroughs of departments are helpful and hosting office hours in those departments can also be beneficial. Participating in university or departmentally sponsored organizations has been an extremely positive experience as well. For example, UNCW hosts a chapter of the Marine Mammal Stranding Network (MMSN) which provides opportunities for students to work with faculty on necropsies and stranding events when they occur in the region. When these situations occur I try to get involved and provide assistance when possible. By doing so, I feel that I have been able to connect individually with students and faculty who then recognize and understand why I'm there to help them.

CONCLUSIONS AND FUTURE RESEARCH

Science librarianship is an exciting occupation within the larger library profession. Having a degree in the sciences is certainly important and worthy of discussion. For those highly specialized libraries serving a small distinct scientific population the argument for librarians having a scientific background is of increased merit. However, smaller institutions serving diverse populations may find it more difficult to recruit librarians with such training. Such institutions seeking to employ a science librarian would do well to consider providing appropriate resources for professional development; particularly if the institution is developing the position from within its current staff; particularly if the position itself is new to the new university. It is my hope that the experiences I have described above will assist in facilitating that process.

Continued professional development is an important issue. Several questions can be addressed with future research both locally (at my institution) and across the field. Given recruitment needs and unequal hiring capabilities among universities, how do these issues impact smaller institutions, particularly those that have demonstrated prolific research and teaching activity? What can smaller universities do to cope with recruitment issues given that many specialists are recruited by larger universities with more competitive salaries? Similarly, it would be interesting to examine the effectiveness of methods used to provide training and development of sci-tech librarians who have no previous formal training or education. As the recruitment and retention issue continues, another exciting area of investigation would be to survey undergraduate and graduate perceptions of science librarianship. Perhaps a multi-university study examining these perceptions would reveal valuable information. Lastly, it may be fruitful to test a Web-based mentoring program that partners an experienced sciences librarian with a new librarian or potential sciences librarian in graduate school as a way of preparing the next generation of professionals for a career in science librarianship. This author, for one, would wholeheartedly welcome such an opportunity.

REFERENCES

Desai, Christina M. 2002. Continuing education needs of science and technology librarians: results of the 2001 STS Continuing Education Committee Survey. *Issues in Science and Technology Librarianship* 34 (Spring). http://www.istl.org/02-spring/article5.html.

Dewey, Barbara I. 1986. Science background required–others need not apply: a study of the science librarian hiring crisis. In *Proceedings of the 49th Annual Meeting of the American Society for Information Science 1986*, ed. Julie M. Hurd and Charles H. Davis, 64-68. Medford, NJ: Learned Information, Inc.

Frank, Donald G. 1989. Education for librarians in a major science-engineering library: expectations and reality. *Journal of Library Administration* 11 (3/4): 107-116.

Frank, Donald G., and Christine Kollen. 1989. Humanities and social sciences librarians in the science-engineering library: utilization and implications for effective collection development and reference services. *Science & Technology Libraries* 9 (3): 63-71.

Gibbs, Anne Beth Liebman. 1993. Subject specialization in the scientific special library. *Special Libraries* 84 (1): 1-8.

Hackenberg, Jill M. 2000. Who chooses sci-tech librarianship? *College & Research Libraries* 61 (5): 441-450.

Hallmark, Julie, and Mary Frances Lembo. 2003. Leaving science for LIS: interviews and a survey of librarians with scientific and technical degrees. *Issues in Science and Technology Librarianship* 37 (Spring). http://www.istl.org/03-spring/refereed1.html.

Haselbauer, Kathleen. 1984. The making of a science librarian. *Science & Technology Libraries* 4 (3/4): 111-116.

Herubel, Jean-Pierre V.M. 1991. To 'degree' or not to 'degree': academic librarians and subject expertise. *College & Research Library News* 52 (7): 437.

Hooper-Lane, Christopher. 1999. Spotlight on the subject knowledge of chemistry librarians: results of a survey. *Issues in Science and Technology Librarianship* 23 (Summer). http://istl.org/99-summer/article1.html.

Krupp, Robert G. 1984. What education is best? *Science & Technology Libraries* 4 (3/4): 105-109.

Liu, Lewis-Guodo, and Bryce Allen. 2001. Business librarians: their education and training. *College & Research Libraries* 62 (6): 555-563.

Liu, Meng Xiong, and Wei Wei. 1993. Science/technology librarians in California: their background, performance and expectations. *Journal of Educational Media and Library Sciences* 31 (1): 28-40.

Lucker, Jay K. 1998. The changing nature of scientific and technical librarianship: a personal perspective over 40 years. *Science & Technology Libraries* 17 (2): 3-10.

Morris-Knower, James. 2001. Phyllostachys aurea–didn't he work with Socrates? Reference work in science libraries by librarians who are not scientists. *Reference Librarian* 34 no. 72: 155-169.

Mosley, Pixey Anne. 1995. Engineers and librarians: how do they interact? *Science & Technology Libraries* 15 (1): 51-61.

Mount, Ellis. 1985. *University science and engineering libraries*. 2nd ed. Westport, CT: Greenwood Press.

Ortega, Lina, and Cecilia M. Brown. 2005. The face of 21st century physical science librarianship. *Science & Technology Libraries* 26 (2): 71-90.

Peterson, Christina, and Sandra Kajiwara. 1999. Scientific Literacy Skills for Non-Science Librarians: Bootstrap Training. *Issues in Science and Technology Librarianship* 24 (Fall). http://www.istl.org/99-fall/article3.html.

Sandy, John H., Mary Francis Lembo, and James E. Manasco. 1998. Preparation for sci-tech librarianship: results of a survey. *Sci-Tech News* 52 (1): 16-17.

Stankus, Tony. 1990. Building confidence and competence: A workshop in science journals for beginning librarians without a science background. *The Serials Librarian* 18 (3/4): 23-45.

Storm, Paula, and Wei Wei. 1994. Issues related to the education and recruitment of science/technology librarians. *Science & Technology Libraries* 14 (3): 35-42.

Stuart, Crit, and Miriam A. Drake. 1992. Education and recruitment of science and engineering librarians. *Science & Technology Libraries* 12 (4): 79-89.

Watson, Erin M. 2005. Subject knowledge in the health sciences library: an online survey of Canadian academic health sciences librarians. *Journal of the Medical Library Association* 93 (4): 459-466.

Wiggins, Gary. 1998. New directions in the education of chemistry librarians and information specialists. *Science & Technology Libraries* 17 (2): 45-58.

Winston, Mark D. 2001. Academic science and engineering librarians: a research study of demographics, educational backgrounds, and professional activities. *Science & Technology Libraries* 19 (2): 3-24.

doi: 10.1300/J122v27n01_07

Why Didn't I Hear About It Sooner? Recruiting Undergraduates into Science Librarianship

Sarah H. Jeong

SUMMARY. This article gives my personal account of how I entered the field of science librarianship. It compares these personal experiences with those of other science librarians using a brief e-mail survey sent to two active science librarian listservs, the Association of College and Research Libraries-Science & Technology Section (ACRL-STS) listserv (STS-L@LISTSERV.UTK.EDU) and the Chemical Information Sources Discussion List (CHMINF-L@LISTSERV.INDIANA.EDU). Two hundred twenty-one responses were received. This article also includes strategies for recruiting undergraduate science majors into the profession. doi: 10.1300/J122v27n01_08 *[Article copies available for a fee from The Haworth Document Delivery Service: 1-800-HAWORTH. E-mail address: <docdelivery@ haworthpress.com> Website: <http://www.HaworthPress.com> © 2006 by The Haworth Press, Inc. All rights reserved.]*

KEYWORDS. Recruitment, science librarianship, undergraduates, survey

Sarah H. Jeong, Science Librarian, Z. Smith Reynolds Library, Wake Forest University, P.O. Box 7777 Reynolda Station, Winston-Salem, NC 27109 (E-mail: jeongsh@wfu.edu).

[Haworth co-indexing entry note]: "Why Didn't I Hear About It Sooner? Recruiting Undergraduates into Science Librarianship." Jeong, Sarah H. Co-published simultaneously in *Science & Technology Libraries* (The Haworth Information Press, an imprint of The Haworth Press, Inc.) Vol. 27, No. 1/2, 2006, pp. 113-119; and: *Recruiting, Training, and Retention of Science and Technology Librarians* (ed: Patricia A. Kreitz, and JoAnn DeVries) The Haworth Information Press, an imprint of The Haworth Press, Inc., 2006, pp. 113-119. Single or multiple copies of this article are available for a fee from The Haworth Document Delivery Service [1-800-HAWORTH, 9:00 a.m. - 5:00 p.m. (EST). E-mail address: docdelivery@haworthpress.com].

Available online at http://stl.haworthpress.com
© 2006 by The Haworth Press, Inc. All rights reserved.
Digital Object Identifier: 10.1300/J122v27n01_08

INTRODUCTION

According to U.S. Census data, more than one quarter of all librarians with a master's degree will reach age 65 by 2009. (Berry, 7) The library profession is facing a crisis in recruitment. Within librarianship, recruiting librarians with an interest in science or a background in science is particularly challenging since, as other articles in this issue show, many librarians have an undergraduate liberal arts degree and may be intimidated by the thought of becoming a science librarian. Creative recruiting efforts are necessary for science librarianship.

I had never heard of the M.L.I.S. degree until after I graduated from college. As a biology major at Duke University, I was encouraged to pursue a Ph.D. or an M.D. degree by my professors. I have also wondered why I had not heard about science librarianship while I was an undergraduate from any alternative source such as career advisors. "Career days in universities, more often than not, pass by without library representation." (Bosseau & Martin, 198) In fact, graduate advisors can be very powerful recruiting tools.

I was actually a perfect candidate for recruitment into science librarianship since I had an undergraduate science degree and did not want to pursue a faculty or medical career. Looking for a profession that was economically and intellectually satisfying, I first started a Master's degree in Elementary Education. Becoming frustrated with my studies in elementary education and looking for an alternate career path, I first heard about the M.L.I.S. degree from my graduate advisor. Prompted by her suggestion, I got a part-time job in a medical library. After working there for a few months, my positive experiences solidified my decision to pursue a career in science librarianship.

The medical library served physicians, medical students, and patients. I especially enjoyed helping patients find health information. I remember one patient who came to the library to find information on a nervous disorder. This person had just been diagnosed with a nervous disorder, and knew very little about it. By helping educate patients, I felt like I had a small, but significant part in empowering them to make informed choices.

I was also drawn to librarianship because it deals with scholarly information. I have always been interested in research, plus I enjoyed interacting with physicians and talking about the latest developments in biomedical research. So upon my matriculation into the M.L.I.S. program, I knew that I wanted to focus my studies on academic science librarianship.

THE PROBLEM

The intellectual and emotional satisfaction of this career choice was a powerful factor in my decision to become a librarian. But it appears, upon reflection, that I learned about this potential career fairly late in my own academic experience–in fact, almost accidentally. Was my experience unique? How had other science librarians learned about the field?

I was interested to learn if other science librarians encountered the same experience of learning about science librarianship after college. In order to find out, I designed a brief survey (questions attached in Appendix A). It was sent as an e-mail to both the Association of College and Research Libraries-Science & Technology Section (ACRL-STS) listserv (STS-L@LISTSERV.UTK.EDU) and the Chemical Information Sources Discussion List (CHMINF-L@LISTSERV.INDIANA.EDU). I chose these two listservs in order to reach a large number of science librarians across the United States. STS-L has 1,082 subscribers, and CHMINF-L has 1,361 subscribers.

THE FINDINGS

Two hundred twenty-one responses were received for Question #1. Interestingly, 39.4% of the respondents said that they heard about science librarianship during graduate school, while 24.4% said that they heard about science librarianship during college (see Table 1). Two hundred seventeen responses were received for Question #2. 32.3% of the respondents said that they heard about the MLS degree during college, while 29.5% said that they heard about the MLS degree after college (see Table 2). One hundred ninety-two responses were received for Question #3.

TABLE 1. Science Librarianship

When did you first hear about science librarianship?	
	Response Percent
• During high school	5.0%
• During college	24.4%
• After college	17.2%
• During graduate school	39.4%
• Other	14.0%

TABLE 2. MLS Degree

When did you first hear about the MLS degree?	
	Response Percent
• During high school	13.4%
• During college	29.5%
• After college	32.3%
• During graduate school	7.8%
• Other	17.0%

The survey results confirm my hypothesis that the majority of science librarians do not hear about careers in science librarianship until after college. One possible explanation is given by Stuart and Drake who observe that "in science and technologically-oriented disciplines students do not have great exposure to traditional library research methods in their undergraduate courses and therefore both student and faculty advisor often give no thought to career possibilities in the library and information science field." (Stuart & Drake, 82) These findings indicate that there is great recruiting opportunity to educate undergraduates about careers in science librarianship.

Undergraduate science majors are often encouraged to explore careers in research, academia, or medicine, but not science librarianship. Another possible explanation for this lack of knowledge and encouragement, in my personal experience, is that there is a communication gap between science librarians and career advisors. While I was in college, I went to the Career Center during college to explore different career possibilities with a science major, and none of the career advisors spoke about science librarianship. Perhaps we are not promoting our profession enough.

SOME SOLUTIONS

The survey included a third, open-ended question asking respondents, "How can science librarians spread awareness about careers in science librarianship to undergraduates?" The responses below show that science librarians recognize a need to reach out to undergraduate students and suggest some creative ways to market ourselves to them:

- "By talking about our background when introducing ourselves in library instruction sessions, and discussing it with our student employees, and by communicating with the office on campus that helps students apply to grad school."
- "Become familiar with your institution's career resources center, and participate in (or recommend colleagues to come to) science career fairs."
- "Encourage undergrads (work study students in the library) to go into the field."
- "Talk to science majors at their undergraduate biology students organizations, chapters of honor societies, and biology seminars."
- "Science librarians need to get on the radar of people who advise/counsel science undergraduate students."
- "By talking to their academic departments–of the many career possibilities that were mentioned to me as a chemistry major by my department, not once did I hear librarianship."
- "Create a fun and exciting atmosphere during instructional sessions. Be visible during job/career fairs. Develop a relationship with Science clubs and be available to speak at their meetings."
- "Initiate a library career day on campus. Collaborate with the campus career service; keep them supplied with a steady stream of brochures from ACRL and other relevant professional groups."
- "Work within the ACRL STS to create a really appealing recruitment brochure, keep a supply on hand in the library and give it directly to anyone that seems likely."
- "Talk one on one with student assistants, encourage them to consider librarianship. Give student assistants meaningful reference projects and responsibilities; train them to think of themselves as reference assistants, not just work-study students passing time as shelvers."

Some professional organizations are trying to reach out to undergraduates to interest them in a career in librarianship. For example, the Association of Research Libraries (ARL) has launched a summer internship program focused on minority undergraduates. Librarian Internship Program at Washington University in St. Louis was launched in June 2004. The Librarian Internship Program is a 10-week comprehensive internship for minority undergraduates from Lincoln University. The internship occurs during the summer between junior and senior year. Librarians at Washington University mentor students during the internship program. At the end of their summer internship, students return to their home institutions for their senior year and work as library aides in their campus libraries. Mentors also prepare students for graduate school in library science.

A very different approach to recruiting undergraduates has been taken by the Ohio Library Council (OLC). It has produced a 10-minute minority-recruitment video entitled, *Looking for Leaders in the Information Age,* aimed to recruit minority college students uncertain about their career path (Verny, 53).

As the results of the survey indicate, there is a clear need for science librarians to build on the creative but small efforts taken by organizations by taking a proactive approach in recruiting science librarians at the undergraduate level. The key is to expose undergraduates to the intellectual, emotional and other satisfactions of science librarianship. "The most important thing we can share with others is our own enthusiasm for our profession" (Echavarria, 19).

REFERENCES

Offord, J. ARL recruits minority undergraduates to research librarianship. April 2004. *ARL* No. 233, 4-6.

Berry, J. W. 2002. Addressing the recruitment and diversity crisis. *American Libraries* 33(2): 7.

Bosseau, D. L., and S. K. Martin. 1995. The accidental profession. *The Journal of Academic Librarianship* 21(3): 198-199.

Chmelir, L. 2003. Got a secret? Pass it on...: Recruiting new librarians. *College & Research Libraries News* 64(6): 395-397.

Echavarria, T. 2001. Reach out to recruit new librarians. *Alki* 17(1): 18-20.

Stuart, C., and M. A. Drake. 1992. Education and recruitment of science and engineering librarians. *Science & Technology Libraries* 12(4): 79-89.

Van Fleet, C., and D. P. Wallace. 2002. O librarian, where art thou? *Reference & User Services Quarterly* 41(3): 215-218.

Verny, C. 2002. Ohio goes recruiting for minority librarians. *American Libraries* 33(7): 52-55.

doi: 10.1300/J122v27n01_08

Appendix A

Survey Questions

1. When did you first hear about science librarianship?

   a. During high school
   b. During college
   c. After college
   d. During graduate school
   e. Other (please specify)

2. When did you first hear about the MLS degree?

   a. During high school
   b. During college
   c. After college
   d. During graduate school
   e. Other (please specify)

3. How can science librarians spread awareness about careers in science librarianship to undergraduates?

Recruiting the Under-Represented: The Science Links Experience

Kawanna M. Bright
Shantel Agnew
Tanya Arnold
LaVerne Gray
M. Nathalie Hristov
Jill Keally
Mark A. Puente
William Robinson

Kawanna M. Bright, MLIS, is Instructional Services Librarian, John C. Hodges Library, University of Tennessee, Knoxville, TN (E-mail: kbright2@utk.edu), Shantel Agnew, MSIS, is Minority Resident Librarian/Research Assistant Professor, John C. Hodges Library, University of Tennessee, Knoxville, TN (E-mail: sagnew@lib.utk.edu), Tanya Arnold, MS, is Coordinator of Student Services, School of Information Sciences, University of Tennessee, Knoxville, TN (E-mail: tnarnold@utk.edu), LaVerne Gray, MSEd, MLIS, is Minority Resident Librarian/Research Assistant Professor, John C. Hodges Library, University of Tennessee, Knoxville, TN (E-mail: lgray@lib.utk.edu), M. Nathalie Hristov, MLIS, is Assistant Professor and Music Librarian for Technical Services, George F. DeVine Music Library, University of Tennessee, Knoxville, TN (E-mail: mhristov@utk.edu), Jill Keally, MSLS, is Assistant Dean and Associate Professor, University of Tennessee Libraries, Knoxville, TN (E-mail: jkeally@utk.edu), Mark A. Puente, MA, MLS, is Minority Resident Librarian/Research Assistant Professor, John C. Hodges Library, University of Tennessee, Knoxville, TN (E-mail: mpuente@lib.utk.edu), and William Robinson, AM, MSLS, PhD, is Associate Professor/Assistant Director, School of Information Sciences, University of Tennessee, Knoxville, TN (E-mail: wrobins1@utk.edu).

[Haworth co-indexing entry note]: "Recruiting the Under-Represented: The Science Links Experience." Bright, Kawanna M. et al. Co-published simultaneously in *Science & Technology Libraries* (The Haworth Information Press, an imprint of The Haworth Press, Inc.) Vol. 27, No. 1/2, 2006, pp. 121-134; and: *Recruiting, Training, and Retention of Science and Technology Librarians* (ed: Patricia A. Kreitz, and JoAnn DeVries) The Haworth Information Press, an imprint of The Haworth Press, Inc., 2006, pp. 121-134. Single or multiple copies of this article are available for a fee from The Haworth Document Delivery Service [1-800-HAWORTH, 9:00 a.m. - 5:00 p.m. (EST). E-mail address: docdelivery@haworthpress.com].

Available online at http://stl.haworthpress.com
© 2006 by The Haworth Press, Inc. All rights reserved.
Digital Object Identifier: 10.1300/J122v27n01_09

SUMMARY. "Science Links" is a program funded by a grant from the Institute of Library and Museum Services to recruit and educate ten diverse students with strong science and technology backgrounds or interests to the field of science librarianship. This paper described the recruitment phase of the project, launched in the summer of 2005. Although national in scope, a key component of the recruitment process was an active public relations campaign that targeted students at Historically Black Colleges & Universities in the southeast. Six librarians from underrepresented groups employed at the University of Tennessee, along with the Co-Principal Investigators for the grant, explain the strategies used to identify and select institutions likely to produce a high number of applicants for on-site visits. Obstacles, challenges, and unanticipated issues faced during the recruitment phase are also addressed. Designed to be a collaborative effort, the program emphasizes the importance of partnerships in achieving success. One expected outcome will be a carefully evaluated model that may be used to recruit future science librarians, with an emphasis on those from minority populations. The initial recruitment phase concluded in February 2006, the deadline for applicants to submit a "letter of intent" to apply to the program. doi: 10.1300/J122v27n01_09 *[Article copies available for a fee from The Haworth Document Delivery Service: 1-800-HAWORTH. E-mail address: <docdelivery@ haworthpress.com> Website: <http://www.HaworthPress.com> © 2006 by The Haworth Press, Inc. All rights reserved.]*

KEYWORDS. Recruitment, minority recruitment, science librarians, science librarianship, science links

INTRODUCTION

The impending shortage of librarians has been well documented. The number of students entering library school is insufficient to replace the librarians predicted to retire during the next 15 years. In 1998, 57 percent of librarians were age 45 or older. Between 2005 and 2019, over 55 percent of librarians will reach age 65.[1]

Libraries report a particularly severe shortage of qualified science librarians. Nearly two-thirds of science-technology librarians lack a science major or minor.[2] Research-oriented academic and special libraries are especially concerned about the limited number of candidates with the LIS degree and undergraduate strength in science or technology.[3]

Lack of qualified librarians for both pure and applied sciences threatens the success of science research initiatives. Librarians play a key role in providing access to the intellectual content needed to advance science projects. The increasing specialization within scientific disciplines creates a need for flexible librarians with subject knowledge who can work comfortably in evolving research frontiers. In these evolving frontiers they will encounter new nomenclature, research methods, and rapidly changing information technology. Cross and inter-disciplinary trends demand librarians who can work across fields and specialties. Active mentoring of LIS students by librarians who work in these rapidly changing environments should help to prepare librarians for the future.

In general, the field of librarianship suffers from a lack of people of color, but no where is the absence more acute than in the pure and applied sciences. Given the importance of pure and applied science in our future, we must remedy this situation. Having visible, successful librarians of color in the field could encourage students to consider the many opportunities of a career in librarianship.

With a grant from the Institute of Museum and Library Services, the University of Tennessee hopes to implement a unique program that seeks to help solve these problems by providing an adoptable model for other ALA accredited LIS schools. Science Links is the name of this program. It is designed to link recruiting, mentoring, a focused curriculum, and placement to ensure that there are more science librarians, particularly from diverse backgrounds.

Launched in fall 2005, Science Links will recruit future librarians, with an emphasis on those from minority populations, who have undergraduate science degrees or substantial coursework in the sciences. The program will provide them with mentoring, financial support, an excellent LIS education, and on-the-job training in nationally recognized science institutions and organizations. Partners in the project include the University of Tennessee (UT) Libraries, Oak Ridge National Laboratory, the Department of Energy's Office of Scientific and Technical Information (OSTI) and Information International Associates, Inc.

Thoughtful recruiting and selection is the cornerstone of the program's success. In addition to a national campaign using posters and brochures targeting minority institutions and scientific organizations, the program has enlisted the help of academic science departments, libraries, and career and guidance centers in Historically Black Colleges and Universities (HBCUs).

The Association of Research Libraries, as recommended by Reese and Hawkins, found personal face-to-face contact by people of color to be the single most effective recruiting approach.[4] Science Links followed that recommendation, providing released time and funding for six minority librarians, four African-Americans and two Latinos, to travel to colleges and universities in the southeast with a high percentage of minority students.

PREPARATION AND RECRUITMENT

The original core group of three Science Links recruiters was augmented in September 2005 with the addition of the three minority residents from the UT Libraries. The Libraries employs, on a professional basis, three early-career librarians from under-represented groups who work in various library departments during a two-year appointment. The residents were invited to take part in the on-site recruitment visits to college campuses for Science Links and to contribute to the creation and distribution of recruitment materials (posters, brochures, etc.). They were paired with three recruiters from the original group to form three two-person teams. Their recent graduate school experience, their familiarity with LIS education (one is a UT SIS graduate), and their own cultural experiences brought additional strength to the recruiting process.

Recruiters agreed that there would be two general strategies for on-site recruitment. The first was to attend graduate-professional school fairs held at some of the targeted institutions. Fairs required registration fees and submission of registration materials to meet deadlines. The second was to visit career counseling centers and academic science departments of other institutions to contact upper division students and/or teaching faculty in scientific disciplines. The latter included contact with the public library system in Memphis by one team to recruit from classified staff working in that large public library system with a large minority representation. The Science Links recruitment team established a self-imposed deadline for the completion of these trips. The first week of November was selected in order to finish traveling before the holidays and the end of the fall terms. Since each recruiter had full-time responsibilities, including desk duty and tasks with deadlines, creating a travel schedule and arranging to be off campus was a challenge.

Additionally, recruiters were encouraged to make recruitment visits during unrelated travels as time and resources allowed. One recruiter, for example, met with career planning personnel from four Hispanic-serving institutions in the Central Texas region while home for the holidays. Another recruiter contacted universities in Puerto Rico while traveling there for a conference.

Before establishing itineraries for recruitment trips, the recruiters helped to create the content and the design of recruitment materials, including a website, brochures, and a poster. Content was evaluated for ease of understanding and clarity of message as well as visual impression. Recruiter involvement in the creation of promotional materials was important for ensuring a thoughtful and persuasive message targeting science majors and members of under-represented groups. After a number of revisions, the team approved the Science Links documentation, and the materials went to press.

An informal brain-storming session identified a list of additional materials that should be gathered and distributed to potential applicants during visits. Recruitment packets were given to each recruiter. Besides the Science Links materials, they included brochures from the School of Information Sciences, the UT Libraries, and information on the city of Knoxville. Feedback from the first team to complete a recruitment trip led the other teams to add brochures from the UT Graduate School. Many prospective students had questions about other UT graduate programs that recruiters, initially, could not answer.

Banners and/or large signs were also needed to identify the recruiters as representatives of the University of Tennessee, the School of Information Sciences, and the Science Links program. The host institutions provided little of these materials and what was provided was not easily visible from a distance. Finally, "freebies" were gathered to attract students to our tables, including candy, water bottles, pens, and bottle openers.

WHERE TO GO?

Identifying institutions to visit began with a complete list of HBCUs. The next step was to determine which states to visit. Given our East Tennessee location, recruiting efforts started with Tennessee institutions and then expanded to neighboring states in the southeast. This strategy allowed each recruiter to select two to three states for investigation. The states initially selected were Tennessee, Arkansas, Mississippi, Alabama, Georgia, South Carolina, North Carolina, Louisiana, Florida, Virginia, and West Virginia.

Each recruiter was asked to list institutions in their states that matched agreed upon selection criteria:

- Five or more BS graduates in pure and applied sciences within the last two years
- A driving distance of eight hours or less
- Proximity to other institutions located within a metropolitan area
- Substantial minority enrollment
- Institutions that exhibited interest after initial contact.

Once this list was completed, recruiters applied additional filtering criteria to maximize recruiter time and focus their efforts. Variables included:

- Total enrollment
- Further indication of interest by career and guidance centers and science departments
- An upcoming career or graduate-professional school fair

Gathering this information was a time-consuming process. Print and on-line college guides provided some useful enrollment information, including total number of students, under-represented populations, as well as the presence of natural science and engineering programs. A few schools, usually the larger ones, provided detailed enrollment and program information on-line. However, some of this information was dated and incomplete. Determining if a career or graduate-professional school fair was scheduled was easy to conclude since this information was almost always on the school's website.

Finding the number of graduates by academic department required much more effort. Often, recruiters were told to contact institutional research offices for current data. These offices were not always responsive or able to find the needed data. Recruiters often contacted individual science departments to ask about their enrollment and graduation rates. Not all departments had this information and often referred the recruiters to other offices on campus.

Once the initial itineraries were established, the next step was to identify appropriate contact persons at each institution. Examining school websites, and then initiating phone calls and e-mails to career counseling staff and science departments took some effort and required follow-up, but proved useful. Persistence was essential. Once the appropriate contact was identified, recruiters informed that person or persons about the Science Links scholarship opportunity as well as library–information science careers. In spite of initial hesitation, campus representatives were eager to host Science Links recruiters once the program details were fully explained. While it was expected that few would be aware of the Science Links program, the relative unfamiliarity of these representatives with the library–information professions on their campuses came as a surprise.

With all of the above collected and evaluated, forty-five institutions were identified as cost-effective prospects. Trip planning required time and effort to ensure that travel costs and time were minimized. Travel costs included:

- Lodging
- Meals
- Vehicle costs (payment per mile for privately owned vehicles or fees for use of university motor pool cars)

When this phase was completed, there were seven trips to visit twenty-three schools. Given the small number of recruiters and the limited time available, recruiters were unable to visit as many schools as they had hoped. However, the recruiters were able to visit a few additional high potential schools beyond the originally designated driving area. Visiting locations such as Baton Rouge was important because of the presence of a large number of students from Louisiana, Mississippi, and Alabama displaced there by Hurricane Katrina. Virginia was important because of a reciprocal program that offers their students in-state tuition in Tennessee.

Hotel reservations were made, and driving routes were mapped using web resources such as MapQuest, Yahoo! Maps, and Google Maps. Directions were compared against one another to find the best routes. When directions varied notably, recruiters consulted travel atlases and then confirmed directions with their school contacts, who also provided specific directions to the campus locations for fairs or presentations. Recruiters learned that it is essential to perform a "dry run" before the event to ensure that there will be no snags with locating the right building or parking.

Two or three day trips allowed recruiters to visit institutions that were reasonably close to each other. Since fairs promised to be the most productive recruiting vehicles, trips were planned around them as often as possible. Fairs usually lasted for five to seven hours and included lunch for the recruiters, which was a notable benefit. Many students were curious about library and information work while others were just interested in the University of Tennessee. Although not the program's primary mission, this was a serendipitous opportunity to spread the good news about the University.

Other visits were set up with local career centers or science programs. Arranging these visits required much more effort, attention to detail, and persistence. In general, recruiting here yielded mixed results since students from all disciplines and many lower division undergraduates approached the information tables. There was no efficient way to determine if the student met the general criteria for the Science Links program short of asking them their academic status and major.

In some cases, arrangements were made to present the Science Links program to science teaching faculty. Since they have direct, regular contact with potential applicants and can encourage and direct them to graduate programs, this method can be ideal. The problem was finding time in an already busy classroom schedule for presentations about the Science Links program. If faculty can be persuaded to market the program to their students, recruiting is likely to be more successful.

The final recruitment effort was to solidify contacts made through campus visits. Several techniques were used including hand-written cards, e-mail messages, and phone calls to potential Science Links applicants, career planning officers, and other campus representatives. Usually, this was done within a week after the recruiters' return to campus. Additionally, some follow-up calls and e-mails were made during the end of the fall term, 2005. This effort may continue and intensify depending on the number of applications received as the program application deadlines approach.

Upon completion of the campus visits, the recruiters compared their experiences. These discussions led to specific suggestions for improvement in future recruiting as well as some changes in the Science Links website and application process.

LESSONS LEARNED

Some aspects of the Sciences Links program made recruiting more challenging. Science Links recruiters obviously looked for students with a strong academic background in the sciences. This decision may have limited the pool of potential applicants since they were primarily encouraging applications from those with either a major or minor in science rather just those with an interest in the discipline.

The search for minority students focused primarily on HBCUs. This strategy not only limited the number of schools to visit, but also decreased the "yield" of qualified applicants since the number of students with the required science background is a relatively small one. Anticipating that some minority students interested in the sciences might also be enrolled in non-HBCU universities and colleges, the recruiters included these schools for on-site visits if they were nearby and offered a reasonable number of minority students as potential applicants. However, to visit all of these schools in the region would dramatically increase the cost of recruiting.

Graduate-professional school and career fairs provided the best and most structured opportunities to contact potential candidates. They attracted students who were specifically looking for graduate school opportunities. The host institutions took care of advertising, often including the name of the program and institution. Fairs are usually in optimal locations, and many HBCUs located in larger metropolitan areas co-host fairs, providing access to an even larger number of students at one time. With adequate advanced planning, these fairs are ideal methods for getting the word out about the program.

Campus career and guidance offices appear to be overworked and perhaps underappreciated. Patience and an understanding, appreciative manner pay dividends in helping to identify contacts and making arrangements to meet potential applicants. The recruiters' experiences suggest that career counselors respond well to a presentation that is a succinct, persuasive statement about the program's importance for the students on that campus, focusing on the unique features and funding support. Since these individuals can facilitate future recruitment efforts, it is also important to allow some time to speak with relevant career or guidance professionals during the on-site visit.

Recruiting is about finding and encouraging people to apply. Having two recruiters per visit may seem like an extravagance. However, it is much more effective. One person can stay at the table while the other runs errands or roams the floor to identify potential candidates. Two people can respond more quickly to questions by different students at the same time. Traveling is also much easier and more comfortable when driving can be shared and a co-pilot can help with directions. Also, if one recruiter is not feeling well, the other can take the lead. The key for the recruiters is to capture needed information about each potential applicant. Complete names, e-mail address, and phone numbers are essential for follow-up communications. An easily completed form is an important asset and reduces the burden on the recruiter. Where eligibility is an issue, there needs to be a field on the form or a code that the recruiter can quickly use to identify a qualified applicant.

Recruiting can be expensive. The cost is not as much financial as it is in time and effort taken away from other responsibilities. Few programs will be able to employ full-time recruiters. If recruiters need to look like those they hope to recruit, that further reduces the number of potential recruiters. Since the best recruiters will likely be productive, professional staff, placing them in the field–even for short periods–can cause problems at home. Enthusiasm and commitment by senior management is essential. Communication with the recruiters' supervisors is essential so that departments can plan for their absence and redirected attention.

Timing is everything in recruiting. It was learned informally that the proposal was funded in June, but the formal announcement came later. Therefore, planning began later than what would have been liked. Since federal funding did not begin until 1 November, well after the beginning of the academic year, temporary funding arrangements had to be made. Identifying institutions for on-site visits did not begin until late August and September, causing recruiters to miss some important career and graduate-professional school fairs. Ideally, planning for academic recruiting trips should occur no later than late May or early June. Finding institutional data, such as the number of science graduates, took much longer than expected as did finding the most appropriate campus contacts. The beginning of the fall term is unusually busy on the campus, and not a good time for gathering information.

Especially in a career fair setting, recruiters may have just a minute or two to make the pitch to a potential applicant. Besides being welcoming and enthusiastic, there is some value in having a hook to generate interest and interaction. For example, one team's hook was "Wanna get paid to go to graduate school?" The ability to establish eye contact, and say a quick word or two is a key ingredient in success. Recruiters discovered that general appeal elements worked better than position titles or names. The "library or librarian" words seemed to turn off students while the kinds of work that librarians do had some appeal. Information tables can be a wonderful way to showcase the program. Their effectiveness depends on the type of institution being visited and the location of the tables. Tables set up in smaller schools near cafeterias were effective in providing an opportunity to speak to a large number of people. It is important to have a good-sized banner or sign and a way to display it. The sign should clearly name your institution and the program. It will attract those who might be interested and eliminate some questions by those who are not. Students like, and often expect, freebies. Pens, water bottles, even library bookmarks attract students and give recruiters an opportunity to interact.

During campus, even class visits, it was difficult for the recruiters to determine if the students were seniors with a strong science interest. Many students who stopped by during the career fairs were not qualified for the program. Setting up a table in the busiest corridor of a science department did help with science interest, but many of these students were not seniors. Tables in college or university centers for career or graduate study fairs provided a large audience as well as competition from the tables nearby. If the school was not an HBCU, there was the added difficulty of explaining that the program focused on minority students. Many students who approached the table were interested in the University of Tennessee, but not Science Links, and were not minorities. Although a reasonably large number of minority students attend non-HBCU colleges and universities, these sites were not as welcoming or as productive as originally hoped.

In addition, many of the students attending career fairs were juniors. The program's target audience was the seniors who would graduate in either spring or summer 2006, but future programs may want to consider another strategy. Recruiting juniors to enter the program following their senior year would have two benefits. One, there would be some time to take particular courses that would strengthen their qualifications, in this case more science courses. Two, juniors may be more open to career choices than seniors. By their senior year, many undergraduates have already decided on a career path.

In some cases, more time should have been planned for each school. Visiting more than one school each day is economical, but it does not allow enough time for set up, interaction, and take down. It is better to limit the visits to one school per day. Spending too much time at one school and arriving late at another can be a disaster. Sending invitations to appropriate faculty members to visit the table and to encourage their eligible students to visit also makes a substantial difference. While requiring some extra effort, this may well increase the "yield."

Originally, the recruiters planned to introduce the Science Links program in science classes. However, teachers were reluctant to lose teaching time and did not always see the relationship between science information work and their particular topic. Developing contacts and building awareness of a program requires more time. Ideally, it is recommend that contact with teaching faculty members occur earlier, more frequently, and on a continuing basis rather than for a program that starts fairly quickly and has a short life.

Recruiting was also affected by the attitudes and values of each school visited. Larger schools have their own graduate programs and recruit internally. Undergraduate students at these schools were more likely to favor the program with which they were familiar. Larger institutions, especially in metropolitan areas, often have many students who do not live or eat on campus. Setting up an information table outside of a campus food court provides high volume pedestrian traffic, but many of these students are freshmen and sophomores who live on campus rather than the juniors or seniors who might be considering graduate school.

Some potential applicants were uncertain about being far away from home and whether Knoxville and the local community would offer a welcoming environment. One suggestion received during a visit to an HBCU institution was to hold a career fair in Knoxville that would enable potential applicants to visit Science Links libraries and the library school. Brief presentations by science librarians and opportunities to speak with librarians of color during this fair would also be recommended. Such an event might dispel doubts or concerns about being welcome in Knoxville.

The relative invisibility of library and information work on the campuses visited was a surprise. Many students were simply unaware of the information professions, including librarianship as a profession requiring graduate study. The lack of visibility and impact of many campus libraries makes recruiting for librarianship much more difficult. Partnering with campus libraries to enhance their visibility would make recruiting much easier in the future.

Graduate school admissions dates normally require all materials to be received in March with decisions made by early April. More flexibility would allow recruitment of individuals who were denied admission or financial aid for other graduate and professional schools and might be open to an interesting alternative. For example, medical librarianship might be attractive to some who were not accepted into medical school.

The opportunities and funding to recruit under-represented groups to librarianship are increasing. For example, another IMLS grant is recruiting African-Americans to become metadata librarians. ALA's Spectrum program is visible and is not limited to a particular aspect of librarianship. A unified recruiting program, a "one stop shop," so that recruiters would be able to present more than one opportunity at the same time would substantially increase recruiting visibility and productivity.

CONCLUSION

In order to know if our recruiting had been successful, we asked those interested in Science Links to send a brief letter of interest by 1 February. On 4 February, we had four letters on file. Although disappointed, we are reviewing our contact lists, making follow-up calls, and making a renewed effort. We agree that a strong follow-up program is needed to ensure that those interested actually apply. In some cases, under-represented students may find the application process–securing references, writing an essay, taking the GRE examination–overwhelming. Helping applicants with that process is essential if recruiting is to be successful.

This was one of the first broad and systematic efforts to test the oft-repeated axiom that face-to-face, personal, contact is an important way to recruit new librarians into the profession, particularly from under-represented groups. While the experiment would have been more effective if we had been able to dovetail our efforts into the campus' academic schedules more optimally, we learned some exciting lessons. As the fall deadline for admissions approaches, we continue to evaluate, refine, and share what we have learned, focusing on the creation of a model that other ALA accredited LIS schools may use to address the shortage of qualified science librarians, especially those from under-represented groups.

NOTES

1. American Library Association, "Library Profession Faces Shortage of Librarians," [online document]. Available from http://www.ala.org/pio/; accessed 26 September 2004.

2. Hooper-Lane, Christopher. 1999. "Spotlight on the Subject Knowledge of Chemistry Librarians: Results of a Survey. *Issues in Science and Technology Librarianship* [online document]. Available from http://www.istl.org/99-summer/article1.html; accessed 16 September 2004; Mount, E. 1985. *University Science and Engineering Libraries* (Westport, Connecticut: Greenwood Press. Referenced in Christopher Hooper-Lane. "Spotlight on the Subject Knowledge of Chemistry Librarians: Results of a Survey." *Issues in Science and Technology Librarianship* [online]. Summer 1999. Available from: http://www.istl.org/99-summer/artilce1.html; accessed 19 September 2004; Liu, M.X. and Wei, W. 1993. *Science/Technology Librarians in California: Their Background, Performance and Expectations*. Presented at the Special Libraries Association Annual Conference, Cincinnati, Ohio. References in Christopher Hooper-Lane. "Spotlight on the Subject Knowledge of Chemistry Librarians: Results of a Survey." *Issues in Science and Technology Librarianship* [Online]. Summer 1999. Available from: http://www.istl.org/99-summer/article1.html; accessed 19 September, 2004; Association for Library and Information Science Education. 2002. *2003 Statistical Report.*

(Reston, VA: ALISE). 68-71; Offord, Jerome Jr. 2004. "ARL Recruits Undergraduate to Research Librarianship [online]. ARL Bimonthly Report, April 2004. Available from: http://www.arl.org/newsltr/233/recruit.html; accessed 17 October 2004; Mosely, Pixie Anne. 1995. "Engineering and librarians: how do they interact?" *Science & Technology Libraries* 15 (1) 51-61. Referenced in Holland, Marita Peterson. 1998. *Science & Technology Libraries* 17 (2): 31-43; 37; National Library of Medicine. 1995. Vol. 5. Referenced in Linda C. Smith. 1998. "Education for Health Sciences Librarianship." *Science & Technology Libraries*, Vol. 17 (2) 1998: 59-80; Winston, Mark D. 2001. Academic science and engineering librarians: a research study of demographics, educational backgrounds, and professional activities. *Science & Technology Libraries*, 19 (2): 3-24; 17; and Jones, Mary Baker, Mary Frances Lembo, James E. Manasco, and John H. Sandy. 2002 "Recruiting Entry-level Sci-Tech Librarians: An Analysis of Job Advertisements and Outcome of Searches." *Sci-Tech News*, (May 2002) 56 (2): 12-16.

3. Capell, Perrie. 2003. "The Hiring Tide Turns For Corporate Librarians' [online]. *The Wall Street Journal Executive Career Site*: Career Journal.com. Available from http://www.careerjournal.com/salary/hiring/industries/librarians/20031022-capell.html; accessed 19 September 2004; Frank, Donald G. 1989. Education for librarians in a major science-engineering library: expectations and reality. *Journal of Library Administration* 11 (3/4): 107-116; Holland, Marita Peterson. 1998. "Modeling the Engineering Information Professional." *Science & Technology Libraries*. 17 (2) 1998: 31-43; Stuart, Crit and Miriam A. Drake. 1992. "Education and recruitment of science and engineering librarians." *Science & Technology Libraries*. 12 (Summer): 79-89; Hansen, Mary J and Jan M. Curtis. "Challenges and Benefits of Chemical Information Service in Industry." 1997. *Science & Technology Libraries*, Vol. 16 (3/4): 209-228; Wiggins, Gary. 1998. "New Directions in the Education of Chemistry Librarians and Information Specialists." *Science & Technology Libraries*, Vol. 17 (2) 1998: 45-58; and Hallmark, Julie. 1998. "Education for the Successful Geoscience Information Specialist." *Science & Technologies Libraries* 17(2): 81-91.

4. Gregory L. Reese and Ernestine L. Hawkins, Stop Talking and Start Doing: Attracting People of Color to the Library Profession (Chicago: American Library Association, 1999): 37.

doi: 10.1300/J122v27n01_09

Making the Science-Library Connection:
A Survey of Sci-Tech Librarians

Linda Eells

SUMMARY. Previous studies have investigated the movement of scientists and library school students into science librarianship (Hackenberg and Chu 2002; Hallmark and Lembo 2003). This survey explores the hypothesis that an individuals' decision to choose science and technology (sci-tech) librarianship as a career is often triggered specifically by an exposure to science libraries or scientific research, and that this exposure often happens relatively late in a student's educational or career trajectory. Identifying specifically what specific experiences or factors were highly influential in attracting practicing librarians to the profession will enable recruiters to focus their efforts on appropriate points along career paths, and help to inform the design of recruiting media that presents an accurate and positive depiction of the profession. The discussion addresses the role of librarians as recruiters for the profession, and includes suggestions for reaching individuals who are not aware of sci-tech librarianship as a rewarding and challenging career option. The study collected in-depth data about the education, work, and personal histories of practicing sci-tech librarians, and included questions that yielded some interesting impressions about the importance of

Linda Eells, MLIS, MS, is Science Librarian, University of Minnesota Libraries (E-mail: lle@umn.edu).

[Haworth co-indexing entry note]: "Making the Science-Library Connection: A Survey of Sci-Tech Librarians" Eells, Linda. Co-published simultaneously in *Science & Technology Libraries* (The Haworth Information Press, an imprint of The Haworth Press, Inc.) Vol. 27, No. 1/2, 2006, pp. 135-158; and: *Recruiting, Training, and Retention of Science and Technology Librarians* (ed: Patricia A. Kreitz, and JoAnn DeVries) The Haworth Information Press, an imprint of The Haworth Press, Inc., 2006, pp. 135-158. Single or multiple copies of this article are available for a fee from The Haworth Document Delivery Service [1-800-HAWORTH, 9:00 a.m. - 5:00 p.m. (EST). E-mail address: docdelivery@haworthpress.com].

Available online at http://stl.haworthpress.com
© 2006 by The Haworth Press, Inc. All rights reserved.
Digital Object Identifier: 10.1300/J122v27n01_10

a science background to sci-tech librarianship, and characteristics of science librarian job requirements and candidate qualifications. doi: 10.1300/J122v27n01_10 *[Article copies available for a fee from The Haworth Document Delivery Service: 1-800-HAWORTH. E-mail address: <docdelivery@ haworthpress.com> Website: <http://www.HaworthPress.com> © 2006 by The Haworth Press, Inc. All rights reserved.]*

KEYWORDS. Surveys/science librarians, recruitment, mentors

INTRODUCTION

Recruiting new talent to the library profession is not a new problem, nor is it a problem restricted to science libraries. "Librarianship is experiencing a labor gap between increasing demand for library and information science professionals and a declining supply of qualified individuals" (Association of College and Research Libraries. Ad Hoc Task Force on Recruitment & Retention Issues 2002). This problem is exacerbated in science libraries, however, by the perceived need for additional training for librarians in the sciences and the difficulty in determining where to focus recruitment efforts to reach potential recruits who possess that science background. Gaining a better understanding of the process that inspires new entrants to join the profession will help recruiters both in library schools and in libraries to think creatively about reaching out to identify talented students and mentor them into the profession.

Previous studies have researched motives for entering the profession. Hallmark investigated science and technology (sci-tech) librarians who became interested in the library profession while working in non-library related science positions (Hallmark and Lembo 2003), and Hackenberg studied library school students and practicing sci-tech librarians (Hackenberg 2000; Hackenberg and Chu 2002). Another population that seems attracted to sci-tech librarianship are students pursuing advanced science degrees (M.S. or PhD), or post B.S. students in search of an interesting job in which their science background will be valued. What event occurred to spark this interest from individuals who had already moved reasonably far down a different career path? This study seeks to gather quantifiable data to demonstrate that an early exposure to libraries is in and of itself insufficient to attract future science librarians to the profession, including those in library school (LIS). It may more specifically be scientific research itself, or at least exposure to a science library, that sparks an interest for many science-minded recruits.

Many undergraduates interested in the sciences may not be exposed to science librarianship early in their life or educational trajectory. For instance, if the undergraduate science curriculum at an institution does not require extensive library research, students may not know what science librarians do or they may have misconceptions about the profession, and so they do not perceive it to be a desirable career option. Perhaps potential recruits' "perception of work in an academic library, shaped by the undergraduate experience . . . is of a traditional, less rewarding relationship with faculty and students. Academic librarians are not usually integral participants in research activity" (Stuart and Drake 1992). Responses indicate that many sci-tech librarians received their first exposure to a science librarian or to scientific library research relatively late in their career or educational trajectory, and that this exposure led directly to the development of an interest in sci-tech librarianship. Recruiters should therefore be encouraged to be more proactive in ensuring that exposure to the profession occurs as early as possible along science student's educational and career paths. Serious recruitment efforts should be focused on high school, undergraduate, and graduate science students in appropriate *non-library* venues, such as career fairs and scientific lectures or conferences; on LIS students with science backgrounds; and on practicing scientists (e.g., scientific laboratory or field employees).

Another factor that is highly relevant to recruitment into the profession is the degree to which science librarians perceive the importance of a science background to sci-tech librarianship relative to library education or library experience. Several questions on the survey illuminated attitudes about this issue, which appeared to be influenced by individual backgrounds as would be expected. The ensuing discussion is especially interesting in light of data showing the proportion of practicing sci-tech librarians who received some science education as part of their library education. Many researchers have suggested that library schools should include more science offerings to address a perceived need for some more subject-specific training for those students interested in pursuing science librarianship. Increased options for sci-tech course courses in library school would enable aspiring sci-tech librarians to focus on appropriate educational and training opportunities for entrance into the profession, and could increase options for hiring authorities attempting to define the educational or experiential qualities to include in job postings.

METHODOLOGY

This study was designed to focus on the education, skills, and views of *practicing* post-MLS sci-tech librarians and information professionals in the health sciences, natural/life sciences, and physical sciences, in all types of libraries (academic, corporate, hospital, and other special). Many of these excellent science librarians do not possess science education or training, but were initially prepared for careers in the humanities, arts, and social sciences. Their opinions provided valuable perspectives to the discussion. Current library school students (pre-MLS) were not solicited or defined as part of the targeted audience, although several responses were received from members of this population. While the opinions of library students are certainly valuable, in trying to define new venues for recruiting efforts it is important to investigate non-traditional target populations. However, in the ensuing discussing regarding recruiting venues, some factors affecting recruitment of sci-tech librarians from the LIS student population will be addressed.

A 28-question survey was designed to gather data that would shed light on when and how librarians became exposed to sci-tech librarianship, their education and experiential background in the sciences, and whether they took science librarianship courses in library school. Also included were questions about recruitment, retention, and basic demographics. While most questions were multiple choice, several open-ended questions were included to gather anecdotal information about experiences that directly attracted respondents to science librarianship, details about mentors or role models, and factors affecting career choices. The survey draft was reviewed by the University of Minnesota's *Survey Research Center*, modified, pre-tested by five science librarians, and modified again. The final survey was produced in Zoomerang™, an online survey instrument. An e-mail solicitation and link to the online survey were distributed to the following discussion groups:

- STS-L (American Library Association, Association of College and Research Libraries–Science & Technology Section)
- ASIS-L (American Society for Information Science & Technology)
- SLA (Special Libraries Association–MN Chapter)
- MIDWEST@uic.edu (Midwest Chapter of the Medical Library Association)
- AGNIC-L (Agricultural Network Information Center)

These listservs were chosen because they are subscribed to primarily by practicing science/technology librarians and information technology professionals. Subscribers were encouraged to forward the solicitation and survey to other science-related listservs to which they had access, and several colleagues mentioned that they had done so. Therefore, it is not possible to calculate the overall response rate as a percentage of the total solicited population, since that population number is impossible to estimate with any degree of accuracy. The solicitation was sent on February 28, 2006 and participants were given ten working days to respond to the survey. A total of 332 responses were received, 80% of those within the first three days. Survey results were compiled by Zoomerang™, which produces several online reports and a .csv file that was imported into Excel for further analysis.

DEMOGRAPHICS

Demographic data collected in the survey included gender and salary information, educational background, years worked in current position, and years worked post-MLS. Many of the degree trends reflect the specialized audience to which the survey was distributed, with an academic focus predominating. Fully 95% possess a master's degree in library/information science, 30% possess a master's degree in another discipline, 6% possess doctoral degrees, and 14% have an uncompleted graduate degree. Many respondents possess some combination of these degrees, so the percentages do not total 100%. Most (78%) work in an academic library, with 48% of those categorizing their environment as a special or subject library, which includes medical school libraries and science and engineering libraries. The remaining responses were from staff in hospital libraries (7%), government libraries (5%), corporate libraries (4%), or "other" (6%). Respondents in the latter category indicated a variety of occupations from consulting to non-profits.

With regard to gender, the data match some previously documented general trends across the profession. The gender distribution corresponded very closely to Hackenberg's 2000 study that included practicing librarians and library school students (Hackenberg 2000). 75.6% of the respondents in her study were females versus 77% in this study, with a distribution of 24.1% males in that group versus 23% males here. Hackenberg did not indicate differences in the gender distributions between library students and practicing librarians, unfortunately, as it would have been interesting to compare the gender data from her groups with the data gathered here.

Q. 22 How many years have you worked as a professional (post MLS) science librarian/information professional?

An interesting gender distribution that is depicted in Table 1 demonstrates both positive and negative trends related to the number of years the librarians in this survey population have worked in the profession (post-MLS). There appear to be an encouraging number of female librarians entering the profession with 23% having worked as a professional for three years or less replacing the 25% of females who have been in this category for more than 20 years. Overall the number of females who received their received their degrees in the past 10 years is equivalent to the number who earned their MLS over 10 years ago. However, the single largest continent of respondents received their MLS more than 20 years ago and is moving toward retirement, including 39% of the males. Somewhat striking is the low percentage of males entering the profession, relative both to the number who have had their degree for more than 20 years and to the percentage of females in that category. Does this correlate to the gender distribution in library schools, and if so, what are the implications of this trend? What is the relationship between the salary trends and the gender balance, for new librarians? What is the impact not only on potential candidates who possess science degrees, but on current sci-tech librarians who may find higher compensation in other professions? Additional correlations and salary trends identified in this survey will be analyzed and discussed in a separate article further investigating issues related to the retention of

TABLE 1. Gender Distribution–Post MLS

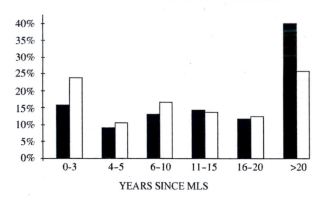

YEARS SINCE MLS

science librarians. Suffice it to say that while data in this survey demonstrate that science libraries are seeking candidates who possess an advanced science education or training, these skilled candidates are likely to be in high demand in non-library venues as well. If the library community identifies an increasing need to hire and retain candidates who possess advanced science degrees, it will need to ensure that competitive compensation is in place to attract and keep them.

SCIENCE LIBRARIANS AND SCIENCE TRAINING

At this point it is appropriate to address the role an advanced degree plays in today's job market, and discuss whether that advanced degree actually does confer some advantage to candidates seeking positions in science libraries. The library profession has long been concerned about whether librarians need to have advanced subject degrees beyond the MLS/MLIS. As recruiters seek to identify when and where to apply their efforts along students' career paths, they first need to know with some certainty that the individuals they recruit are correctly suited for the positions for which they are being recruited. What education or experience should they possess relative to the education that employers seek, and how can they obtain that education? A number of authors have discussed the difficulty science libraries face in recruiting candidates with science backgrounds into the profession (Storm and Wei 1994; Stuart and Drake 1992; Winston 2001). This study investigated attitudes from the field about whether candidates actually need a science background to be effective science librarians. If so, how should we focus recruiting resources more effectively to ensure that individuals with science backgrounds are being recruited? Various opinions and sides of the controversy were documented and discussed thoroughly in Mayer and Terrill's excellent 2005 study of the issue (Mayer and Terrill 2005). However, it is difficult to draw direct correlations from their results to a scientific population due to the fact that fewer than 10% of their respondents received their advanced subject degree in the sciences. Therefore, a few questions in this survey were designed to gather direct impressions specifically from practicing science librarians about the importance of either a science degree or science experience to their work.

Do you need a science background to be a good science librarian? Among this survey population, the answer would be a resounding "yes" when discussing how job descriptions are written for current science library positions. The large majority of libraries represented in this sample are inclined to require, recommend, or prefer a science degree in their job postings for science librarians. When asked what *science* degree requirement is stated in job postings for science librarians, only 16% indicated that their library does not require, recommend, or prefer a science degree. 19% indicated that a B.S. or M.S. in the sciences was required, and fully 66% said the advanced science degree is not required but it is "recommended or preferred." These results contrast strikingly with respondents in Mayer's study (Mayer and Terrill 2005), 46% of whom indicated that an advanced subject degree is required or preferred for their job. Again, most of Mayer's study respondents received their advanced subject degrees in humanities, social sciences, education, and fine arts. This particular comparison does suggest the existence of a stronger requirement for advanced subject degrees for science librarians than for arts, humanities, and social science librarians.

The need for some level of science education was reiterated by respondents when asked what they personally thought was more important for science librarians to possess: a science degree; a library degree; library experience; or the combination of "science education *and* library education or experience." The last choice received the highest response rate, at 49%, followed by "library degree" at 29%. Only 9% of the respondents selected "science degree" as most important for a science librarian. This is an interesting assessment of perceptions from the field, so to speak, on whether a science background is indeed requisite for science librarians. The low response rate for a science degree alone also appears to provide an answer for Storm and Wei, who questioned whether, "according to traditional beliefs, the possession of a science degree is the most important criterion in the evaluation of potential candidates for sci/tech library positions," noting that this would result in losing as potential recruits humanities and social sciences librarians who could serve very effectively as science librarians (Storm and Wei 1994). While these results demonstrate that science librarians clearly feel the science background is important, they also emphasize the great importance these librarians continue to place on the library degree and/or experience. Most of the respondents to this survey did have that library experience, with 96% having worked in a library prior to receiving a library degree, 35% of those in a volunteer or internship capacity (paid and unpaid).

The degree status of respondents had a decided impact on how they responded to this question. Of those with doctoral degrees, for instance, 42% responded that a science degree is the most important, with another 42% indicating that both the science education and library education are equally important. The caveat to this result is that the number of respondents possessing a doctorate was relatively quite small, at only 6% of the sample population. Among respondents with master's degrees, 11% indicated that a science degree is most important, with 53% choosing the science education/library education or experience combination.

Overall, these opinions appear to reflect the percentage of respondents who actually possess the preferred combination of degrees in reality, at least among this particular survey population. Fully 95% of all respondents possess an MLS/MLIS, and 50% indicated a science focus to their degree work. The latter result demonstrates a significant increase over the 32% who reported a scientific educational background in Mount's 1983 survey of sixteen sci-tech college and university libraries (Mount 1985). Not surprisingly, those who have completed post-baccalaureate degrees are most likely to have received that degree in a scientific field, with 55% of those possessing a non-MLS/MLIS master's degree and 68% of those with doctorates indicating a science major. These results should be encouraging to those who feel that "one of the primary issues in science librarianship involves the academic background we bring to the job," and that "the scarcity of librarians with science degrees continues to concern the information profession" (Hooper-Lane 1999).

However, data also demonstrate that a significant percentage of practicing sci-tech librarians did not pursue or obtain a science education. Of those respondents who specified the disciplinary focus to their higher education, 26% pursued degrees a non-scientific field such as history, English, linguistics, or French literature. Perhaps these individuals obtained positions as science librarians somewhat serendipitously, or perhaps they actively pursued these positions. In any event, the lack of a science education does not preclude excellence in the profession. "The scientific method can be learned and a librarian can be literate in relevant aspects of the sciences without having a formal subject background in science or engineering" (Storm and Wei 1994). Comments received by the author over the course of this study reflect the controversy and highlight the need for greater specificity in the discussion, specifically with regard to the definition applied to "science librarianship."

> The problem is that the library profession by its very nature is split between those who have subject knowledge and those who don't. [My organization] will take a curious person with high interest and knowledge of tools if the right subject specialist isn't available. I truly fell into R&D long ago and have been happily taking care of

nerds and geeks ever since . . . And it's all about language anyway.
I don't walk the walk, I talk the talk!

–Jane Kaufenberg, Honeywell Corp.

In the past few years I've chaired search committees to hire science
librarians, and in three instances we hired librarians who didn't
really have science education or work experience but who were
willing to learn how to do it. They've proven to be tops at instruction and reference, so it's all worked out OK.

–Flora Shrode, Utah State University

The focus on instruction and reference in the latter comment is interesting. Clearly, the qualifications libraries seek will be dependent on the
specific, local nature of the job. "Many variables can factor into the
decision to get an advanced-subject degree, including type of library,
personal career goals, whether to be a generalist or a specialist, area of
librarianship (e.g., reference, collection development, cataloging, etc.),
and personal commitment" (Mayer and Terrill 2005). Even if we limit
our discussion to science librarianship, it is important to note that there
is no standard definition of a "science librarian," a fact recruiters need to
consider and address as they design recruiting media. That definition
will be quite different depending on specific situations and job postings.
A library in a small institution serving primarily an undergraduate population might post a different position and attract job candidates with
broader backgrounds than would a large research institution also serving a large population of graduate students and research faculty. The
former may find general reference and instruction skills and the ability
to support basic research in a broad range of disciplines more important.
The research institution may post a subject specialist position that
would be more likely to attract candidates who possess an advanced science degree. Those candidates may have a preference for working with
the graduates and faculty on advanced research projects, and a tendency
to be less interested in general reference and instruction. This is a gener-
alization, however, that has yet to be documented.

Attracting scientists and science students to the library profession is
perhaps the highest hurdle to recruiters, but it is also very important to
ensure that library schools are able to then train those students to use the
specialized information sources and tools they will need to succeed in
the profession. The library school curriculum has changed significantly
over the past two decades due to technological advances that have

added extra layers of complexity to information-seeking tools, although training in advanced tools is still not offered to many library students. This is especially true of tools used in the sciences. Fred Stoss, long a proponent of reaching out to scientists as recruits, noted that, "[o]ur need for scientists as science librarians has grown in the past decade. From a biologist's perspective, the data and information aspects of the Human Genome Project have left many science librarians in the wake of the development of a new generation of genomic, bioinformatics, proteomics, and other molecular biology data and information tools" (Stoss 2005). A related concern is that employers needing a combination of information seeking skills and scientific background may seek talent elsewhere if they cannot find it in the pool of readily available candidates nearby. In a global community, we may be falling behind our peers internationally in terms of the skills and knowledge we have to offer.

Data from this survey suggest that LIS schools are aware of this issue and are addressing it by offering more science librarianship courses in their curricula. Most survey participants had access to science courses in library school, with 59% reporting that they took a science librarianship-related course, 26% reporting that they did not, and only 15% reporting that science librarianship courses were not offered at their institution. LIS programs need to continue to be aware of this factor and to ensure that graduating librarians possess the training and skills valued by the research community, including those working in academia and in special, hospital, and governmental institutions. While more library schools have pursued the notion of collaborating with colleagues in college and university science departments to offer joint degree programs, the majority still do not offer joint programs or certificate programs in bioinformatics or chemical information, for example. Those library schools that have established joint programs, such as Indiana University in Bloomington Indiana (http://www.slis.indiana.edu/degrees/joint/smaster.html), have been very successful at placing their students in academic libraries, health systems libraries, and corporations such as Quest and Oracle.

INTEREST BLOSSOMS

Ensuring that graduating science and library school students are adequately prepared to enter science libraries is important, but these candidates first must be made aware of science librarianship as a career option. Data emphasizes the urgency and importance of recruiting greater numbers of science librarians into the profession, yet serendipitous exposure to libraries in general is not necessarily sufficient to attract scientifically inclined individuals. How do we reach those potential recruits, and where should we insert our efforts along their career or life trajectory? Several articles have studied sci-tech librarians and investigated who chooses this profession, and why (Hackenberg and Chu 2002; Hallmark and Lembo 2003). Science librarianship as a second career is a documented phenomenon; however these studies did not directly correlate a sparked interest in the profession with first exposure to science libraries or to science library research. This study seeks to investigate more closely what event or specific experience triggered practicing librarians' first interest in the profession. Was the interest in science librarianship sparked when they first needed to use a library, any library, or did that interest blossom later when they were exposed more specifically to *science* libraries or *science* research? If the latter, this would enforce the hypothesis that potential recruits to science librarianship are not aware of the advanced technology, challenges, and rewards of science librarianship until they are directly exposed to a science library or to science research. They may even be interested in librarianship but have not consciously made the connection between their science background and a related library career. Does data support the hypothesis that interest in the profession correlates to exposure to science librarianship or science research, and that this exposure first occurs when individuals are pursuing a science education, working in a science library, or working in a non-library science position? Although the connection seems to be a logical assumption, it has not been documented. Verification of this link will enable recruiters to focus their resources in the appropriate places along the life trajectories of individuals possessing an innate interest in the sciences.

Two questions in the survey were designed to address this issue. Question 1 asked respondents to "indicate what degree you were working on, or position you were in, when you *first needed to use a library* on a regular basis?" Question 5 then asked them to "indicate what degree you were working on, or what position you were in, when you *first became interested in science librarianship*?" Correlations between responses to these two questions were informative and helped to define more precisely when and where science librarians first became interested in this challenging profession. There appears to be very little correlation between when an individual first needs to use a library and the development of their interest in science librarianship. Rather, this interest appears to be triggered when individuals have to more specifically perform *science* research, or work in or use a *science* library. Fifty-three percent of all respondents indicated that they were in high school when they first needed to use a library on a regular basis; however only 3% of that group indicated that they became interested in science librarianship "pre-BS." It is difficult to assess the significance of this data without knowing what percent of all librarians became interested in library work while still in high school. Fifteen percent of those who first used the library in high school became interested in science librarianship while working on their BS, 28% while working on their MLS/MLIS, another 28% when working in a science position (non-library related), and 10% when working on an MS or PhD in science. Of the remaining 16%, six percent had some degree work or experience in the sciences, while the remainder simply indicated that they were offered a position. Of the 36% of all respondents who first needed to use a library regularly while pursuing their bachelor's degree, only 19% actually became interested in the profession at that point in their education. Twenty-three percent were working in science positions and 13% were working on advanced science degrees when their interest blossomed. Fully 32% became interested while in library school, not surprisingly, and the remaining 13% chose "Other" or "Pre-BS."

Of all respondents, regardless of when they first needed to use a library, 24% were working in a science position when they first became interested in science librarianship. This "second career" phenomenon is not new, nor is it limited to science librarians, as demonstrated in Pearson and Webb's 1987 survey in which over 70% of library school students indicated that they worked full-time in another profession before they decided to enter librarianship (Pearson and Webb 1988). As a practicing science librarian who chose this profession as a second career, I have often been struck by the number of colleagues who "discovered" librarianship while in pursuit of a science degree, or while working in a science position. A personal note received by the author eloquently articulates one librarians' personal philosophy about this phenomenon:

> I consider myself extremely fortunate to have been able to try careers in the real world before finding my destiny as a science librarian.
>
> –William Garrabrant, Science Librarian Emeritus

In the sciences, these careers in the real world include "the science journalist . . . the high school chemistry teacher . . . the graduate student who asks a question about biosensors at the reference desk, and . . . the secretary with a degree in zoology" (Vazakas and Wallin 1992).

Especially interesting were comments provided by a few of the 15% who chose "other" when asked to indicate what degree they were working on or what position they were in, when they first became interested in science librarianship. These comments inspire some additional thoughts about focusing and refining recruitment efforts (emphases added by the author):

- I had finished a bachelor's degree and decided not to continue in graduate school in my science major. I was browsing the school catalog looking for options and saw description of dual master's degrees for librarianship and history of science. This description said that the program might be good for science librarians. *I didn't know there was such a profession* and it sounded interesting.
- I wasn't working on a degree when I became interested in science librarianship. I applied for a residency program at a large university and happened to get an interview with the health sciences library. *I didn't even know the institution had a science librar[y]* when I applied.

These quotes highlight the major branding or image problem faced by library school and science library recruiters. As documented in OCLC's recent report *Perceptions of Libraries and Information Resources*, "roughly 70% of respondents, across all geographic regions and U.S. age groups, associate the library first and foremost with books" (De Rosa et al., 2005). Potential recruits to the library profession are among that 70% who have a dated perception of the field. Most people do not know what librarians actually do, especially science librarians. Many survey respondents stated that did not even know science libraries existed until someone told them, they read an article, or they happened to work in a position that exposed them to the field. A career counselor commented that, "[w]hen Hollywood depicts a librarian, the information conveyed may be totally different than when a career counselor describes a librarian, or when a librarian describes a librarian" (Vaughters 1992). Many comments about experiences or events that attracted respondents to the career included reference to the discovery of what it is librarians actually do:

- Discovered Manfred Kochen's article on what is an information scientist. Changed my life.
- The roommate of a (biology) grad-school colleague was in library school, and I'd hear her descriptions of what she was doing/learning.

- I was always interested in science and librarian [sic], while in college I realized there was such a thing as a science librarian.
- I was doing research on a paper as an undergrad. The science librarian helped me and I thought, "what a great job. Exposure to science without having to go through the drudgery of post-docs or being a P.I." Also, while I was working as a lab tech, after graduating with my BA, my favorite part of the job going to the library and pulling articles for my boss.

What were some of the other reasons these sci-tech librarians become interested in the field? Question 6 was designed to find the answer, asking, "What experience or event(s) happened to . . . attract you to science librarianship as a career." Responses to this open-ended question were difficult to categorize, however a few general themes emerged and are compiled in Table 2.

Comments from respondents in each category are quite enlightening, and many support the notion that actual exposure to research, to a science library, or to a science librarian are critical factors in attracting new talent to the profession.

Worked in a Library

Those whose first exposure to the profession came by working in a science library included an interesting mixture of support staff, science undergraduate and graduate students, and LIS students.

- I was working in a university medical library and became aware of how scientific information resources and services were ahead of the other disciplines (e.g., Medline was on cd-rom at that time, whereas

TABLE 2. Attractors to a Science Librarian Career

Q.6 What experience or event(s) happened . . . to attract you to science librarianship as a career?	
Worked in a library	22%
Performed research for grad school or job	25%
Job Opportunity	21%
Recommendation/Mentor	13%
Other/Blank/NA	19%

MLA was still in print). My science and engineering reference course was the most challenging and most interesting of all my studies in library school and I was especially intrigued by the challenges of chemical information.

- A 6-week fill-in at a sci/tech library.
- By working in clerical positions in an agricultural sciences library, I discovered I had a knack for reference work.

Performed Research for Grad School or Job

This category included independent researchers, scientists, faculty members, and graduate students:

- While working as a researcher I found that I enjoyed and had a natural knack for the "library"/information science side of research. Before I knew it I was freelancing for several faculty members and the rest is history.
- Finding relevant articles on a chemistry research project in the library. They solved a laboratory mystery.
- I was doing collections work for biology for the university library and hence got to know all the librarians well–at this time I was also losing interest in being a professor with its heavy demands of research and grant chasing . . . (former Zoology professor).
- The realization that there was an enormous body of chemical information available for improving problem-solving and decision-making processes of chemists, which would result in improving their personal productivity and the success of their organizational work affiliation.
- As I was completing the thesis for the MA in BioPsychology, I was inspired by the Science Librarian helping me with the lit review. She had a masters beyond the MLS, and I saw an exciting career to pursue!

Job Opportunity

A surprising number of practicing sci-tech librarians fell into this category. In some cases they simply wanted a job, any job. In many others, they believed or had been told that the job market in libraries was very good for individuals with a science background.

- Career change, interested in research and, to be honest, knew it would be a quick degree back into computers and science from a very different field.
- I originally thought I would go into Information Systems, but then I found out about the great need for science librarians.
- Discovery that having a science degree and getting a library degree was marketable.

Other

This category includes serendipitous events and those difficult to categorize elsewhere, usually because respondents were non-specific about what attracted them to this profession over any other career choice.

- Was teaching guitar to a librarian, became interested in the profession.
- Deciding not to pursue a career in mathematics.
- I needed to find a different career. I was a chef previously.

Recommendation/Mentor

The number of individuals reporting that a particular individual or mentor was instrumental in attracting them to the profession was not particularly large for this group, with 13% indicating that they decided to enter the profession based on someone's recommendation. Some respondents stated that the recommendation of others was influential, although they may not have viewed that as mentoring per se:

- My advisors knew I didn't want to be a bench chemist and suggested this as an alternative. I was majoring in Chemistry.
- School advisor strongly advised me to use my Bachelor of Science in Nursing degree and 12 [years?] experience as a practicing RN.
- My mother suggested it because she did not think I would find a job as an entomologist and I have 2 cousins who are librarians.
- It was simply a suggestion by a friend who didn't know anything more than I knew at the time about librarianship.

However, some comments do reflect a direct mentoring relationship and highlight the importance of librarians as recruiters:

- The teacher of the above course became my mentor and inspired me. She was our Agriculture Librarian. Subsequently I met and became friends with more science librarians at the university.

- I had an undergraduate degree in Biology. My father had just finished his MLS (as a second career choice) and taken a position as an Engineering librarian. He encouraged me to go into science librarianship.
- Encountered some very good librarians.
- Excellent mentors when I worked as a paraprofessional, plus ability to combine interest in librarianship and health sciences.
- I was encouraged by science librarians to consider librarianship as a profession.

The importance of correcting misperceptions or of increasing awareness about the nature and rewards of science librarianship today cannot be overstated to this audience, especially given data indicating that practicing librarians are such important recruiters of candidates to the field. This is not a new concept; in 1985 Barbara Dewey studied "the notion of librarians' influence as a primary factor in a student's choice of librarianship as a career and the implications of the general occupational image in librarianship as it relates to career choice" (Dewey 1985). This sentiment is reiterated throughout the library literature, with Vazakas and Wallin commenting again in 1992 that, "Academic librarians are in a unique position to reach many students who have not yet declared their majors or have no idea about what they would like to do after they graduate" (Vazakas and Wallin 1992). More recent articles about the recruitment of librarians have also mentioned the importance of librarians as recruiters for the profession (Hewitt, Moran, and Marsh 2003; Lucker 1998).

Responses to this survey confirm the impact practicing librarians can have by promoting a challenging, positive image, and by mentoring individuals into the profession. Question 10 asked, "If you had a mentor or role model who encouraged you to enter librarianship, please indicate that person's title and/or relationship to you." This direct question elicited stronger support for the importance of mentoring as a factor, than did the more broadly worded Question 6. Thirty-four percent of the respondents indicated that a mentor or role model had some impact on their decision to enter librarianship. This number could be much larger if librarians believe that they are the single greatest recruitment tool available to the profession, and act on that belief. As library schools and science libraries think about the role of personal mentoring in recruiting efforts, perhaps they should consider re-scoping or adopting the "Each One Reach One" slogan previously used by the ALA in the 1990s to focus their recruitment efforts on diverse populations.

WHERE TO RECRUIT? TRADITIONAL
AND NON-TRADITIONAL VENUES

As we seek to refine our recruiting efforts, it is important to focus resources on appropriate target populations while not overlooking more obvious or traditional possibilities. In the latter category are library school students, who have already been recruited into the profession and are more likely than any other population to be exposed to the various options or avenues open to them as they seek to define a specific direction to follow in their career in the information sciences. Recruiters should not overlook the many potential recruits to science librarianship who are in library school but who may harbor their own misconceptions about the nature of science positions. "Each year, many new students enroll in an MLS program because they have a general interest in the LIS field, but the majority of incoming students do not know what kind of an environment they want to work in post-graduation" (Hewitt, Moran, and Marsh 2003). Some comments indicated that LIS students were not necessarily aware of science librarianship as a career option when entering library school.

- I was looking for a new job and decided to go back to school because I wanted my MLIS. I did not consider science librarianship until after I graduated.
- When I met with the Dean regarding admission to the M.L.S. program & he saw I had degrees in Ag Ed, he said, "So you want to be an Ag Librarian?" To which I replied, "There's [sic] Ag Librarians?" Manuscripts brought me to librarianship. I didn't realize there were librarians with that specific a subject focus . . .
- I have an undergraduate degree in Geology, so when I started library school, I realized that I loved reference, and that I could combine reference work with a science focus.

In fact, these LIS students were represented in every category of responses to Question 6 (Table 3), which indicates that recruiters for science librarians may not be reaching this population as well as we might assume. LIS faculty and recruiters should consider more creative mechanisms to ensure that library students are aware of science librarianship as a rewarding career option.

Recruiters also need to reach science-minded individuals who may not necessarily want a "hard" science career but who are intrigued by science librarianship once they see it as an option. Stuart even suggested that libraries consider dropping the library degree requirement for sci-tech positions and, "focus their energy on developing recruitment programs which identify and attract freshly minted scientists and engineers directly into the ranks" (Stuart and Drake 1992). Some of his other suggestions were to focus on students currently enrolled in BS programs in science, and to collaborate with department heads and academic advisors to investigate the development of career path alternatives that involve technical and scientific information work, for those students who are interested in the sciences but do not enjoy the lab environment. Providing support for this suggestion were several survey participants who mentioned that an academic advisor or faculty member influenced their decision to enter the profession:

- I realized I enjoyed talking about other people's science research rather than working on my own; When I finished my MSc., a faculty member advised me to find a career where I could use both my science background and work with people.
- My graduate advisor suggested that I look into librarianship. I got a job at a hospital library and I enjoyed it, so I decided to become a librarian.

Recruiters should design brochures geared specifically to this population and post them in places frequented by these students, such as departmental bulletin boards or study areas in science and engineering classroom buildings. The idea of focusing recruiting efforts in arenas outside of the traditional library world is not new. Nearly 20 years ago J. Adam Edwards asked, "How easy is it for a science graduate, looking for scientific jobs or science-based courses, to come across details about LIS work or courses" (Edwards 1987)? He noted that advertisements are often either entirely missing from career guides aimed at science students, or they are buried in the social science sections of guides, or they include descriptions that do nothing to accurately describe what science librarians actually do. It is discouraging to note that while technology has revolutionized the tools used by information scientists over the past 20 years, especially in the sciences, impressions of what librarians actually do have not changed at all. We need to ensure that advertisements are informative and inspire interest in the profession, since advertising outside of the library does reach some students:

- I was finishing my MSc. (Chemistry) and I saw a poster advertising an information session on the MLIS degree at my school. The free lunch attracted me so I went.

In addition to pinpointing when and how people get exposed to science librarianship as a career choice ". . . having a knowledge base of how students learn and make decisions about careers can be extremely helpful" (Vaughters 1992). Vaughters, a career counselor, notes that recruiting materials need to appeal to different learning styles, and that students in difference phases of their education will be seeking different kinds of information about career options (i.e., first year freshmen versus graduate students). She also suggests targeting students in multiple venues, including where they live and study, and utilizing career planning professionals to take advantage of their expertise in recruiting efforts. Career counselors are well positioned to reach students seeking creative ideas about career options that meet their talents and interests, as one survey respondent noted:

- High school counselor asked me what subjects I liked in school–I picked library and genetics–she looked up careers that would match those subjects and came up with only one–medical librarianship.

When considering where to target potential recruits, libraries should not forget another interesting population that emerged from this study: the contingent of sci-tech librarians who first became interested in the field while working in a library as a member of the paraprofessional staff or as a student. Libraries should think creatively about how to support the movement of interested, talented individuals who are already working in their libraries into professional positions. Some libraries are already doing so:

- The library director where I was working picked a group of support staffers and underwrote all our expenses for library school.

All of the factors discussed above need to be incorporated into future recruitment efforts if science libraries are to be successful at filling the open positions coming over the horizon.

FURTHER RESEARCH

This study yielded a wealth of data to be mined for further research, and inspired ideas for other avenues of inquiry. One very important related issue that was not discussed extensively here is retention. This study included several questions designed to investigate whether sci-tech librarians are frustrated by an inability of libraries to place a high enough dollar value on those who have science backgrounds to compete well with their other career options. Data was gathered on factors impacting job satisfaction in the library profession, the pursuit of other job opportunities, and reasons why librarians might be considering a career change, as well as demographic salary information. This data is so rich that it deserves a separate discussion. However, a preliminary analysis of the data suggests that most practicing sci-tech librarians are satisfied with the profession and are not actively seeking new opportunities elsewhere. Also, while salary and compensation are definitely very important retention factors, others that are equally or more important include, "a sense of accomplishment/effectiveness," a "sense of respect/recognition from colleagues, management, and clientele," and "autonomy: independence in setting goals and establishing priorities."

Other concerns to be addressed involve recruits who are currently in library school. Further study and analysis is needed to understand patterns in library school students moving into science librarianship. What are the trends in the inclusion of science information courses in library school curricula? How might all of these trends impact future recruitment efforts? Finally, if exposure to science librarians and the work they do is a significant key in motivating individuals to pursue librarianship as a career option, as has been demonstrated here, how might the movement of students at all levels toward online research and away from in-library research impact recruiting for all academic libraries? Alternately, with the relatively recent emphasis on increasing information literacy and writing skills in all subject areas, undergraduate science curricula may reflect a corresponding increase in research and writing requirements. If so, what might be the impact of that changing dynamic on future recruitment efforts for sci-tech Librarians? Might science students "get the bug" and learn to love the hunt for information earlier in their careers?

CONCLUSION

The library profession will continue to evolve rapidly as we strive to adapt to the profound changes every library and information center, regardless of type or specialty, will continue to experience due to technological advances. We "need to attract and keep bright, creative, and energetic people involved in research, academic, and special libraries as well as in the science departments of public and academic libraries," which "will require more recruiting among high school students and college undergraduates" (Lucker 1998). Responses to this survey support the notion that a science background is an important qualification for candidates interested in science librarianship, although the MLS/MLIS is of primary importance as the terminal professional degree. Responses also support the theory that exposure to science research and science libraries, rather than serendipitous exposure to libraries in general, is a significant factor in inspiring potential recruits to pursue careers as science librarians. Therefore, the single most important method for attracting sci-tech candidates to the profession is to identify scientifically inclined individuals and ensure that they are exposed to science librarianship as early in their career trajectory as possible. This can occur via advertising in non-traditional venues, or by focusing on individuals working or volunteering in a science library, or by increasing active mentoring efforts by science librarians. Recruitment methods, models, and venues must change to reflect the changing nature of the profession. Library schools must work harder to ensure that students are provided with both the opportunities for obtaining subject specific knowledge and the tools that will enable them to excel in libraries as well as in the corporate world, where knowledge management skills are increasingly important. "Promoting LIS work as a career for the science graduate is thus but one small part of promoting LIS work in the whole of society" (Edwards 1987). Everyone in the library profession, regardless of the size or type of library or information center in which they work, is responsible for changing perceptions about the skills needed to work in libraries, and the challenges and rewards that can be found here.

REFERENCES

Association of College and Research Libraries. Ad Hoc Task Force on Recruitment & Retention Issues. 2002. *Recruitment, retention, and restructuring: Human resources in academic libraries.* Chicago: Association of College and Research Libraries.

De Rosa, Cathy, Joanne Cantrell, Diane Cellentani, Janet Hawk, Lillie Jenkins, and Alane Wilson. 2005. *Perceptions of libraries and information resources: A report to the OCLC membership.* Dublin, Ohio: OCLC Online Computer Library Center, Inc.

Dewey, Barbara I. 1985. Selection of librarianship as a career: Implications for recruitment. *Journal of Education for Library and Information Science* 26 (1): 16-24.

Edwards, J. Adam. 1987. Selling information science to scientists: The role of careers guides in the promotion of library/information science. *Library Association Record* 89 (12): 641-645.

Hackenberg, Jill M. 2000. Who chooses sci-tech librarianship? *College & Research Libraries* 61 (5): 441-450.

Hackenberg, Jill M., and Barbara Chu. 2002. Why does one choose sci-tech librarianship? Findings of a survey. *Science & Technology Libraries* 23 (1): 3-16.

Hallmark, Julie, and Mary Frances Lembo. 2003. Leaving science for LIS: Interviews and a survey of librarians with scientific and technical degrees {computer file}. *Issues in Science & Technology Librarianship* 37, http://vnweb.hwwilsonweb.com/hww/jumpstart.jhtml?recid=0bc05f7a67b1790eb24c0e7097de0bd0d4c6d8b 53e8 efdfe439c0ea07d6d17c101cd52721b7acddf&fmt=C.

Hewitt, Joe A., Barbara B. Moran, and Mari E. Marsh. 2003. Finding our replacements: One institution's approach to recruiting academic librarians. *Portal* 3 (2): 179-189, http://vnweb.hwwilsonweb.com/hww/jumpstart.jhtml?recid=0bc05f7a67b1790eb24 c0e7097de0bd0d4c6d8b53e8efdfebe969ed092fd8d818045fd9c3f782e5d&fmt=C.

Hooper-Lane, Christopher. 1999. Spotlight on the subject knowledge of chemistry librarians: Results of a survey. *Issues in Science & Technology Librarianship* Summer (23), http://vnweb.hwwilsonweb.com/hww/jumpstart.jhtml?recid=0bc05f7 a67b1790eb24c0e7097de0bd088ee4f971e9e39b50a0a2d0031be143ebb82052b2e edbdc8&fmt=C.

Lucker, Jay K. 1998. The changing nature of scientific and technical librarianship: A personal perspective over 40 years. *Science & Technology Libraries* 17 (2): 3-10.

Mayer, Jennifer, and Lori J. Terrill. 2005. Academic librarians' attitudes about advanced-subject degrees. *College & Research Libraries* 66 (1): 59-73.

Mount, Ellis. 1985. *University science and engineering libraries.* Contributions in librarianship and information science. 2nd ed. Vol. 49. Westport, Conn.: Greenwood Press.

Pearson, Richard C., and T. D. Webb. 1988. The new librarians: How prepared are they? *Library Journal* 113 (14): 132-134.

Storm, Paula, and Wei Wei. 1994. Issues related to the education and recruitment of science/technology librarians. *Science & Technology Libraries* 14 (3): 35-42.

Stoss, Fred. 2005. Recruiting scientists into our profession. *STS Signal* 20 (2): 6.

Stuart, Crit, and Miriam A. Drake. 1992. Education and recruitment of science and engineering librarians. *Science & Technology Libraries* 12 (4): 79-89.

Vaughters, Sharon. 1992. Promoting careers in library and information science. *College & Research Libraries News* 53 (6): 386-389.

Vazakas, Susan M., and Camille Clark Wallin. 1992. Where are all the science librarians? *College & Research Libraries News* 53 (3): 166-171.

Winston, Mark D. 2001. Academic science and engineering librarians: A research study of demographics, educational backgrounds, and professional activities. *Science & Technology Libraries* 19 (2): 3-24.

doi: 10.1300/J122v27n01_10

Science Librarianship in Africa

Innocent Awasom

SUMMARY. Science librarianship is a relatively new specialty in the library profession in Africa as the bulk of the early librarians had a background in the Arts and Humanities. Unfortunately there is a dearth of science librarians on the continent and the need for science librarians is more crucial to help support meaningful scientific research and development on the continent. Why does the gap exist? What are Library and Information Science (LIS) schools doing to entice, attract, enroll, motivate, and train science librarians? What are the professional associations doing to promote the cause of science librarianship? What are academic and research libraries doing to retain and stop science librarians from invading or migrating to other niches. This paper attempts to provide answers to the above questions with input and insight from across the continent. doi:
10.1300/J122v27n01_11 *[Article copies available for a fee from The Haworth Document Delivery Service: 1-800-HAWORTH. E-mail address: <docdelivery@ haworthpress.com> Website: <http://www.HaworthPress.com> © 2006 by The Haworth Press, Inc. All rights reserved.]*

Innocent Awasom, M.Inf.Sc., is Science Librarian, Texas Tech University in Lubbock. He has liaison responsibilities for Agriculture, Chemistry and Mathematics (E-mail: awasom.afuh@ttu.edu).

The author would like to express his gratitude to Drs. Vero Ngole and Wole Olatokun of the University of Botswana and Ibadan respectively, Ngang Cornelius of the University of Yaoundé, Demissew Tsigemalak of the University of Addis Ababa, and Seynabou Mbengue of EBAD Senegal for the data used in this study.

[Haworth co-indexing entry note]: "Science Librarianship in Africa" Awasom, Innocent. Co-published simultaneously in *Science & Technology Libraries* (The Haworth Information Press, an imprint of The Haworth Press, Inc.) Vol. 27, No. 1/2, 2006, pp. 159-171; and: *Recruiting, Training, and Retention of Science and Technology Librarians* (ed: Patricia A. Kreitz, and JoAnn DeVries) The Haworth Information Press, an imprint of The Haworth Press, Inc., 2006, pp. 159-171. Single or multiple copies of this article are available for a fee from The Haworth Document Delivery Service [1-800-HAWORTH, 9:00 a.m. - 5:00 p.m. (EST). E-mail address: docdelivery@haworthpress.com].

Available online at http://stl.haworthpress.com
© 2006 by The Haworth Press, Inc. All rights reserved.
Digital Object Identifier: 10.1300/J122v27n01_11

KEYWORDS. Science librarianship, recruitment, retention, training, academic libraries, Africa

INTRODUCTION

Academic and research libraries in the West are going through a phase where the major concern is recruiting younger practitioners into the profession because a large percentage of the currently working librarians might be retiring in the next decade or two. Africa on the contrary is faced with a different set of problems that need urgent attention by the academic and research institutions if they want to be productive and stay competitive in the emerging global economy. Universities are expanding in response to the youthful population attaining higher education age much faster than before but unfortunately the information infrastructure is not expanding at a rate proportionate to the college age population. Libraries and information centers which are supposed to be catering for the research and teaching needs face the greatest challenges (Rosenberg, 1997). For example Cameroon prior to 1993 had one state university (Yaoundé University) and five specialized university centers. A presidential decree in 1993 changed this situation, bringing the total number of full fledged universities to six. That meant the upgrading of library facilities that previously served a restricted clientele to a broad based service expectation without the necessary manpower in place to run them (Awasom, 2003).

In most of Africa, educational counseling is such that the smarter kids are generally oriented towards the sciences to such professions as medicine, pharmacy, engineering, agriculture and related research. Librarianship unfortunately has not been one of the trendy professions. The fact that the early librarians were mostly from the arts and humanities and that the professions is plagued by considerations of status and low moral, means that there has been very little appeal for students to think of it as a career option. However with scholarship growing increasingly interdisciplinary, there is a greater need for management of specialized information. The raising stature and need for science librarians, coupled with an increasing attractiveness of the field as a second career option for science graduates, is creating a potential pool for recruits.

Again because of vertical and horizontal movement of the workforce in response to economic pressures, the recruitment and retention of quality staff remains a very big issue. Therefore this study takes a look at some library schools as well as their curriculum, their staffing situation and its impact on the training of science librarians. What are the LIS institutions doing to recruit students with scientific background? What innovative strategies are libraries using to recruit and retain a new generation of professionals and entice them from migrating to other niches.

What are the professional associations doing to counter poor opinions and revamp the morale of the profession? This paper attempts to provide answers to the above concerns with input and insight from the Consortium of African Schools of Information Science (CASIS) and from across the continent.

Articles in professional literature abound in the developed world on recruitment and retention of librarians. However not much is available on African librarianship much less on science librarianship. Formal LIS education in Africa is a relatively recent phenomenon. (Aiyepeku, 1997). The bulk of the literature on African librarianship is from the leading centers in sub Saharan Africa, Nigeria and Ghana for West Africa, Botswana for South Africa and Uganda and Kenya for East Africa. Scholarly publications on African librarianship abound in western journals for reasons of prestige, recognition and visibility (Ehikhamenor, 1990). This does not however overlook a number of local and regional publications that existed for a brief period and died out with the downward trend of African economies in the late eighties while some have thrived with donor support (Aina, 2002; Mabawonku, 2002).

In contrast to the state of library science education in the U.S and Europe, Nwakanma, 2003 critically examines the problems of the development of the library profession and he advocates for the development of local publishing so that results could be easily available to impact local development. Badu, 2004 looks at career development pathways while Onatola, 2000 examines both career development and job mobility among academic librarians in Nigeria which is a reflection of what obtains on the continent. Success in any chosen career is a function of the initial motivating factors that led to that choice of a career and this has an influence on further recruitment and retention in the long run (Nzotta, 1983). Ngulube, 2000 looks at staff retention in Zimbabwe while Tiamiyu and Aiyepeku (2004) take a cursory look at the pioneer graduates from the Africa Regional Center for Information Science. This is the only institution that puts a premium on recruiting to a large extent of students with scientific backgrounds.

As can be seen, there is a dearth of information on the recruitment and retention of specifically science librarians in Africa. This study is an attempt to fill this void. It takes a look at some library schools, their staffing capacity and curriculum as a reflection of their ability to train and produce science librarians for the many academic and research libraries. Recruitment, retention and mobility of science librarians is also examined to give a snapshot of the prevailing situation on the continent.

METHODOLOGY

The design of the study takes into consideration what is happening in the libraries and library schools and places these activities in a more general context. In this regard, a survey was mailed out to select libraries and LIS schools in Africa in November 2005 to obtain information about recruitment and retention strategies for librarians in general and science librarians in particular. It also followed up on techniques that have been successful and what motivating factors keep the professionals in place. As a follow up, an online version was sent to colleagues on a discussion list of the special libraries association and alumni association to obtain information about professional mobility. Despite the above, the response was poor and so personal e-mails as well as phone interviews were used to complement the information obtained.

Fortunately some libraries and LIS have a web presence and so information was obtained from there to complement some of the data that came in. The main problem in the data collection was the low rate of return that necessitated numerous phone calls and e-mail reminders to get the necessary information. For best results it would have been better to have a researcher on the ground or to do an investigator–monitored questionnaire.

RESULTS AND DISCUSSIONS

Respondents

Data was received from three of the four major schools of LIS that make up the Consortium of African Schools of Library and Information Science (CASIS) and the fourth was obtained from the Internet. Seventy five colleagues from libraries and library schools on two list serves responded to the survey. This number may be small compared to the total number of subscribers, but it none the less presents an insight into the current state of science librarianship in Africa. Calculations of a response rate may therefore not be useful as it may not be known exactly how many of the list subscribers are science librarians.

Library School Training

Of the 8 institutions that offered courses in LIS only 1 (12.5%) had over 50 % of the teaching staff having a background in the sciences. That is the Regional Center for Information Science (ARCIS) University of Ibadan. The bulk of the LIS faculty there have degrees in the physical sciences notably Informatics (71.42%). At some of the responding institutions, there were instructors with no scientific background or training but the curriculum had courses in scientific and technical information management. One might wonder how effectively they could teach such specialized courses if they do not have a good command of the basic principles and subject matter in the fields being served (see Table 1).

TABLE 1. Library and Information Science School Staffing Strengths

Name of Institution	Staff Educational Background					
	Degree/ Dip offered	Arts	Social sciences	Sciences	Total	% in the Science
ARCIS, University of Ibadan–Nigeria	P.G	2	2	10	41	71.42
ESSTIC, Univ. of Yaoundé II–Cameroon	UG and PG Diploma	6	6	4	16	25
EBAD–Senegal	UG and PG				33	
Moi University Kenya	UG and PG	12	12	4	28	14.5
EASLIS, Univ. of Makerere–Uganda	UG and PG	3	7	-	10	0
University of Botswana	PG	14	5	7	26	26.9
University of Ghana	UG	5	2	1	8	12.5
Univ. of Ngaoundere–Cameroon		1	1		2	0

PG = Post Graduate (PG Diploma, Masters, and PhD); UG = Undergraduate (Diploma and Certificate)

Academic Background of Science Librarians

The idea of having a background in the sciences as a prerequisite for assuming and effectively executing the functions of a science librarian has generated controversy in library circles. Some opine that to produce good results, a good scientific base is very necessary (Lucker, 1998) Others think that having other skill-sets plus the willingness or zeal to learn through conferences, and hands on the job can make up for the lack of a science degree (Morris-knower, 2001).

Table 2 shows the academic background of science librarians. And it shows the University of Botswana having the highest (14.63 %) staff with a science background. However, much depends on the general background of the librarian, for if specialization was early in his educational training, then it might be difficult to come to terms with scientific concepts and formula. Students start specializing very early in Africa and this does not help them in the long run as they become too narrow in their perspective. Moreover everyone needs basic mathematics and science in every day life. Fortunately, this weakness has been identified and forward looking nations like Nigeria, Senegal and Kenya are changing their curriculum, expecting students to do all subjects up till high school with minors and majors determining their career path. That way students in the sciences are not completely blank in the arts and vice versa.

TABLE 2. University Libraries Staffing Strength

Institution	Educational Background						
	Diploma or less	Arts	Law	Social science	Science	Total	% Science
University of Ngaoundere	10	1	1	1	1	14	7.14
University of Yaoundé	28	6	1	3	1	39	2.56
University of Buea	21	5	3			29	0
University of Ghana		13		2		15	0
Makerere University Uganda	8	2				32	0
University of Botswana	4				6	41	14.63
Univ. of Addis Ababa Ethiopia	7					17	0

In Africa where the image of the librarian is not the best, having a science librarian who cannot comfortably respond to queries will further alienate patrons from library services and the reverse is true. Moreover, because some faculty do not treat librarians as colleagues despite sometimes similar qualifications, being able to discuss intelligently and with mastery of the subject matter with them works to the benefit of the librarian, the library and the profession. Therefore it is urgent that libraries and LIS institutions attract people with a broad scientific base especially these days when the government is not funding research institutes and numerous science graduates are migrating into other fields.

Status of the Library Profession

A lot of attention is given to science education but unfortunately the library profession in Africa has not taken advantage of this to change the mentality of library patrons. If the smart students are counseled towards the sciences and then end up being science librarians then it may begin to influence the minds of the younger generation. Professional associations could play a strong role in influencing the public point of view in Africa, patterned after the success of associations in the U.S and Europe (e.g., ALA's @ Your Library Campaign). Unfortunately the professional associations in most parts of Africa are plagued by problems of leadership. Many of the associations are moribund or if existing are on life support or are highly politicized rendering them ineffective.

In the survey, library staff were asked if any of them belonged to library associations. Few of the librarians (20%) belonged to local library associations and (5%) belonged to international associations but had their dues subsidized or paid for by colleagues in the West. This is understandable because of the weak currency situation.

The library schools have to take the lead in reorganizing the library associations and get the younger generation in library school involved. Through this they can improve visibility which may lead to the reorganization at the national and regional levels. Soon one might see the desired multiplier effect especially when people start attending conferences nationally and internationally. Laudable initiatives by the SLA through the Global 2000 Fellows for Africa saw the emergence of a crop of leaders from the library community in Africa who are now championing the cause of African librarianship. The International Association of Agricultural Information Specialists (IAALD) also invited a number of science librarians to the World Congress in the USA in 2005 and these leaders are shaping the culture of science librarianship in Africa. They are the nucleus of the African Chapter of the IAALD and are organizing a follow up IAALD conference in May 2006. Another laudable initiative is that of the physics, Astronomy and Mathematics Division (PAM) of the SLA which each year invites a science librarian to its annual conference. The last two have been from Africa and they are changing the future of librarianship in their countries. Thus the collaboration between Library Associations in the West and in Africa has raised consciousness and visibility which might ultimately attract younger science graduates to the profession.

Recruitment of Science Librarians

In the professional market place, the professions which attract and retain the most talented people are those who market their profession well and succeed in capturing the minds and psyche of those entering the professional world. The recruitment of science librarians falls into the realm where library schools, university libraries as well as professional associations have to work hard to gain recruits into their ranks. Library schools in Africa tend to rely on students just applying to become librarians and this is not yielding the desired results. At the launching of the African Regional Center for Information Science (ARCIS), University of Ibadan, grants were made available (with funding from IDRC Canada) to attract science graduates from the region and this worked pretty well. LIS institutions can work with institutional libraries to offer paid internships to students especially those with science backgrounds. Graduate school applicants having worked as library interns stand a better chance compared to those with no such advantage. Nzotta, 1983 confirms that having worked in a library plays a crucial role in students' choice of librarianship as a career.

LIS schools should have brochures with eye-catching messages to target high school students, college graduates and others in the work force looking for a career change. Most people in Africa want to be computer literate and where else to have this training for free than in library schools. Here it is incorporated into the curriculum and this training makes them ready to work not only in libraries in particular but also in information centers or any where that there is need for information/ knowledge management.

Unlike in the West, career mobility is not frequent in the developing countries. It is very common to see librarians start and end their careers in the same institution. Sometimes rising to management positions is more related to political affiliations than to competence and experience.

Recruitment Methods

As no formal vacancy notices are put out advertising available vacancies, respondents were asked to identify the method they used to get their current job with 1 being most to 5 being the least applicable (see Table 3).

The results show that there is no formal structure that job seekers can tap into. What is required is the ability of the individual to use his/her initiative as well as aggressive marketing skills to sell his/her potential. That applicants use the "broadcast method" is an indication to the LIS schools to devout more attention to preparing graduates for the job market through courses in communication that would include job-hunting skills, preparing CV's and resumes, etc.

Word of mouth came in second place and the absence of a search committee in many institutions raises questions of credibility. Instituting a search committee with a clear position criteria and expectations would result in the selection of the best candidate. Internship programs and practical training is another way of letting students have a feel of the profession and institutions that have a good internship program usually record a high rate of employment of its graduates (Tiamiyu and Aiyepeku, 2004).

Strategies for Recruitment

At the African Regional Center for Information Science (ARCIS), University of Ibadan, 3 faculty members said that they were attracted to the profession by the prospect of further education. Librarianship is a profession where continuous professional development is a sine qua non for promotion. Therefore the science librarian not only keeps abreast with developments in his area of specialty but also knows how to manage effectively such information. This is a convincing argument to use to attract science students. The avenues and support for further

TABLE 3. Methods of Recruitment of Librarians

Recruitment Method	%	Ranking
Application broadcasting	95	1
Word of mouth	90	2
Internship program	75	3
In-house information	60	4
Use of newspapers and web sites	35	5

education exists for science librarians and this should be used to advertise the profession.

Many librarians have commented on the fact that in the course of their education, relatives taking them to the library, a certain public reference librarian helping them to find information, access a paper for a research project, etc., made them choose librarianship as a career (Nzotta, 1983). Mentoring therefore plays a critical role in shaping the destiny of many a student and professionals. Many students look for internship opportunities in academic and research libraries and if academic and research institutions mount an aggressive campaign targeting mostly science and technology students for a couple of years and letting them see how exciting it can be to work in scientific and technical information management, I am sure down the line, we will begin to see an increase in the number of science librarians in the continent. This approach has proven successful in the United States (Roland, 2000).

Another strategy that can be used by institutions is tuition remission for library paraprofessional staff or others interested in taking relevant courses towards a degree in the sciences. That way they acquire the necessary knowledge that would be applicable in their jobs. They get an education and are paid for it while the institution benefits with more knowledgeable staff, a win-win situation for all parties.

Retention

Even though jobs are hard to come by in Africa, the few science librarians have a different story to tell. On the contrary, they are very mobile and usually use their first job as a stepping stone to another more lucrative position usually in the private sector. This has been the case especially with systems librarians.

Colleagues were asked what major consideration made them to stay at their current job and the results are displayed in Table 4. Faculty status

TABLE 4. Factors Favoring Retention

Retention criteria	%	Ranking
Faculty status	95	1
Professional Development	90	2
Geographic location	80	3
Cost of living	60	4
Benefits package	59	5

is given a very high premium. This is not only because of the fact that it brings the benefits of recognition and prestige but it is also associated with "perks" like book and research allowances, sabbaticals, scholarships opportunities, etc. This is in agreement with Rosenberg's (1997) earlier findings. Professional development is closely associated with faculty status but has the added advantage of leave of absence policy for all librarians. A nuance however exists in the categorization of professional librarians. While those with an undergraduate degree, B.Sc., B.L.S are professional librarians, they are not conferred faculty status while those with a second graduate degree have an added advantage compared to those with just the Library graduate degree. This is because they have been involved with research and can interact with more expertise with faculty and graduate students. In a recent IAALD World Congress meeting, one of the participants opined that he was forced to do a second masters because his colleagues in the faculty of Arts were given courses beyond library instruction, better remunerated, considered senior librarians and faculty, and had more respect within faculty circles than the rest of the librarians.

Professional development which ranked second includes opportunities for study leave for advanced degrees with or without pay depending on longevity, organization of in-house conferences and workshops with the international ones being highly dependent on external donor support and the proactive nature of the individual librarian. Institutions supporting librarians attending conferences abroad was a major attraction and staff retention rate was higher there.

Geographic location ranked third and had a division along age lines. Younger librarians needed to be in an area where there will be good school facilities for their children as well as opportunities for continuous education. Cost of living is a direct reflection of the benefit package and only in the private sector does any substantial benefit exist. With government's facing economic crises, having the regular salary is good enough.

The strategies proposed for the recruitment and retention of librarians range from "catching them young" to "dangling the carrot" but from a practical point of view, a staff who has been in a position over a period of time learns to master the collection, is comfortable working with colleagues and faculty and knows to a great extent the total environment. New staff will have to learn all of the above. It could then be implied that retention is far less costly than recruitment and should be pursued more vigorously by library administrators.

CONCLUSION

The study shows that science librarianship is still in its infancy in Africa. No clear cut policy exists on recruitment into LIS schools. More is done through informal networks. The same can be said for strategies for retention of professional staff. Administrators seem to feel since jobs are hard to come by, staff may be content and lucky to have one. This is a pointer to the lack of knowledge about personnel needs. This is very disturbing as the youthful population is rising and there is need for qualified and professional librarians, not charlatans.

Research institutions in most African countries depend heavily on government and donor support that is increasingly diminishing and as a result there are many science graduates left without jobs in the teaching or research fields. Therefore, LIS schools should develop an aggressive marketing strategy coupled with other incentives such as scholarships, part-time positions, and on-the-job-training to reach out to science graduates. According to Ngang Cornelius, Chemistry librarian at the University of Yaoundé "the harvest is plentiful but the workers are few." The few science librarians in Africa have to step up to the plate and be mentors and advocates for the profession. They should lobby and inform library and university administrators of the deplorable state of science librarianship in particular and librarianship in general in their respective institutions.

There is need for more research to better understand the internal processes of recruitment and retention in African academic libraries. The findings in this survey are a call for LIS schools and professional associations on the continent. They should pursue more active partnership in this era of globalization with their counterparts in the U.S.A and other developed countries.

The current state of science librarianship in Africa leaves much to be desired but there is hope in the few existing networks. According to Quinn, 2005, taking a positive approach to librarianship and fostering a positive culture within institutions may result in a variety of benefits in the area of mentoring, productivity, recruitment and retention of staff.

REFERENCES

Aina, L.O. 2002. African Journal of Library, Archives and Information Science as a resource base for information science research in Africa. African Journal of Library, *Archives and Information Science* 12(2): 167-175.

Aiyepeku, W.O. 2003. African regional Center for Information Science (ARCIS)–Organizational Brief.

Aiyepeku, W.O. and Kolamofe, H.O. 1997. Africa. In Courrier Yvess (ed.) World Information Report 1997/98. Paris: UNESCO Pub.

Awasom, I.A. 2003. Academic and research libraries in Cameroon: Current state and future perspectives. In Zeleza and Olukoshi (eds.) African Universities in the 21st century Vol. 2. Dakar, Senegal: Council for the Development of Economic and Social Research in Africa.

Badu, E.E. 2004. Academic Library development in Ghana: Top managers' perspective. African Journal of Library, *Archives and Information Science* 14(2): 93-107.

Beyer, H.E. 2004. Finding leadership and mentoring opportunities. LIScareer, March 2004. www.liscareer.com/beyer_mentoring.htm (Accessed March 25th, 2006).

Bothmer, J.E. and Lacroix, M.J. 2004. Recruitment and Retention at the Creighton University Libraries. *Nebraska Library Association Quarterly* 35(2):11-13 www.nebraskalibraries.org/nlaquarterly/2004-2-BothmerLacroix.htm.

Ehikhamenor, F.A. 1990: Productivity of physical scientists in Nigerian universities in relation to communication variables. *Scientometrics* 18 (5/6):437-444.

Engel, Debra: Resources about Librarian recruitment and retention. www.rose.edu/faculty/ssaulmon/Debraresources.htm. (Accessed on March 24th, 2006).

Lucker, J.K. 1998. The changing nature of scientific and technical librarianship: A personal perspective over 40 years. *Science & Technology Libraries* 17(2):3-10.

Mabawonku, I. 2001. Trends in library and information science research in Africa, 1999-2000. African Journal of Library, *Archives and Information Science* 11(2):78-88.

Morris-Knower, J. 2001 Phyllostachys Aurea–didn't he work with Socrates? Reference work in science libraries by librarians who are not scientists. *The Reference Librarian* 34(72) 155-169.

Nzotta, B.C. 1983. Choice of Librarianship as a career: The case of the post graduate class of 1978. *Nigerian Journal of Library and Information Studies* 1(1):1-11.

Ocholla, D.N. 2000: Training for library and information studies. A comparative overview of LIS education in Africa. *Education for Information* 18(1):33-52.

Onatola, A. 2000. Career development and movement of librarians in a Nigerian university library. African Journal of Library, Archives, and Information Science 10(1):63-68.

Ortega, L and Brown, C. 2005. The Face of 21st century Physical Science Librarianship Science and Technology Libraries 26(2):71-90.

Quinn, B. 2005. Enhancing Academic Library performance through positive psychology. *Journal of Library Administration* 42(1):79-101.

Roland, K.C. 2000. Training Future science Librarians: A Successful Partnership Between Academia and the United States Environmental Protection Agency. Issues in Science and technology Librarianship. Spring 2000 www.istl.org/00-spring/article3.html.

Rosenberg, D.B. 2002. Current issues in Library and information services in Africa www.inasp.info/pubs/bookchain/profiles/rosenberg.html (Accessed March 20th, 2006).

Rosenberg, D.B. 1997. University libraries in Africa. A review of their current state and future potential. Vol.1 London: International African Institute.

doi: 10.1300/J122v27n01_11

New Models of Recruitment
and (Continuing) Education
for Sci-Tech Librarianship

Linda C. Smith

SUMMARY. This paper discusses the role of library and information science (LIS) educators in recruiting and retaining sci-tech librarians. Strategies include increasing access to degree programs using Web-based technologies; enriching course offerings that contribute to the preparation of sci-tech librarians; partnering with experienced sci-tech librarians who can serve as guest speakers, practicum and internship supervisors, and course instructors; and developing continuing education offerings, especially for Web-based delivery in partnership with professional associations. In the era of e-science and e-learning, LIS educators have a responsibility to contribute to recruitment and retention of sci-tech librarians ready to take on new challenges and opportunities. doi: 10.1300/J122v27n01_12 *[Article copies available for a fee from The Haworth Document Delivery Service: 1-800-HAWORTH. E-mail address: <docdelivery@haworthpress.com> Website: <http://www.HaworthPress.com> © 2006 by The Haworth Press, Inc. All rights reserved.]*

Linda C. Smith, PhD, is Professor and Associate Dean, Graduate School of Library and Information Science, University of Illinois at Urbana-Champaign, 501 East Daniel Street, Champaign, IL 61820 (E-mail: lcsmith@uiuc.edu).

[Haworth co-indexing entry note]: "New Models of Recruitment and (Continuing) Education for Sci-Tech Librarianship" Smith, Linda C. Co-published simultaneously in *Science & Technology Libraries* (The Haworth Information Press, an imprint of The Haworth Press, Inc.) Vol. 27, No. 1/2, 2006, pp. 173-184; and: *Recruiting, Training, and Retention of Science and Technology Librarians* (ed: Patricia A. Kreitz, and JoAnn DeVries) The Haworth Information Press, an imprint of The Haworth Press, Inc., 2006, pp.173-184. Single or multiple copies of this article are available for a fee from The Haworth Document Delivery Service [1-800-HAWORTH, 9:00 a.m. - 5:00 p.m. (EST). E-mail address: docdelivery@haworthpress.com].

Available online at http://stl.haworthpress.com
© 2006 by The Haworth Press, Inc. All rights reserved.
Digital Object Identifier: 10.1300/J122v27n01_12

KEYWORDS. Continuing education, education of sci-tech librarians, online education

INTRODUCTION

In an article titled "Where are all the science librarians?," Vazakas and Wallin (1992, 166) noted that recruitment "can take place at the levels of undergraduate student, library school student, library professional, and professionals outside librarianship." The focus of this paper is on the potential roles of library and information science (LIS) educators in recruitment and retention of sci-tech librarians and how developments in technology are enabling new strategies for fulfilling those roles. LIS educators can contribute through recruiting students with potential interest in sci-tech librarianship, providing a faculty advisor who is familiar with career opportunities and trends in sci-tech librarianship, and offering courses and related experiences that prepare students to pursue those opportunities.

Hallmark and Lembo (2003), reporting on interviews with scientists-turned-librarians, found that their respondents "had no idea that the LIS profession was so interesting, challenging, and enjoyable, nor were they aware of the revolution brought about by information technology." Those surveyed by Hackenberg and Chu (2002) to determine why people chose to be sci-tech librarians reported a variety of reasons, with fewer than half having a background in the sciences. LIS educators have an important responsibility to make those with science backgrounds aware of new career possibilities where they can build on their science background, as well as to equip those without a science background but with an interest in science to work effectively in sci-tech libraries. As elaborated in this paper, this can be done in partnership with working sci-tech librarians, but having a member of the LIS faculty who is knowledgeable and enthusiastic about career possibilities in sci-tech librarianship ensures that there is a key point of contact to guide such students in planning their program of study and conducting a job search.

STRATEGIES FOR RECRUITMENT AND RETENTION

Accessibility

A barrier to recruitment of students into LIS education has been the relatively small number and limited geographic distribution of the accredited programs. There are currently only 56 universities with accredited programs in the U.S. and Canada (American Library Association 2006) and many states lack even one such program. While there is a long history of distance education efforts on the part of some schools (Barron 2003), the Internet has enabled many more "environments in which the learner and teacher are separated by time and space, but are connected by technology and commitment" (Barron 2002, 4). This is consistent with larger trends in higher education with a growing number of courses and degree programs available online (Allen and Seaman 2005). Statistics compiled by the Association for Library and Information Science Education (Daniel and Saye 2005, 123-124) show substantial off-campus enrollments for many of the accredited schools.

Because of the growth in degree programs delivered online, prospective students seeking to prepare for careers in sci-tech librarianship no longer need to be co-located with a university offering the LIS degree. This allows individuals already working in libraries in support staff roles as well as others seeking to change career paths (e.g., from work as a laboratory technician into librarianship) to continue working while pursuing the degree. An obvious concern is whether the online degree is comparable in quality to the face-to-face experience on a campus. When properly designed, online education can match or surpass face-to-face learning. While there is much research that demonstrates this (e.g., Russell 1999), Kassop (2003) offers a concise list of potential advantages of online education: (1) student-centered learning; (2) writing intensity; (3) highly interactive discussions; (4) geared to lifelong learning; (5) enriched course materials; (6) on-demand interaction and support services; (7) immediate feedback; (8) flexibility; (9) an intimate community of learners; and (10) faculty development and rejuvenation.

Coursework

While much of the coursework needed as preparation for work in sci-tech librarianship is not specific to that specialization, LIS educators seeking to prepare sci-tech librarians should ensure regular availability of at least one science reference or science bibliography course. Such a course benefits not only those who already have sci-tech librarianship as a career goal, but also can serve as a recruiting tool stimulating interest in sci-tech librarianship among students who do not already have a science background. Of course to be of widest benefit, such courses should be offered online. One such course, offered by the University of Illinois at Urbana-Champaign (UIUC), is described later in this paper.

Ardis (2003) discusses her experience teaching a science reference course simultaneously face-to-face and online, concluding that she "may actually slightly favor distance education as a method of teaching." Detlefsen (2004) describes the specialization in medical librarianship offered online through the University of Pittsburgh's LIS program.

In a compilation of articles on the education of professionals for scientific and technical information management, Hallmark and Seidman (1998, 1) note that "a central theme is that of the influence of technology on our profession and the resulting changes in curricula for programs of library and information science." While that is largely reflected in enhancements of existing courses and the addition of new courses to the LIS curriculum, some LIS programs are also becoming involved in cross-campus initiatives to contribute to education in emerging specializations. For example, Wiggins (1998) discusses development of a program in chemical informatics at Indiana University and the survey of bioinformatics programs compiled by Hemminger, Losi, and Bauers (2005) includes a program offered by the University of North Carolina at Chapel Hill School of Information and Library Science.

Partnerships

LIS full-time faculty members have responsibility for curriculum development but can benefit from working in partnership with experienced sci-tech librarians in educating new recruits. This can take the form of involving professionals as guest speakers in courses, as supervisors of practicums or internships in sci-tech libraries, and/or as instructors of the science reference course. In a face-to-face course, guest speakers are generally limited to those individuals who can easily drive to campus and meet with the class at a specified time. In online education, guest speakers or "visiting experts" (Yontz 2002) can be located anywhere and interact with students in the class either synchronously or asynchronously, depending on what the technology used for online delivery allows. This enables a much wider range of professionals to share their expertise. Likewise those interested in teaching a full course may be able to serve as adjunct faculty online even though they are not located near a university offering an LIS degree program.

LIS programs generally rely heavily on libraries in their geographic region to host students in practicums or internships, offering valuable hands-on experience. Wixson (2006) describes how she promotes chemistry librarianship through practicum experiences for students at the University of Wisconsin-Madison School of Library and Information

Studies. Roland (2000) characterizes one particularly successful long-standing partnership between the U.S. Environmental Protection Agency and the School of Information and Library Science at the University of North Carolina at Chapel Hill, enabling MS students to acquire practical experience working in a science library while taking classes. Given employer preferences for practical library experience (Kim and Kusack 2005), online degree programs need to assist their students at a distance in locating practicum and internship opportunities wherever they may live.

Retention through Continuing Education for New Roles

Surveys of continuing education needs of science and technology librarians, as reported by Desai (2002) and Christianson (2004), demonstrate an interest in such topics as improving liaison relations with academic faculty, information literacy in the sciences, the effect of electronic sources on library collections and services, and alternative approaches to scholarly communication. Desai (2002) concludes:

> Developing procedures for selecting and making accessible the growing collection of electronic resources is an ongoing challenge. Since many patrons now choose to access these resources from outside the library, librarians must manage the electronic resources in such a way as to make them easier to find through the library's web site rather than through traditional reference. This in turn leads to expansion of the instructional role of librarians: they must provide instruction in traditional as well as new media, such as web tutorials, if they are to reach all patrons whether they are located in the library building or beyond its walls. Survey respondents are highly interested in acquiring the skills needed for these expanded roles.

While face-to-face conference sessions and workshops remain important for continuing education, professional associations are also exploring Web-based continuing education offerings as an alternative to assist their members in preparing for new roles. For example, Medical Library Association members Garrison, Schardt and Kochi (2000) discuss development of a Web-based continuing education course on the subject of the librarian's role in evidence-based medicine. An evaluation comparing outcomes of face-to-face and Web-based offerings of this course (Schardt, Garrison and Kochi 2002, 456) found that distance education learners "appear to have retained twice as much knowledge as the class-room students" due to more time for learning and reflection, individual attention from instructors, and motivation to actively participate. The flexibility in scheduling and elimination of travel expenses associated with online continuing education offerings may enable more librarians to engage in lifelong learning activities and to better prepare to fill new roles. Where appropriate, LIS educators with experience in delivering courses online can partner with professional associations on course design and delivery.

CASE STUDY: LEEP

The Graduate School of Library and Information Science (GSLIS) at the University of Illinois at Urbana-Champaign (UIUC) has a long history of offering courses in science reference and preparing sci-tech librarians, with Frances Briggs Jenkins (1951-71), George S. Bonn (1971-76), and Linda C. Smith (1977-present) taking the lead in this effort. In Hackenberg's (2000) survey on "Who Chooses Sci-Tech Librarianship?," she found that in response to the question on what LIS school was attended, the University of Illinois was the one university listed most frequently. Until 1996 students had to pursue the MS degree in residence in Urbana-Champaign, with many benefiting from concurrent assistantships working in one of the science libraries on campus (e.g., Agriculture, Biology, Chemistry, Engineering, Mathematics, Veterinary Medicine). In 1996 the LEEP (originally standing for Library Education Experimental Program) online enrollment option was introduced, enabling students from around the U.S. and beyond to complete the MS degree online. Requirements are the same as those for students pursuing the degree on campus. It is a 40-hour program with two required courses (LIS 501 Information Organization and Access; LIS 502 Libraries, Information and Society) and the remainder selected from available elective courses. At present, more than one-half of GSLIS students enrolled in the MS degree program are in the LEEP option. While a cohort of LEEP students begins each July, students are free to enroll part-time or full-time to complete the degree. Courses conform to the University academic calendar (16-week fall and spring semesters and an 8-week summer session). On-campus students can and do enroll in LEEP courses on a space-available basis. Required face-to-face time is limited to the initial 10-day on-campus session (which has acquired the label "boot camp" because it is an intense period of study and technology training) and brief visits each semester associated with other courses. GSLIS instructional technology staff are responsible for all aspects of technical support. Library support is provided by the Academic Outreach librarian (for document delivery) and the Library and Information Science Library staff (for reference, instruction in use of library resources, and electronic reserves). The program focuses on communication and community in its design (see the collection of papers in Haythornthwaite and Kazmer (2004) for more details).

Development of the LEEP virtual classroom environment has been accomplished in-house. Technologies currently in use support the following activities: asynchronous discussions via electronic bulletin boards; live session interactivity (class presentations via RealAudio by faculty, students, and guest lecturers with simultaneous navigation of associated slides stored on the Web; text chatting for class discussion and asking questions; chalkboard; break-out rooms for small group discussion); and collaborative document creation and editing. Faculty are free to combine Web-based distribution of course materials, live synchronous sessions, and asynchronous bulletin board discussions in ways that help students meet the learning objectives of their particular course. With limited time for face-to-face (usually one day) and live sessions (two hours per week in a regularly scheduled slot), lectures can no longer serve as the primary means of presenting content. Course design includes the syllabus (sequencing of topics and readings), assignments (individual, group), and allocation of content delivery and learning activities (face-to-face, synchronous, asynchronous). Smith et al. (2001) offer a more detailed discussion of changing models of teaching and learning in LEEP. In this paper the focus is on how this virtual classroom environment can be used to teach future sci-tech librarians in the course LIS 522 Information Sources and Services in the Sciences (a syllabus can be found at http://leep.lis.uiuc.edu/spring06/LIS522LE/index.html).

In Spring 2006, 25 students were enrolled in the course, including two who were pursuing their MS at the University of Texas at Austin and enrolled in the course through the WISE consortium (http://www.wiseeducation.org). UIUC students included several students at a distance (as far away as Hong Kong) as well as a few on campus. Some students were already working in science libraries (e.g., Archer Daniels Midland corporate library, John Crerar Library of the University of Chicago, St. Louis University Health Sciences Center Library) or as graduate assistants in campus branch libraries (Agriculture, Engineering, Health Sciences). Other students at a distance held positions in academic, public, and school libraries or non-library positions. Students' prior education ranged from bachelor's degrees in the humanities to Ph.D. degrees in the life sciences. They thus brought diverse backgrounds and experience to the learning community that the class developed.

Weekly live synchronous sessions were scheduled from 6:45-8:45 pm central time. The first third of the course introduced the scientific publication cycle and various types of materials; the remainder covered sources and services by discipline, illustrating similarities and differences as one moves from the physical to the life sciences. The live sessions were enriched considerably by the participation of a range of guest speakers, most of whom were UIUC alumni. Their locations ranged from New Hampshire to California. Topics and presenters included: (1) special materials (Leora Siegel, Manager of the Library, Chicago Botanic Garden); (2) mathematics (Kristine Fowler, Mathematics Librarian, University of Minnesota); (3) astronomy and physics (Lee Robbins, Head, Astronomy and Astrophysics Library, University of Toronto); (4) chemistry (Chuck Huber, Chemical Sciences Librarian, University of California, Santa Barbara); (5) engineering (Mel DeSart, Head, Engineering Library, University of Washington); (6) environmental sciences (Amy Schuler, Librarian, Institute of Ecosystem Studies); (7) biological sciences (Linda Coates, Librarian, San Diego Zoo); (8) agriculture (Nan Hyland, Public Services Librarian, Mann Library, Cornell University); (9) health sciences (Lora Thompson, Associate Director/Education and Information Services, Biomedical Libraries, Dartmouth College); and (10) future of sci-tech librarianship (David Stern, Director of Science Libraries and Services, Yale University). The on-campus session for the course held in early March benefited from participation of UIUC science librarians, including a panel on issues in collection development (with librarians addressing geology, biology, and environmental science) and a panel on new approaches to services (with librarians addressing chemistry, biotechnology, and engineering).

Assignments involved both individual and group work and encouraged use of print collections to which students had access as well as fully exploiting the many databases and full-text electronic resources to which students had access through the UIUC Library's Online Research Resources portal (http://www.library.uiuc.edu/orr). Library support is critical to the quality of online LIS courses (Searing 2004). Student work on some individual assignments was shared with the class as a whole via posting to class bulletin boards, so that all students could benefit from what individual students learned through their literature searches, database reviews, web site evaluations, and compilation of webliographies. One group project, the electronic journal club, involved small-group discussion of articles from the LIS journal literature on topics such as new roles, expanded services, and issues in scientific publication. The activity was modeled on the Medical Library Association's discussion group program (http://www.mlanet.org/education/discussiongroups/) for continuing professional development and gave students an opportunity to explore topics introduced in class in more depth. The other group project allowed students to pick a discipline and prepare a guide for others in the class outlining types of information needed in the discipline, major professional associations (and government agencies, if applicable) and their publishing programs, and major databases. While it is too early to determine whether completion of this course will lead to placement of these students as future sci-tech librarians, a number of students who have enrolled in the LEEP version of this course in the past are now working in science or medical libraries. In any case all should be better prepared to work with sci-tech materials and to handle sci-tech questions in any setting.

CONCLUSION

Any discussion of recruitment and retention of sci-tech librarians in the 21st century should take into account what is happening in the practice of science:

> Whether it's *e-research* in Australia, *cyberinfrastructure* in the United States, the *grid* in Europe, or *e-science* in the United Kingdom, a transformation is clearly occurring in research practice, a transformation that will have a profound impact on the roles of information professionals within higher education. Research is becoming more multidisciplinary, more collaborative, and more global. (O'Brien 2005, 65)

In e-research, primary research data must often be managed. O'Brien (2005) argues that information professionals within higher education must contribute to this activity to remain relevant. Likewise a recent National Science Board (2005) report on *Long-lived digital data collections: Enabling research and education in the 21st century* defines collaborative roles for data managers and data scientists (including librarians). In this context UIUC has recently received support from the National Science Foundation to develop a graduate program for scientific communication specialists who understand some aspects of the practice of science and who are skilled in the associated computational and information management tasks (http://sci.lis.uiuc.edu/Papers/Summary.pdf). At the same time academic librarians are investigating ways to integrate library resources and services in e-learning initiatives (OCLC E-Learning Task Force 2003). These are just some of the opportunities and challenges to which those being educated now as sci-tech librarians will need to respond in the future.

With their research, curriculum development, and teaching responsibilities, LIS educators have a significant role to play in helping to recruit and prepare new librarians as well as in offering continuing education opportunities for working librarians. Technology enables marshalling of distributed expertise in new ways to support these efforts. Initiatives like the WISE consortium for coursesharing can enable LIS students to enroll in an online science reference course when one is not offered by their home institution. Experienced librarians can serve as guest speakers in or instructors of online courses. LIS educators can collaborate with representatives of professional associations to offer new continuing education opportunities online. The multidisciplinary, collaborative, and global character of e-research can inspire similar efforts in recruiting and educating the sci-tech librarians of the future.

REFERENCES

Allen, I. Elaine and Jeff Seaman. 2005. *Growing by degrees: Online education in the United States, 2005*. Needham, MA: Sloan Consortium.

American Library Association. 2006. *Library & information studies: Directory of institutions offering accredited master's programs*. Chicago: Office for Accreditation, American Library Association.

Ardis, Susan B. 2003. A tale of two classes: Teaching science and technology reference sources both traditionally and through distance education. *Issues in Science and Technology Librarianship* Spring 2003, http://www.istl.org/03-spring/article7.html.

Barron, Dan. 2002. Distance education in library and information science: A long road traveled. *Journal of Education for Library and Information Science* 43(1): 3-5.

Barron, Daniel D., ed. 2003. *Benchmarks in distance education: The LIS experience*. Westport, CT: Libraries Unlimited.

Christianson, Marilyn. 2004. The 2003 STS continuing education survey: Selected analyses of science librarians' interests. *Issues in Science and Technology Librarianship* Fall 2004, http://www.istl.org/04-fall/refereed.html.

Daniel, Evelyn H. and Jerry D. Saye, eds. 2005. *Library & Information Science Education 2004 Statistical Report*. Oak Ridge, TN: Association for Library and Information Science Education.

Desai, Christina M. 2002. Continuing education needs of science and technology librarians: Results of the 2001 STS Continuing Education Committee survey. *Issues in Science and Technology Librarianship* Spring 2002, http://www.istl.org/02-spring/article5.html.

Detlefsen, Ellen G. 2004. Getting on the Fast Track, or how to get an MLIS through distance education, with a specialization in medical librarianship. *Medical Reference Services Quarterly* 23(4): 87-94.

Garrison, Julie A., Connie Schardt and Julia K. Kochi. 2000. Web-based distance continuing education: A new way of thinking for students and instructors. *Bulletin of the Medical Library Association* 88(3): 211-217.

Hackenberg, Jill M. 2000. Who chooses sci-tech librarianship? *College & Research Libraries* 61(5): 441-450.

Hackenberg, Jill M. and Barbara Chu. 2002. Why does one choose sci-tech librarianship? Findings of a survey. *Science & Technology Libraries* 23(1): 3-16.

Hallmark, Julie and Mary Frances Lembo. 2003. Leaving science for LIS: Interviews and a survey of librarians with scientific and technical degrees. *Issues in Science and Technology Librarianship* Spring 2003, http://www.istl.org/03-spring/refereed1.html.

Hallmark, Julie and Ruth K. Seidman, eds. 1998. Sci/tech librarianship: Education and training. *Science & Technology Libraries* 17(2): 1-91.

Haythornthwaite, Caroline and Michelle M. Kazmer, eds. 2004. *Learning, culture and community in online education: Research and practice.* New York: Peter Lang.

Hemminger, Bradley M., Trish Losi, and Anne Bauers. 2005. Survey of bioinformatics programs in the United States. *Journal of the American Society for Information Science and Technology* 56(5): 529-537.

Kassop, Mark. 2003. Ten ways online education matches, or surpasses, face-to-face learning. *Sloan-C View*, http://www.sloan-c.org/publications/view/v2n4/tenways.htm.

Kim, Hak Joon and James Michael Kusack. 2005. Distance education and the new MLS: The employer's perspective. *Journal of Education for Library and Information Science* 46(1): 36-52.

National Science Board. 2005. *Long-lived digital data collections: Enabling research and education in the 21st century.* Arlington, VA: National Science Foundation.

O'Brien, Linda. 2005. E-research: An imperative for strengthening institutional partnerships. *Educause Review* 40(6): 64-76.

OCLC E-Learning Task Force. 2003. *Libraries and the enhancement of E-learning.* Dublin, OH: OCLC.

Roland, Kristen Conahan. 2000. Training future science librarians: A successful partnership between academia and the United Stated Environmental Protection Agency. *Issues in Science and Technology Librarianship* Spring 2000, http://www.istl.org/00-spring/article3.html.

Russell, Thomas L., comp. 1999. *The no significant difference phenomenon: as reported in 355 research reports, summaries and papers.* Raleigh, NC: North Carolina State University.

Schardt, Connie M., Julie Garrison, and Julia K. Kochi. 2002. Distance education or classroom instruction for continuing education: who retains more knowledge? *Journal of the Medical Library Association* 90(4): 455-457.

Searing, Susan E. 2004. All in the family: Library services for LIS online education. *Journal of Library Administration* 41(3/4): 391-405.

Smith, Linda C., Sarai Lastra and Jennifer Robins. 2001. Teaching online: Changing models of teaching and learning in LEEP. *Journal of Education for Library and Information Science* 42(4): 348-363.

Vazakas, Susan M. and Camille Clark Wallin. 1992. Where are all the science librarians? *College & Research Libraries News* 53(3): 166-171.

Wiggins, Gary. 1998. New directions in the education of chemistry librarians and information specialists. *Science & Technology Libraries* 17(2): 45-58.

Wixson, Emily. 2006. Promoting chemistry librarianship through library science graduate school practicum experiences: Field projects to inspire future chemistry librarians. *LiveWire* 7.2 (ACS Publications online newsletter), http://pubs.acs.org/4librarians/livewire/2006/7.2/librarianspr.html.

Yontz, Elaine. 2002. When donkeys fly: Distance education for cataloging. *Cataloging & Classification Quarterly* 34(3): 299-310.

doi: 10.1300/J122v27n01_12

Holding on to Our Own:
Factors Affecting the Recruitment
and Retention of Science Librarians

Allison V. Level

Joanna Blair

SUMMARY. The graying of the library profession means that recruiting and retaining librarians is essential to maintaining quality services and ensuring that libraries have a store of potential leaders. Science librarian positions often draw smaller pools of applicants than social science or humanities positions, making it even more important that good hires are retained. We examine programs that contribute to recruitment and retention as well as some of the trends in science librarianship and the impact on science librarians. The differences in the needs and practices of new librarians versus mid-career science and technology librarians are also discussed. Solutions to the shortage of science librarians need to include creative recruitment, support for research and professional development,

Allison V. Level, MEd, MLS, is Assistant Professor and Natural Resources Librarian (E-mail: Allison.Level@colostate.edu), and Joanna Blair, MLIS, is Assistant Professor and Biological Sciences Librarian (E-mail: Joanna.Blair@colostate.edu), both at Morgan Library, Colorado State University, 501 University Avenue, Fort Collins, CO 80523.

[Haworth co-indexing entry note]: "Holding on to Our Own: Factors Affecting the Recruitment and Retention of Science Librarians" Level, Allison V., and Joanna Blair. Co-published simultaneously in *Science & Technology Libraries* (The Haworth Information Press, an imprint of The Haworth Press, Inc.) Vol. 27, No. 1/2, 2006, pp. 185-202; and: *Recruiting, Training, and Retention of Science and Technology Librarians* (ed: Patricia A. Kreitz, and JoAnn DeVries) The Haworth Information Press, an imprint of The Haworth Press, Inc., 2006, pp. 185-202. Single or multiple copies of this article are available for a fee from The Haworth Document Delivery Service [1-800-HAWORTH, 9:00 a.m. - 5:00 p.m. (EST). E-mail address: docdelivery@haworthpress.com].

Available online at http://stl.haworthpress.com
© 2006 by The Haworth Press, Inc. All rights reserved.
Digital Object Identifier: 10.1300/J122v27n01_13

and promotion of involvement in national organizations. doi: 10.1300/J122v27n01_13 *[Article copies available for a fee from The Haworth Document Delivery Service: 1-800-HAWORTH. E-mail address: <docdelivery @haworthpress.com> Website: <http://www.HaworthPress.com> © 2006 by The Haworth Press, Inc. All rights reserved.]*

KEYWORDS. Science librarians, recruitment, retention, new librarians, mid-career librarians, college and university, academic

INTRODUCTION

The library literature has a patchy examination of science librarians as a group. However, two factors may converge in the coming years to make retention and recruitment of these individuals increasingly important. First of all, studies indicate that there is a shortage of librarians with science subject degrees (Winston, 2001; Frank, 1989; Mount, 1985). Secondly, the graying of the profession suggests that demand for qualified librarians will increase in the near future (Association of College and Research Libraries [ACRL] Ad Hoc Task Force on Recruitment & Retention Issues, 2002; Wilder, 1995). These two factors may mean that the already small applicant pools for science librarian positions will become even smaller, resulting in increased pressure to recruit new individuals and to retain those already in the profession. Retention at the institutional level will be especially important to ensure that an organization has a store of potential leaders in science librarianship and sufficient institutional knowledge to train the next generation of science librarians.

In a recent *Denver Post* article, it was reported that almost 50% of professional librarians in the United States are expected to retire in twelve years (Whaley, 2002). With a median age of 47, librarians need to increase their focus on succession planning. In a report by the ACRL Ad Hoc Task Force on Recruitment and Retention Issues, it was noted that, "based on data from various library surveys as well as U.S. Department of Labor census information, the library profession is clearly facing the potential loss to retirement of approximately 60% to 65% of all current librarians by the year 2020" (p. 293). Predictions for the near future are also grim, Stanley Wilder's (1995) demographic study of academic librarians predicts retirement of 24% between 2005 and 2010.

Estimates in Canada mirror the U.S. situation and predict that 21% of Canadian librarians will retire between 2003-2013 (8R Steering Committee,

2003). A human resources steering committee, charged with evaluating the major staffing issues in Canadian Libraries, has identified recruitment and retention as numbers one and two on their list of challenges and note that "at the sector level, institutions will have greater problems in replacing staff, as well as replacing their knowledge and experience" (p. 55).

Staff shortages are likely to have an amplified effect on science librarians because few librarians also possess science subject degrees and this qualification is in demand. Winston (2001) found that only 35.5% of academic science librarians have a degree in biology, physics, chemistry, or engineering. This echoes a 1983 survey of academic librarians that found that only 32% of science librarians had degrees in science or engineering (Mount, 1985). Hackenberg and Chu (2002) found that 40% of librarians had no background in the sciences at all, such as, elective science courses or science librarianship courses. Furthermore, it has been found that the requirements listed in job ads for science librarians has increased steadily since 1976 and that increasingly, technological skills are a requirement (Osario, 1999). In a content analysis of job postings for science and engineering librarians, Osario (1999), found an average of 29 requirements listed in 1976 and an average of 73 listed in 1998.

The increasing number of required skills in science and engineering librarianship coupled with the desire for applicants who possess a science degree often results in small applicant pools for open positions. "For decades the job market has been excellent for qualified librarians who are also versed in one or more of the sciences . . . such candidates are typically scarce and in high demand" (Hallmark & Lembo, 2003, para. 1).

The shortage of science librarians highlights the need to increase recruitment efforts into the profession and to make the workplace as appealing as possible in order to attract science librarians and keep them once hired. Many organizational opportunities contribute to both recruitment and retention. Some of these opportunities may include continuing education, funding for professional development, mentoring programs, or a library culture that supports new ideas. These features will be discussed here as they apply to science librarians. Although we will focus primarily on academic libraries, most principles can be applied to all library environments.

RECRUITMENT

Recruitment of academic library specialists is an increasingly difficult task. Many people with undergraduate degrees in the sciences, engineering, or technology often opt for higher paying jobs and careers in science or business, with some moving to the educational sector to become secondary school science teachers. Science librarians, like many others in the profession often choose this path as a second career. Science librarianship covers specialized fields including biology, agriculture, engineering, chemistry, physics, natural resources, physical sciences, and natural sciences. Recruiting librarians for jobs in these specialized areas can be challenging.

In his article about effective leadership of science libraries, Frank (2004) says, "Recruiting and hiring professionals to provide information services in science/technology libraries is occasionally problematic. Locating professionals with the expertise or academic credentials needed to communicate effectively with scientists and engineers is particularly difficult. Comparatively few librarians possess academic degrees in science or technology. Professionals in positions of leadership need to be more creative or innovative in efforts to recruit and hire" (p. 414).

> I have a job that gives me passion for what I do, working with departments for which I have a subject background, the community of students, faculty and staff at [my college], the freedom to explore new opportunities and for collaboration with teaching faculty, a great group of science librarians to work with. My job is what I make it and I am grateful to be able to keep my job interesting, challenging, and rewarding. (Science librarian with 25 years experience)

As Hewitt (2003) describes, "More and more libraries are experiencing extremely small applicant pools and/or failed searches. This is quite a change from the situation a few years ago when there were sometimes hundreds of applicants for an opening in a college and university library" (p. 179). Recruitment is a key issue for the entire profession and is not limited to the science specialist. For academic libraries as a whole, there needs to be a shift in traditional recruiting practices. "Librarians need to think about a variety of types and times of recruiting. There have even been some attempts to attract pre-college age students to the library profession; for example, some academic librarians make a point of attending high school career days, and the ACRL sponsors a 'Shadow Day' in an attempt to introduce high school students to the career possibilities in academic librarianship" (Hewitt, p. 181).

As a profession, those currently working in science and technology libraries need to do a better job at recruiting in non-traditional ways.

As Larry Hardesty (2003) remarks, "We have many warning signs that a major recruitment and retention storm does loom on the horizon. We know that a large percentage of experienced academic librarians will reach retirement age within the next few years, and academic institutions could lose much of the senior leadership of the academic librarian profession. Attracting and retaining experienced academic librarians will become increasingly challenging" (p. 4). While teaching library research, librarians should mention librarianship as a career option to those in undergraduate classes, attend career day sessions of the sciences, and encourage science librarians to participate in science education programs for middle grade and high school students. Another non-traditional recruitment tool could be to target those working in science who may be ready for a career change. Many librarians enter the profession as a second career, and scientists may be ready for a change from the laboratory. We need to be more proactive at reaching this group through outreach activities by professional organizations and library schools.

Where possible, library schools should offer a work experience for MLS students in science libraries, either in companies or on campus. One example of this partnership was between the University of North Carolina (UNC), Chapel Hill and the United States Environmental Protection Agency (EPA) library. A UNC student worked as an EPA intern and said, "I feel I greatly benefited from my experience as an intern, and learned much about providing quality information services to scientific researchers" (Roland, 2000, para. 1). This type of collaboration would encourage the student with a science specialization to continue to keep that subject expertise and work within an information setting that would benefit from the specialized knowledge.

We need to be proactive at promoting our institutions, long before we are promoting job openings at conferences and via listservs. For the large and prestigious universities, there will always be a long list of people wanting to work in that location. For the mid-size, smaller, or ARL universities not in the top 50%, schools will have to rely on more than name recognition and extensive science collections as an employment enticement. Training programs, mentorship opportunities, and tuition reimbursement will all serve to make a workplace more attractive to a new recruit.

RETENTION

The smaller pool of qualified applicants, the increasing demands of the job, and the graying of the profession, all highlight the need for institutions to retain current, experienced, science librarians. Recruitment of qualified individuals to fill vacant positions is important but working toward retaining science librarians who have institutional knowledge and are able to take on leadership roles within the institution is paramount to uninterrupted quality service. Furthermore, institutional characteristics that feed into retention will likely make the workplace more attractive to a potential recruit.

The cost of attrition can be felt in several ways in a library. There is the cost to morale when co-workers take on additional responsibilities while a search for a replacement takes place. There is a cost in staff time when conducting the search as well as the cost of the search itself. The net result is a decline in the effectiveness of the organization (Dee, 2004). Further costs result from the time and energy put into training and orientation. Large companies spend millions of dollars to reduce staff turnover because of the savings realized through uninterrupted productivity and saved training costs (Mullich, 2005). The difficulties associated with hiring qualified science librarians may result in searches with high costs as well as longer orientation periods if the new hire does not meet all of the desired qualifications and requires additional training. There are real cost advantages to keeping employees motivated and engaged at their institution.

> I have stayed in the same department but my job has changed over the years and there is never a dull moment. As the library moves forward both technologically and physically there have been many opportunities and challenges that keep the job exciting. Figuring out how to move the collection and maintain a high level of service, going from a card catalog to an online system, to a gopher, to web based. There has always been administrative support to be involved on the local, national, and international level. (Science librarian with 20 years experience)

Very little has been written on retention of science librarians as a group but there is a body of research discussing what keeps academic librarians in the profession. Millard (2003) found that academic librarians in Canada with more than 15 years experience were motivated to stay in librarianship primarily by career commitments, whereas organizational commitment was not a high motivator. This shows that there is room for improvement within the workplace and organizations need to do more to motivate science librarians to remain in their positions.

It is important that organizations recognize that "[r]etention strategies need to differ for different stages of a person's career" (ACRL Ad Hoc Task Force on Recruitment and Retention Issues, 2002, p. 17). Therefore, a wide variety of strategies should be employed to cater to the needs of different employees. Outlined here are organizational characteristics that both new and mid-career science librarians find valuable for maintaining enthusiasm and professional interest.

MENTORING

Everyone has experienced the "new job" uncertainties at some point in their career. For science librarians new to the field or in a new job, participating in a mentoring program can be a valuable way to exchange knowledge and experiences. On the local level, more and more libraries have established mentoring programs within their organizational structure. Mentoring new librarians in a tenure-track situation is especially important to retention since achieving tenure is essential to retention.

Mentoring programs may also aid recruitment efforts since the presence of such a program will demonstrate a high level of support available for new staff. The literature suggests that one of the most successful aspects of formal mentoring programs is orienting new librarians to the institutional culture, demystifying the advancement process, and improving retention (Black & Leysen, 2002; Munde, 2000). Another advantage that has been reported is that new librarians "see tenured faculty as individuals eager for the protégée's success, and . . . see their mentor as a colleague and advocate instead of as one more supervisor who need[s] to be pleased and satisfied" (Kuyper-Rushing, 2001, p. 444).

> I feel fortunate to work at a library where colleagues, including my supervisor and the library director, are supportive and welcoming. Within my first year, I had opportunities to work on many exciting and interesting projects including implementing a library blog, instant messaging reference service and library portal. I have also been encouraged to join professional organizations and attend national conferences both as a participant and as a speaker. (Science librarian with 2 years experience)

Despite the success of many formal mentoring programs there is some evidence that this is not the preferred delivery method of information. The STS Continuing Education Survey has mentoring listed seventh out of a list of eight options for continuing education delivery (Desai, Christianson & Burright, 2004). Furthermore, a 2002 survey of new librarians showed that new librarians preferred informal mentoring relationships and did not want to be involuntarily matched up (Black & Leysen, 2002). The preference for informal mentoring relationships underlines the importance of having experienced librarians at the institution available to support new science librarians outside of a formal program. Equally important may be supporting a new librarian's ability to seek out informal mentoring relationships at the state or national level.

Providing support to establish mentoring relationships applies equally to the mentors. Seasoned librarians also benefit from the mentor/protégé relationship. When Louisiana State University Libraries started a formal mentoring program, the mentors were encouraged to create goals for themselves as part of the mentoring process (Kuyper-Rushing, 2001). The mentor may benefit from learning new subject knowledge or new skills from the protégée or simply from the rewards of helping a colleague succeed.

> We do not have a formal mentoring program, but from the very start, my colleagues have made it clear that I can ask them for guidance, and I really appreciate their willingness to help. (Science librarian with 1.5 years experience)

For veteran librarians, becoming a mentor to those new to the field should be a contribution that they would want to make. Mentoring can be an avenue to networking, understanding the resources needed in the discipline, and understanding key issues that are at the forefront of the profession. On the national level, the American Library Association, ACRL–Science and Technology Section (ACRL–STS) Continuing Education Committee sponsors a Science and Technology Library Mentors Program (see http://www.ala.org/ala/acrl/aboutacrl/acrlsections/sciencetech/stsmentors/stsmentors.htm). Librarians may volunteer to be a mentor and provide a brief description of their work experience, subject areas, and projects. Mentors can decide if they prefer to be contacted via e-mail or phone and if they want to arrange for a meeting at conferences. The mentors are then listed alphabetically, geographically, and by areas of expertise. Science and technology librarians with experience in the field have a responsibility to share their knowledge and experience and help maintain a pool of quality science librarians.

CONTINUING EDUCATION

The ever-changing nature of libraries means that continuing education is essential to staying current and serving our clients. Continuing education may be immediately important to new science librarians since over half of new hires do not have degrees in the sciences (Winston, 2001). This figure may worsen if the predictions of librarian shortages holds true and institutions are forced to hire more science librarians with little experience in sciences. Training opportunities are essential to the orientation process in these cases. "If academic libraries are to hire inexperienced individuals with only entry-level credentials, several practitioners point out the need for more development and training opportunities for these individuals. In fact, they stressed this need for both experienced, as well as beginning, librarians in this time of rapidly changing developments" (Hardesty, 2003 p. 3).

> As a new librarian I also appreciate all of the training opportunities. I have participated in as many Continuing Education opportunities as time has allowed. I have taken advantage of the job-related training opportunities, brown-bag lunches, computer courses, and webinars. I have also taken advantage of the tuition waiver of 6 credits a year to pursue other interests in credit courses. (Science librarian with 1.5 years experience)

Furthermore, even those with subject degrees "must . . . react to the constantly changing nature of knowledge itself, particularly in the sciences" (Paster, 2004, p. 38). A 2001 survey of science librarians showed that improving knowledge of subject resources is a top priority, particularly in chemistry and engineering (Desai, 2002). Providing release time for continuing education and waived tuition to take credit courses in subject areas will help new science librarians get up to speed and seasoned librarians stay up to date.

Interviewees should ask if funding for professional development and training is available in the position. Resources for training and staying current with trends and technologies are critical for science and technology librarians. Even veterans in the profession need to "sharpen the saw" in order to stay current with new trends and technologies. Science librarians who work a lot with instruction may want to apply for the ACRL Information Literacy Immersion Institutes. There is usually a track available for new librarians and a track for librarians developing an information literacy program.

Academic libraries seem to now recognize the return on investment of continuing education. Lynch (2001) reports that the percentage of library staff payroll spent on professional development increased from 1.04% in 1995 to 1.26% in 2001. The largest increase in spending was seen in academic libraries. A survey of reference librarians showed that a supportive supervisor was the single most positive influence on participation in continuing education (Chan & Auster, 2003).

Also of note is the general trend of "new information professionals [who] actively seek out change and new opportunities to increase and upgrade their technology skills so that they can remain professionally engaged and competitive . . ." (Stambaugh 2004, p. 32). This outlook is so strongly supported at the University of Georgia Libraries that they have committed to providing continuing education as a retention tool (Cetwinski, 2000).

> I just keep my eye pealed for something new and interesting. I like the challenge of keeping up with the changes, so my institution has allowed me to, through my own initiative, to engage in cutting-edge projects. In times of rapid change, you cannot sit back and wait for things to come to you. You must stay engaged and 'out there.' (Science librarian with 18 years experience)

On top of trying to learn the most recent digital innovation, ". . . the challenge now lies in staying current. The rapid turnover in daily tools requires a constant renewal of both technical knowledge and subject expertise" (Paster, 2004, p. 38). Making sure that new librarians have several avenues to pursue for professional development and continuing education will contribute to improved job performance and retention. Librarians, of all types, cite professional competence and patron service as the prime motivating factors for participating in continuing education (Chan & Auster, 2003). Organizations should offer these opportunities so that librarians at all levels feel they are effective in their positions.

PROFESSIONAL ORGANIZATIONS

Participation in professional organizations offers important opportunities to network, learn, and share knowledge. In a survey of new librarians Black and Leysen (2002) found that participation in professional service is an indicator of successful orientation to the profession of librarianship. They also found that 20% of library directors provide more support for entry-level librarians to attend professional conferences than mid-career librarians (Black & Leysen, 2002). A survey of 311 sci-tech librarians generated a list of 103 professional organizations to which the librarians belonged (Hackenberg, 2000). This figure is supported by Mark Winston's (2001) finding that 91.1% of academic science librarians are members of a professional association other than ALA. This diversity of organizational memberships suggests that both new and seasoned librarians value membership in professional organizations and would be attracted to organizations that support professional membership in terms of travel funds and professional leave.

The new science librarian may have a greater need to interact with peers outside of their own institution. In some cases a science librarian may not have a counterpart at their institution and relies on professional organizations for contact with similar librarians. New science librarians may also be the only entry-level librarian at their institution and might benefit from a network of other entry-level employees. "An interesting finding uncovered a feeling of isolation on the part of entry-level librarians. Many felt alone and disregarded because they did not possess the experience of others on the staff" (Black & Leysen, 2002, p. 15). This feeling of isolation may also be the case for seasoned librarians who are solo librarians.

Some organizations that would be of interest to science and technology librarians include, ACRL-STS, the Special Libraries Association (SLA) divisions, and specialty organizations such as the United States Agriculture Information Network (USAIN) and American Society for Engineering Education (ASEE). It is common for new librarians to pay dues and join organizations, but newer librarians need to go one step further and apply to committees and participate fully in the organization.

> I have the freedom to pursue projects based on my own initiative.... I love being able to work on projects that are interesting to me and that I think will help my faculty and students. Solid professional development funding to attend conferences certainly helps, too, but my autonomy helps me implement what I learn at conferences. (Science Librarian with 3 years experience)

Professional associations themselves are developing an interest in recruitment and retention not just to ensure the nation's libraries continue to have professional staff, but also to ensure a steady stream of members to help the association fulfill its mission and mandate. With memberships in the hundreds, organizations like ACRL-STS, USAIN, may also be hurt by mass retirements. Veterans to science and technology librarianship routinely run for office or volunteer to serve on or chair a committee. For people in tenure-track positions, national service may be an expectation of the job. But as a matter of contributing to the professional "village," libraries and senior librarians need to identify ways to acclimate new sci/tech librarians into the advantages and responsibilities of professional involvement.

According to a survey of academic librarians, support for professional meetings is the most commonly funded professional development activity and an analysis showed that institutional support increases the attendance rate of librarians at conferences (Havener & Stolt, 1994). The same study shows that the professional service rate for those librarians with institutional support is almost double that of librarians without institutional support. This exemplifies the importance of institutions getting involved in the professional development of employees. The return on investment for the supporting institution may be realized in improved retention of science librarians who use this as a means of professional support and continuing education.

SUPPORT FOR RESEARCH

A 2003 survey of junior academic librarians found that new librarians identified publishing as one of the areas where they needed help (Millet, 2005). This finding complements Black and Leysen's (2002) study suggesting that participation in research is an indicator of successful orientation to the profession of librarianship. A survey of academic librarians indicated that only 15% of academic librarians received support for research (Havener & Stolt, 1994). Not surprising, the Havener and Stolt (1994) study showed that librarians at institutions that provide support for research publish more than librarians at institutions that do not provide support.

> I attribute my 25 + -year tenure as librarian in a research library to a supportive environment in which faculty, administration and students believe that "research begins not in the laboratory, but in the library." I have consistently been allowed the administrative freedom to pursue those ideas, projects and services that are of interest to me. This support has resulted in a highly satisfactory career and a library that is valued by our customers. (Science librarian with 25 years experience)

Adequate support for the new science librarian may extend beyond the availability of funding for research or professional leave time dedicated to research. New science librarians may need help becoming familiar with the body of research in their field, especially if they are part of the large percentage of science librarians that do not have a background in science. They may also need help with the project management aspect of research and publication (Millet, 2005). Keeping a research project on track may be one area where mentorship is particularly valuable for the new science librarian. New librarians may want to look for opportunities to partner with veteran librarians in research activities that will benefit all participants. Veteran librarians may also be able to point new librarians to grant writing opportunities as an avenue for specialized research in the sciences. Seasoned librarians should keep in mind the value that their guidance can have to the new science librarian and the value to the profession if this leads to improved retention.

OPPORTUNITIES FOR ADVANCEMENT

"Simply providing opportunities for professional development is not enough . . . Supportive managers are those who . . . take an interest in the career goals of their staff" (Chan & Auster, 2003, p. 281). The University of Georgia Libraries recognize that training today needs to "address individual career objectives" (Cetwinski, 2000). This type of encouragement has a dual advantage because it will contribute to retention and will help provide skills for potential leaders.

In the working world of today, few people stay in the same job at the same institution for their entire career. Once in the field of science and technology librarianship, brand new subjects and responsibilities give way to subject and organizational mastery and content plateauing. As Montgomery (2002) describes it, content plateauing occurs when work is mastered and there is not much else new to learn. Montgomery goes on to describe structural plateauing, where due to organizational constraints, there is no opportunity for upward mobility. Several years in the same position without new opportunities on the horizon may lead to restlessness within the organization.

Librarians with experience in the field should keep an eye out for opportunities for advancement and leadership. This can often mean moving out of a strict science specialization and taking on more administrative or supervisory work. Having a science expert in a position of leadership as coordinator, assistant dean, or dean can work to the advantage of the other science and technology specialists. Administrators with in-depth knowledge of issues in scientific publishing will be advantageous when negotiating big-deal packages in the sciences. The science background and expertise of the manager will also carry over when looking at the macro level issues at the library or university. The organization can facilitate these moves by offering the training needed for individuals to advance to supervisory roles. The organization will benefit by keeping the individual's institutional knowledge and subject expertise.

PLANNING FOR THE FUTURE

The higher education landscape is changing and so too are academic libraries. Science and technology specialists need to keep up with the large-scale environmental changes as well as developments in the disciplines. One developing trend is the closing or redistribution of subject or departmental libraries, often in the sciences, and the merging of those collections and resources into the main library. Other trends include downsizing departments or freezing positions (Harralson, 2001). If campuses have several subject or service points, even those are being combined. In Zabel's article about trends in reference services she notes, "[c]onsolidation of service points and even of libraries is an emerging trend in large research libraries in response to staff losses due to budget reductions and retirements. In some cases, service points have simply been merged in an existing facility. Some of these consolidated service points have been expanded to include the help desk function (assistance with computing questions). In other cases, institutions have merged separate subject libraries for greater efficiencies" (2005, p. 9).

> We do peer training sessions where we take turns presenting to each other, and these are very helpful as we have one reference desk, and we need to answer questions that are not in our subject areas. (Science Librarian with 1.5 years experience)

This merger of the collections or the access points means science and technology specialists need to remain involved in the scholarly communication and information transfer within the discipline. As Moyo explains, "The scholarly communication patterns themselves have changed, with more electronic publishing taking place, and more players involved in creation of electronic information products. Librarians now need to interact with other agencies involved in facilitating access to electronic information: database vendors, journal publishers, government agencies, etc. Librarians have to seek new alliances within the academic community" (2004, p. 229).

Continued communication with faculty and researchers in the sciences will be critical as changes to the dissemination of information will be ongoing. In addition, most science librarians will still provide instruction or research assistance for the sciences, even if they have additional reference or service point responsibilities that include broader and more general topics. Cardina and Wicks (2004) reviewed changes in the responsibilities and duties of academic reference librarians over time. Some clear trends include the use of more technology to perform tasks, more subject-based and general library instruction, and fewer mediated online searches. These trends indicate that science librarians will be maintaining traditional roles and continuing to expand their skills and responsibilities.

In planning for the future workforce in science and technology, we must begin recruiting for the profession earlier. While in library school, many students seek out internships and job rotation experiences that will allow them to see inside a specific type of library or environment. Hewitt discusses the Carolina Academic Library Associates (CALA) program which, "is intended to be an enhanced pre-professional experience for students who want to prepare for careers in academic librarianship. It is designed to be a tool for recruitment into academic librarianship, and also to better prepare students who choose to work in academic libraries. It is a practice-based supplement to a student's academic coursework" (2003, p. 183). If the shortage of qualified science librarians continues, it will become even more important to link practical work or internship opportunities with the library science academic program.

CONCLUSION

Rather than lament the current shortage of qualified recruits, science and technology librarians and library administrators need to work on creative solutions. New and veteran librarians need to plan and work together on strategies to encourage those with science specializations to see librarianship as a viable career path. Libraries may also want to consider growing their own science librarians by offering release time for online credit courses in science librarianship or courses within science disciplines.

Individuals with science degrees can often find higher pay outside librarianship so efforts to make the workplace appealing can provide important reasons for science librarians to take a job or stay in their positions. Libraries should also prepare for business-like talent heists. If science librarians are in high demand, poaching of experienced science librarians could transpire. Holding on to talent in-house should be a priority. Funding for professional development, support for new ideas, and opportunities to change the scope of one's job are methods of improving the long-term productivity of the library. Paramount to the orientation of new recruits is the availability of a pool of experienced science librarians to provide training and guidance. It is clear that new hires are more comfortable and more successful when they are oriented to the profession and have access to experienced professionals who can guide them in their careers.

The recruitment and retention strategies need to be unrelenting because the large-scale retirements are predicted to occur for decades. Science librarians in various stages of their career need to contribute to this effort and act as ambassadors to the field through mentorship programs, one-on-one interactions, and at career day events. Administrators can help by creating environments that support continued learning and provide opportunities for innovation and advancement. Most of us can agree that science librarianship is a rewarding and worthwhile career choice. To make positive changes for the future, those currently involved in librarianship must work to spread that message.

REFERENCES

Association of College and Research Libraries. Ad Hoc Task Force on Recruitment & Retention Issues. 2003. Recruitment and retention: a professional concern. In Dave Bogard (ed.). *The Bowker Annual Library and Book Trade Almanac* (pp. 291-302). Medford, NJ: Information Today, Inc.

Association of College and Research Libraries. Ad Hoc Task Force on Recruitment & Retention Issues. 2002. *Recruitment, retention, and restructuring: Human resources in academic libraries.* Chicago: Association of College and Research Libraries.

Black, William K. and Joan M. Leysen. 2002. Fostering success: The socialization of entry-level librarians in ARL libraries. *Journal of Library Administration* 36(4): 3-27.

Cardina, Christen and Donald Wicks. 2004. The changing roles of academic reference librarians over a ten-year period. *Reference & User Services Quarterly* 44(2):133-42.

Cetwinski, Thomas. 2000. Using training for recruitment and retention. *Georgia Libraries Quarterly* 37(1): 5-10.

Chan, Donna C. and Ethel Auster. 2003. Factors contributing to the professional development of reference librarians. *Library & Information Science Research* 25(3):265-286.

Dee, Jay R. 2004. Turnover intent in an urban Community College: Strategies for faculty retention. *Community College Journal of Research and Practice* 28: 593-607.

Desai, Chris. 2002, Spring. Continuing education needs of science and technology librarians: Results of the 2001 STS Continuing Education Committee survey. *Issues in Science and Technology Librarianship* 34, Retrieved February 1st, 2006, from http://www.istl.org/02-spring/article5.html.

Desai, Chris, Marilyn Christianson and Marian Burright 2004. STS continuing education survey 2003: *Results*. STS Continuing Education Committee. Retrieved February 2, 2006, from http://www.lib.auburn.edu/sci-tech/resguide/forestry/STSSurvey2003.htm.

8Rs Steering Committee. 2004. Preliminary findings from the 8Rs study: Staffing crisis or business as usual? *Feliciter* 50(2): 54-56.

Frank, Donald. G. 1989. Education for librarians in a major science-engineering library: Expectations and reality. *Journal of Library Administration* 11(3/4): 108-116.

Frank, Donald. G. 2004. Effective Leadership in Postmodern Science/Technology Libraries. *Science & Technology Libraries* 24(3/4): 107-116.

Hackenberg, Jill. M. 2000. Who chooses sci-tech librarianship? *College and Research Libraries* 61(5): 441-50.

Hackenberg, Jill. M. and Barbara Chu. 2002. Why does one choose sci-tech librarianship? Findings of a survey. Science & Technology Libraries 23(1): 3-16.

Hallmark, Julie and Mary Francis Lembo. 2003, Spring. Leaving science for LIS: Interviews and a survey of librarians with scientific and technical degrees. *Issues in Science and Technology Librarianship* 37, Retrieved February 1st, 2006, from http://www.istl.org/03-spring/refereed1.html.

Hardesty, Larry. 2003, September. Recruiting and retaining academic librarians: A calm before the storm? *Library Issues* 24(1): 1-4.

Harralson, David M. 2001. Recruitment in academic libraries: Library literature in the 90s. *College & Undergraduate Libraries* 8(1): 37-68.

Havener, Michael W. and Wilbur A. Stolt. 1994. The professional development activities of academic librarians: Does institutional support make a difference? *College & Research Libraries* 55(1): 25-36.

Hewitt, Joe. A., Barbara B. Moran and Mari E. Marsh. 2003. Finding our replacements: One institution's approach to recruiting academic librarians. portal: *Libraries and the Academy* 3(2): 179-189.

Kuper-Rushing, Lois. 2001. A formal mentoring program in a university library: Components of a successful experiment. *Journal of Academic Librarianship* 27(6): 440-446.

Lynch, Mary Jo. 2001. Spending on staff development. ALA Office for Human Resource Development and Recruitment. Retrieved January 28, 2006, from http://www.ala.org/ ala/hrdr/libraryempresources/spendingstaff.htm.

Millard, Donald M. 2003. Why do we stay? Survey of long-term academic librarians in Canada. *portal: Libraries and the Academy* 3(1): 99-111.

Millet, Michelle S. 2005. Is this the ninth circle of hell? *Library Journal* 130(5): 54.

Montgomery, Denise L. 2002. Happily ever after: Plateauing as a means for long-term career satisfaction. *Library Trends* 50(4): 702-716.

Mount, Ellis. 1985. *University Science and Engineering Libraries*. (2nd ed.). Westport, Connecticut: Greenwood Press.

Moyo, Lesley M. 2004. Electronic libraries and the emergence of new service paradigms. *The Electronic Library* 22(3): 220-230.

Mullich, Joe. 2005. Attacking attrition. *Workforce Management* 84(3): 46-48.

Munde, Gail. 2000. Beyond mentoring: Toward the rejuvenation of academic libraries. *Journal of Academic Librarianship* 26(3): 171-175.

Osario, Nestor L. 1999, Fall. An analysis of science-engineering academic library positions in the last three decades. *Issues in Science and Technology Librarianship* 24, Retrieved January 28, 2006, from http://www.istl.org/99-fall/article2.html.

Paster, Luisa. R. 2004. Current issues in staff development. In J. Simmons-Welburn & B. McNeil (Eds.). *Human Resource Management in Today's Academic Library: Meeting Challenges and Creating Opportunities*. (pp 37-46). Westport, CT: Libraries Unlimited.

Roland, Kristen C. 2000, Spring. Training future science librarians: a successful partnership between academia and the United States Environmental Protection Agency. *Issues in Science and Technology Librarianship* 26, Retrieved February 10th, 2006, from http://www.istl.org/00-spring/article3.html.

Stambaugh, Laine. 2004. Recruitment and selection in academic libraries. In J. Simmons-Welburn & B. McNeil (Eds.). *Human Resource Management in Today's Academic Library: Meeting Challenges and Creating Opportunities*. (pp 27-36). Westport, CT: Libraries Unlimited.

Whaley, Monte. 2002, November 11. Librarian slots stack up in state pay, age, image take toll in schools. *Denver Post* B-01.

Wilder, Stanley. 1995. *The age demographics of academic librarians: A profession apart: A report based on data from the ARL annual salary survey*. Washington, D.C.: Association of Research Libraries.

Winston, Mark D. 2001. Academic science and engineering librarians: A research study of demographics, educational backgrounds, and professional activities. *Science & Technology Libraries* 192(2): 3-24.

Zabel, Diane. 2005. Trends in reference and public services librarianship and the role of RUSA part one. *Reference & User Services Quarterly* 45(1): 7-10.

doi: 10.1300/J122v27n01_13

Networking, Networking, Networking: The Role of Professional Association Memberships in Mentoring and Retention of Science Librarians

Jeanne R. Davidson
Cheryl A. Middleton

SUMMARY. The authors surveyed new and veteran science and engineering librarians to determine the roles membership and participation in professional organizations play in mentoring and/or retention to the field. The authors compare activity and membership levels in several subject-oriented organizations and discuss the perceived benefits members receive from these professional activities as well as the challenges these memberships present. The networking that occurs as part of participation in subject-oriented library associations provides mentoring that may not be available to science librarians any other way. doi: 10.1300/J122v27n01_14 *[Article copies available for a fee from The Haworth Document Delivery Service: 1-800-HAWORTH. E-mail address: <docdelivery@ haworthpress.com> Website: <http://www.HaworthPress.com> © 2006 by The Haworth Press, Inc. All rights reserved.]*

Jeanne R. Davidson is Physical Sciences Librarian, and Cheryl A. Middleton is Interim Head of Undergraduate Learning & Library Information Access, both at Oregon State University.

[Haworth co-indexing entry note]: "Networking, Networking, Networking: The Role of Professional Association Memberships in Mentoring and Retention of Science Librarians." Davidson, Jeanne R., and Cheryl A. Middleton. Co-published simultaneously in *Science & Technology Libraries* (The Haworth Information Press, an imprint of The Haworth Press, Inc.) Vol. 27, No. 1/2, 2006, pp. 203-224; and: *Recruiting, Training, and Retention of Science and Technology Librarians* (ed: Patricia A. Kreitz, and JoAnn DeVries) The Haworth Information Press, an imprint of The Haworth Press, Inc., 2006, pp. 203-224. Single or multiple copies of this article are available for a fee from The Haworth Document Delivery Service [1-800-HAWORTH, 9:00 a.m. - 5:00 p.m. (EST). E-mail address: docdelivery@haworthpress.com].

Available online at http://stl.haworthpress.com
© 2006 by The Haworth Press, Inc. All rights reserved.
Digital Object Identifier: 10.1300/J122v27n01_14

KEYWORDS. Science librarians, professional organizations, mentoring, retention, personal networking

INTRODUCTION

Libraries of all types are grappling with recruitment and retention issues. Recruitment is less of an issue if those hired are retained for longer periods. Mentoring and ongoing professional development are often critical to retention, although few studies have examined the direct relationship between the two. Detlefson and Olson (1991) surveyed M.L.S. graduates and concluded that "those who leave the field for other occupations were more often individuals with no previous experience in libraries and those with an educational background in fields other than humanities." In addition, they determined that those with advanced degrees in science (along with law and business) were among those most likely to leave the field. If those with science degrees had received additional mentoring, personal networking and/or professional development in the library profession might they have been more likely to stay in the field? What resources do new, or even experienced, sci-tech librarians have and/or need for professional development and/or mentoring?

For science and technology (sci-tech) librarians, recruitment and retention issues are compounded by several factors. The specialized subject areas often intimidate new librarians who may not have a science background. In addition, many science librarians work in branch libraries or special libraries with few staff and fewer people to help with questions that may arise. In these circumstances they may be called upon not only to understand the discipline, but also to be adept at all areas of librarianship. Frustration with any or all of these circumstances or lack of confidence in one's ability to perform adequately might prove discouraging to the new sci-tech librarian and negatively affect retention. For these librarians, professional development and/or mentoring opportunities beyond the library may be essential for their success in serving their scientific clientele. While this study does not directly examine retention, a closer look at whether sci-tech librarians find professional organizations useful for professional development and mentoring may establish a baseline from which further connections can be drawn between mentoring and retention.

Participation in professional organizations is often encouraged as a primary resource for professional development and mentoring (see, for example, Frank (1997), Fisher (1997), and Harvey (2005)). Indeed, many institutions require librarians to participate in regional or national level associations for promotion, tenure, or other advancement. The Association of College and Research Libraries' (ACRL) "Guidelines for the Appointment, Promotion and Tenure of Academic Librarians" (2005) specify that to be promoted to associate professor or professor, librarians should demonstrate achievements in "other professional endeavors." In addition, the criteria for tenure are "closely allied to the criteria for promotion in academic rank." Just how effective or useful *are* professional associations in meeting the needs for professional development and/or mentoring? In trying to answer this question, the authors examine several related questions in this article, including:

- What do librarians really gain from participation in professional organizations? What form(s) does participation take?
- How often is participation required for promotion, tenure or other advancement?
- *Are* professional associations a good resource for mentoring?
- How is participation financed, institutionally or personally? Is it and should it be considered a good investment?

BACKGROUND

Professional library associations have recognized the need to provide professional development for their members for many years (see, for example, Ritchie (2002); Roper (2006)). Formal and informal mentoring appears to be an increasingly important benefit of professional membership if one looks at the number of organizations that provide this for their members. For example, the Medical Library Association (MLA) began developing a formal mentoring program in 1999 (Kwasik et al., p. 20), ACRL initiated a new member mentoring program in 2001 and SLA and ACRL-STS have had mentoring programs since the 1990s. Anecdotal evidence indicates that these mentoring programs do improve retention of new librarians.

The few studies that have examined retention do not concretely link professional development or mentoring with staying or leaving the field. For example, Millard (2003) attempted to determine factors influencing retention of academic librarians in Canadian institutions through a survey of librarians who had been in their positions for more than 15 years. Respondents in her survey indicated that professional development opportunities and funding were valued, although other factors

were considered to be of more importance. In their study of MLS graduates Detlefson and Olson identified attitudes, demographic characteristics and educational backgrounds but their questions did not address
whether professional development or mentoring would have impacted
those who had left the field.

The library literature includes definitions of mentoring along with
descriptions of formal and informal mentoring programs, many of which
draw a connection between professional development/mentoring and
retention in the field. In their description of a mentoring program targeted toward new, entry-level underrepresented librarians Acree et al.
(2001) asserted that "[f]or most librarians, professional development is
a key component of the ongoing effort to maintain employment and enhance careers." Bullington and Boylston (2001) linked retention with
mentoring in their call for participants in the ACRL New Member
Mentoring Program.

Although professional associations tout professional development
and mentoring as critical benefits for their members, very little research
assesses the actual value members find in these programs. Ritchie and
Genoni (1999) discussed mentoring for librarians and based on their
experience with the Australian Library and Information Association,
concluded that, "Professional associations, however, including some in
the [library and information science] LIS field, have demonstrated that
they are capable of providing a far more active and targeted form of
mentoring, by overseeing the implementation of formally structured
and facilitated mentoring programmes." In addition, ACRL's Ad Hoc
Task Force on Recruitment and Retention Issues (2002) identified "providing ongoing training and development opportunities both within the
library and outside the library" and "creating multiple opportunities for
mentoring" as key strategies for improving retention in the profession.

Research by Frank (1997) and Kamm (1997) are among the few studies that examine the actual value librarians attach to their participation
in professional associations. Both of these authors' research included
all types of librarians in their studies. Based on three focus groups,
Frank concluded that participation in professional organizations positively impacts librarians' career development. He suggested that organizations provide relevant information, aid in leadership development,
improve communication skills, increase opportunities for research and
publication and establish a professional community for participants. He
also recognized the challenges presented by the costs of participation
and the limitations imposed on librarians working in libraries with a
small staff.

Kamm's survey tried to assess the reasons why librarians join professional organizations and how they determine which one(s) to join. Not surprisingly, she found that librarians' reasons for joining vary, including necessity for promotion or feeling that participation at this level is the only way to participate in political action beyond the home institution. She acknowledged that little research has been done on the types of organizations to which librarians belong. She concluded that, "In the end, opting to join a professional body and deciding which one(s) is a subjective choice for most librarians. Finances, job constraints, and the goals of the organization affect that decision."

METHODOLOGY

While these studies shed some light on the role of professional organizations, they clearly do not address the particular needs of sci-tech librarians. To address these questions and gaps in the literature, the authors developed a web-based survey in consultation with Oregon State University's Survey Research Center. The survey contained 26 questions, including several open-ended questions for respondents to elaborate on particular questions. The questions were divided into sections to elicit information related to: demographics, association membership(s), type(s) of participation activity, conference attendance, and mentoring experience (as a mentor or mentee). Based on a suggestion from the Survey Research Center, a final open-ended question solicited any additional comments from respondents.

The authors solicited responses to the survey through an invitation to participate sent to a mixture of large library-centric organizations, specialized library organizations and discipline-specific professional organizations via their respective e-mail distribution lists. The request for response went to the following lists: STS-L (ACRL Science & Technology Section), SLA PAM (Special Libraries Association Physics, Astronomy and Math Division), SLA Sci-Tech (Special Libraries Association Science & Technology Division), MLA (Medical Library Association), ASEE-ELD (American Society of Engineering Education Engineering Libraries Division), CHMINF-L (Chemical Information Sources Discussion List). Following distribution to these lists, the invitation was also posted to one science librarian's blog. While these lists are open to anyone by subscription, they are all sponsored by professional organizations and so respondents may be more active in professional associations than the sci-tech librarian population as a whole.

The authors also invited survey responses directly from approximately 155 science librarians at Oregon State University's peer institutions in an attempt to broaden the number of responses. Librarians were identified from library staff directories on the web at each institution. The authors realize a weakness in this strategy in that all participants from the peer institutions are librarians at larger academic institutions. However, the authors considered the benefits of the potential increase in survey responses and of broadening the survey pool beyond communication channels tied to professional associations would alleviate any potential biases. The peer institutions include:

- University of Arizona
- Colorado State University
- Iowa State University
- Michigan State University
- North Carolina State University
- Purdue University
- University of California, Davis
- University of Oregon
- Washington State University
- University of Washington

RESULTS

The survey received 265 responses. Respondents are primarily academic librarians (227; 86 per cent) followed by corporate librarians (19; 7.2 per cent), government librarians (11; 4.2 per cent) and other special libraries (7; 2.7 per cent). Most respondents are self-identified subject specialists (170; 64.9 per cent) although the comments associated with this question indicate that respondents commonly have mixed responsibilities, including administration, public services, and technical services. In some instances respondents have more specific responsibilities such as patent searcher, project manager or web editor. Respondents represent a range of longevity in their current positions as noted in Table 1. Over 69 per cent (182) of respondents have a sci-tech education or background.

Respondents overwhelmingly belong to professional associations. Only 16 (6.1 per cent) do not have membership in any professional library organizations. Not only do these librarians belong to professional organizations, most (197; 80.7 per cent) consider themselves to be active members of at least one organization. Table 2 shows the number indicating membership in various professional organizations along with the percentage of those members who consider themselves active in that organization.

Table 3 identifies the organizations survey participants indicated as the associations in which they are most active. To facilitate examination of the results, the authors used the following categories for the various other associations participants identified:

- State/Regional library associations (including Canadian or those from other countries)
- Discipline-based associations such as American Association of Colleges of Pharmacy
- Other library-focused associations, such as LITA (Library & Information Technology Association), ASIST (American Society for Information Science & Technology, IFLA (International Federation of Library Associations), etc.

TABLE 1. Years in Current Position

Years in current position	Number	Percentage
Less than one year	28	10.7
1 year to 5 years	103	39.3
6 years to 10 years	50	19.1
More than 10 years	81	30.9

TABLE 2. Organization Membership and Participation

Organization	Member	Active	% Active
ALA	146	63	43
ACRL	142	62	44
ACRL STS	130	56	43
ASEE Engineering Libraries Division	49	37	76
SLA (any division)	130	92	71
Medical Library Association	18	11	61
Other Associations	137	84	61

TABLE 3. "Most Active" Organizations

Organization Name/Type	Number
ALA	16
ACRL	14
ACRL STS	21
ASEE Engineering Libraries Division	24
SLA (any division)	72
Medical Library Association	7
State/Regional Library Associations	13
Discipline-based Associations	26
Other Library-focused Associations	9

Active participation in chosen organizations takes many forms. The most common activities are identified in Table 4. The variety of activities identified by respondents is represented by the following categories:

- Conference activity includes presenting papers, organizing programs or workshops, facilitating discussion groups or other conference-related activities
- Publishing includes providing content for journals, newsletters, web sites, blogs or other association publications
- Editorial work includes newsletter/bulletin editorial work, blog, website or listserv maintenance or moderator
- Mentoring

The majority of active members attend the organization's national conferences as often as they are held (162; 82 per cent). In most instances, conference attendance is paid for as a combination of institutional support and individual investment (121; 61 per cent). In only 16 cases (8 per cent) does the individual pay the entirety; and for 60 respondents (30 per cent) the institution pays for the individual to attend. Of the 127 respondents whose institutions require participation in professional organizations for retention, promotion and/or tenure, 85 (75 per cent) are funded through a combination of personal and institutional investment. The institution pays the entirety in only 21 cases (18 per cent).

The 184 responses to the question "What do you gain most from your professional activity in this organization?" overwhelmingly identify networking opportunities and continuing education/professional development as the primary benefits to participation. Of the 184 comments,

151 include "networking" or some phrasing related to interaction or communication with colleagues to exchange ideas and provide support. The next most common response (109) relates to ongoing learning, keeping up with the field, learning new skills, best practices, etc. Respondents also identify leadership development, improvement of presentation skills and informal mentoring as important aspects of participation. Only two respondents indicated that they did not gain much from their participation in the organization(s).

The responses to the questions related to mentoring are given in Table 5. Although a larger percentage of librarians have acted as mentors, it is still the minority of librarians who are participating in mentoring activities, either as recipient or provider. Of the 91 librarians who received mentoring, 41 received mentoring either through programs sponsored by an outside professional organization (10) or by the librarian's home institution (31). Twenty three respondents indicated mentoring was informal. From the 36 associated comments, it is clear that most mentoring occurs through informal channels, either at the home institution by a more senior librarian, or by contacts made through participation in a professional organization.

Outside organizations seem to be more helpful to librarians that have acted as mentors to others than they are to those being mentored. Of the

TABLE 4. Organization Participation Activities

Activity	Number
Attend conferences	188
Committee work	174
Contributor to e-mail list(s)	136
Hold office	103
Conference activity	23
Publish	10
Editorial work	12
Mentoring	2

TABLE 5. Mentoring Activities in Current Position

Activity	Yes	No
Received mentoring	91 (35%)	169 (65%)
Acted as mentor	114 (44%)	144 (56%)

113 librarian mentors responding, 66 provided mentoring through programs sponsored by the home institution (34) or through a professional organization (32). Thirty-five mentored others through other means. The associated comments indicate that the mentoring varies in duration. It can be short-term as a "conference buddy," of medium duration such as mentoring an intern or much longer-term, such as relationships with junior colleagues.

Sci-tech librarians clearly prefer personal interaction with other librarians as their primary means of getting the 'just-in-time' mentoring needed to answer questions they may have (see Table 6). The comments included in the follow up question primarily related to how the other people contacted had been identified. It is interesting to note and somehow very reassuring that another strategy for answering questions for 22 librarians included doing research–reading the literature, looking at web sites, using subject guides, etc.

Table 7 represents how respondents came to know the "colleague elsewhere" whom they ask for assistance. In many instances contacts came from more than one source. Clearly, conference attendance and professional organizations play an important role in linking individuals for mentoring relationships. The authors placed responses into the following categories:

- Conferences/Professional Organizations include responses in which the librarian had met contacts through conference attendance, committee work or had used the membership directory to identify someone to ask.
- Consortia/Local organizations/Branches represent responses where contact was facilitated through activity in a consortium or through local or regional librarian groups, both formal and informal.
- Previous position includes responses where contacts were employees, employers or colleagues from work at a previous institution.
- E-mail list includes responses in which contacts were identified through monitoring a subject or organizational e-mail distribution list.
- Library school includes those whose primary contacts were classmates, mentors or instructors from library school.
- Other responses included personal friends, vendor representatives, and identified colleagues at peer institutions.

Most comments in the final open-ended question reinforce the value individuals find in professional organizations, especially for continuing

TABLE 6. Strategies for Answering Sci-Tech Librarianship Questions

Strategy	Number (n = 253)
Ask a peer at my institution	194 (77%)
Send question to association e-mail list	180 (71%)
Contact a colleague elsewhere	167 (66%)
Other	37 (15%)

TABLE 7. Connection to Colleagues Elsewhere

Means to identify colleagues to ask	Number (n=146)
Conferences/Professional Organizations	90 (62%)
Previous Position	41 (28%)
Consortia/Local Organizations/Branch Libraries	19 (13%)
E-mail list	20 (14%)
Library School	13 (9%)
Other	5 (3%)

education and professional development, either directly through conference participation or indirectly through the networking and contacts made. Several also commented on professional organizations as the key to development of the profession as a whole. However, it is also clear that cost of membership and participation is of concern. Because of the number or the nature of subject areas they cover, some sci-tech librarians expressed the need to be members of multiple organizations and find the expense involved to be burdensome. In addition, some felt the cost of memberships and conferences are overwhelming librarian salaries, especially those salaries received by new librarians.

DISCUSSION

A closer look at membership and active participation in the various organizations is revealing. Figure 1 provides a graphical representation of membership in the various organizations and the proportion of members identifying themselves as active participants. The authors did not count membership in the American Library Association (ALA) or its Division, the Association of College and Research Libraries, (ACRL) because these are required for membership in ACRL's Science and

FIGURE 1. Membership and Active Participation

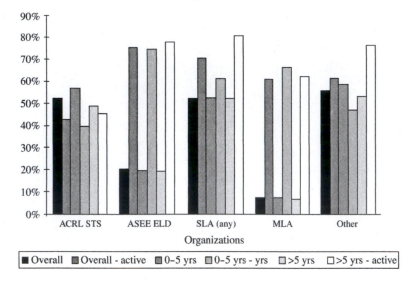

Technology Section (ACRL-STS). Our focus is on ACRL-STS and the other sci-tech oriented organizations. ACRL-STS, SLA (Special Libraries Association) and the variety of organizations represented by the "Other" category (described above) have significant proportions of memberships. Although ACRL-STS has relatively high membership numbers, especially among newer librarians, fewer members consider themselves active members. Membership numbers in ASEE-ELD (American Society of Engineering Education Engineering Libraries Division), SLA and MLA (Medical Library Association) are similar across all types of members. These organizations also show the highest proportion of consistently active members. The high proportion of active members among librarians who have been in their positions for 0 to 5 years in ASEE-ELD and MLA would indicate that these organizations represent good opportunities for active participation for newer librarians in these fields. Librarians who have been in the same position for more than five years appear to be more actively involved in ASEE-ELD, SLA, MLA, and the "Other" organizations category.

Activity and/or membership in professional organizations are clearly important to sci-tech librarians. Respondents in our survey belong to an average of two organizations each, ranging from none to seven memberships. Of the 265 respondents, 166 are members of more than one organization and 72 are members of more than two. In addition, 53 considered themselves to be active participants in more than one organization. Because the authors did not count ALA and ACRL as noted above, counts for number of memberships and active association participation might actually be higher than what is reported here.

In examining subsets of the results based on membership in each of the four primary organizations considered here, MLA and ASEE-ELD were the least likely as secondary organizations for membership, probably due to the specific nature of clientele for each of these groups (Figure 2). STS, SLA and the "Other" category (representing a variety of organizations as discussed above) are quite common as secondary affiliations, varying from 40 to 67 per cent. Because these organizations represent a broader cross-section of librarianship for academic libraries, special libraries or regional associations, respectively, they are complimentary to the primary organization.

MENTORING

The authors did not define the term "mentoring" as used within the survey, either for formal or informal mentoring. Comments received in the survey indicate that the "networking" professional organizations provide is often considered a form of informal mentoring. While several of these

FIGURE 2. Alternate Memberships

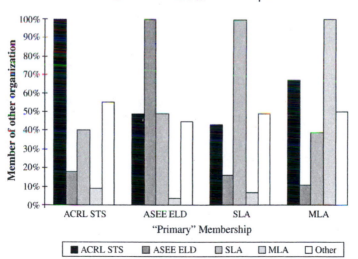

organizations have formal mentoring programs, new librarians don't seem to know about them. Only 10 respondents indicated they had received mentoring through a program sponsored by a professional organization. As shown in Figure 3, the proportion of new librarians receiving mentoring is growing. From comments in the survey, however, it appears that most of the mentoring is informal or through institutional programs. In addition, those librarians who have been in the field longer appear to take their role as mentors seriously, as more than 50 per cent act as mentors to others. Those respondents who do not belong to any professional organizations participate significantly less in mentoring activities.

Keeping in mind that respondents are often members of multiple associations and membership does not mean mentoring was received only through that particular organization, Figure 4 can be used to gain an impression of which organizations are providing the best opportunities for mentoring activity. ASEE ELD members appear to be the most engaged as mentors and mentees. However, looking across all the organizations, the proportion of members acting as mentors is not as variable and is consistently higher than the proportion receiving mentoring.

Frank's (1997) and Kamm's (1997) studies both raised the issue of solo librarians not having the time and/or flexibility to actively participate

FIGURE 3. Participation in Mentoring Activities

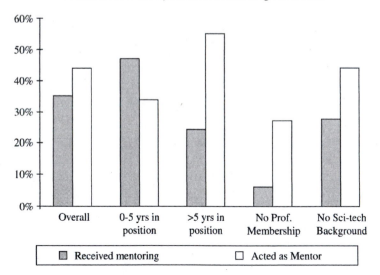

FIGURE 4. Mentoring Activity by Organization

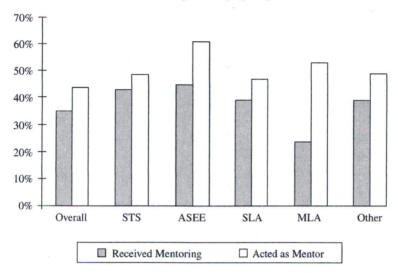

in professional organizations. Responses from this survey, however, indicate many sci-tech librarians consider their participation in professional organizations to be critical for keeping up with the field even if they are solo librarians or in small branches. As a matter of fact, of the 19 librarians who clearly identified themselves as branch librarians, 16 consider themselves actively involved in at least one professional organization. Overall, sci-tech librarians find the contacts they make to be excellent resources for questions that arise that no one else in their organization has the experience or expertise to answer.

Several respondents in this survey considered costs of memberships to be challenging, especially for those librarians whose responsibilities include several subject areas, each of which might have its own disciplinary organization. As Kamm noted in her study, "While . . . the cost of joining/participating in professional associations is an important element for some librarians, those with other motivations for taking part in professional organizations will find the means to do so." The results from the current study show that sci-tech librarians consider their activities in professional organizations to be of sufficient importance that they will and do share the cost of participation with employers. It is clear that institutions also consider librarian participation in professional organizations to be important because 92 per cent either pay or share the costs for participation (although the level of institutional contribution when sharing expenses for participation cannot be determined here).

Of the respondents to our survey, 127 (49 per cent) are required to participate in professional organizations for retention, promotion and/or tenure. Requirements for promotion and/or tenure often include demonstrated professional achievement in scholarship and service to the profession. Virgo (1991) noted the challenges of finding a critical mass of researchers working on related topics. She noted that:

> Associations, through their conferences and publications, provide the opportunity for informal discussion, the exchange of ideas, and the mentoring of younger researchers in the profession. These occasions provide nurturing support, reinforcement, and new ideas that are critical for a researcher working in relative isolation. (p. 194)

The results of our survey reinforce Virgo's conclusion that professional associations provide this critical mass of support for sci-tech librarians in research and professional development in areas directly applicable to their work. Another facet of promotion and tenure is service and leadership in the profession. Respondents in our survey identified opportunities for leadership as important benefits to their membership and activity in professional associations.

CONCLUSION

The results of this study have direct ramifications for librarians, the libraries they work in, and for the professional associations themselves. It is clear that sci-tech librarians consider their involvement in professional associations to be valuable personally as well as for the contribution they can make to their institution and to the field as a whole. This study supports the conclusion drawn by Ritchie and Genoni (1999) that professional associations play a valuable role in mentoring members. However, it is also evident that formal mentoring opportunities sponsored by professional associations are not used as much as they could be. Organizations with formal mentoring programs need to find additional ways to inform members, especially new members, about these programs. Further investigation is needed to find out more about how new members find out about these programs and how they are using them. Do members know about the formal mentoring programs that already exist and choose not to use them because the informal opportunities are preferred? If informal contacts made through conference attendance are the preferred means to professional growth for new librarians, these organizations may want to investigate options for subsidizing attendance at conferences for new members or providing other incentives to attract new members.

Sci-tech librarians consider professional associations invaluable to professional growth and continued learning in the field. As noted above, many of the librarians in this study are active members in several associations. However, others commented that they would be involved in more if they could afford it, particularly associations related to their particular disciplines. In addition, librarians early in their careers, when participation is expected and professional growth is most needed, found the expense involved to be daunting especially because their salaries are lower. Additional research into funding models for participation in professional organizations is needed. As noted above, librarians clearly are willing to share costs of participation. Hiring institutions, particularly those which require active participation for promotion or retention, should look at the benefits this participation brings to the institution and examine their funding models to ensure that sci-tech librarians have the means to participate in the professional associations most relevant to their work.

While this study shows that sci-tech librarians clearly value the collegiality, networking and mentoring professional associations provide, additional research needs to be done to examine whether these mentoring opportunities for sci-tech librarians have influenced their choice to remain in the profession, particularly in the decision to remain in the field of sci-tech librarianship. This question may only be answered by identifying those who are no longer in the field and finding out why they left.

REFERENCES

Acree, Eric Kofi, Sharon K. Epps, Yolanda Gilmore, and Charmaine Henriques. 2001. Using professional development as a retention tool. *Journal of Library Administration* 33 (1/2): 45-61.

American Library Association. 2006. A Guideline for the appointment, promotion and tenure of academic librarians. http://www.ala.org/ala/acrl/acrlstandards/promotiontenure.htm (accessed 03 May, 2006).

Association of College & Research Libraries Ad Hoc Task Force on Recruitment and Retention Issues, 2002. *Recruitment, Retention, and Restructuring: Human Resources in Academic Libraries.* Chicago, IL: American Library Association.

Bullington, Jeffrey S. and Susanna D. Boylston. 2001. Strengthening the profession, assuring our future. *College & Research Libraries News* 62 (4): 430-431.

Detlefsen, Ellen Gay and Josephine E. Olson. 1991. The librarian and the leaver: who leaves the profession? *Journal of Education for Library & Information Science* 31 (4): 275-293.

Fisher, William. 1997. The value of professional associations. *Library Trends* 46 (2): 320-330.

Frank, Donald G.1997. Activity in professional associations: the positive difference in a librarian's career. *Library Trends* 46 (2): 307-319.

Harvey II, Carl A. 2005. Get involved! *Teacher Librarian* 32 (4): 32-34.

Kamm, Sue. 1997. To join or not to join: how librarians make membership decisions about their associations. *Library Trends* 46 (2): 295-306.

Kwasik, Hanna, Pauline O. Fulda, and John P. Ische. 2006. Strengthening professionals: a chapter-level formative evaluation of the Medical Library Association mentoring initiative. *Journal of the Medical Library Association* 94 (1): 19-29.

Millard, Donna M. 2003. Why do we stay? Survey of long-term academic librarians in Canada. *portal: Libraries and the Academy* 3 (1): 99-111.

Ritchie, Ann. 2002. Continuing professional development and workplace learning 1. IFLA's contribution. *Library Management* 23 (8/9): 442-443.

Ritchie, Ann and Paul Genoni. 1999. Mentoring in professional associations: continuing professional development for librarians. *Health Libraries Review* 16: 216-225.

Roper, Fred W. 2006. The Medical Library Association's professional development program: a look back at the way ahead. *Journal of the Medical Library Association* 94 (1): 8-18.

Virgo, Julie A. C. 1991. The Role of professional associations. *In*: McClure, Charles R., and Peter Hernon, eds., *Library and Information Science Research: Perspectives and Strategies for Improvement.* Norwood, NJ: Ablex Publishing: 189-196.

doi: 10.1300/J122v27n01_14

APPENDIX–SURVEY QUESTIONS

The survey was conducted using the SurveyMonkey software (http://www.surveymonkey.com/). Text of the questions is included below.

1) In what type of institution do you work?

   ☐ Academic
   ☐ Corporate
   ☐ Government
   ☐ Other, please specify

2) What is your primary role in the library?

   ☐ Subject specialist/bibliographer
   ☐ Administrator
   ☐ Technical Services
   ☐ Other, please specify

3) How long have you been in this position?

   ☐ Less than 1 year
   ☐ 1 to 5 years
   ☐ 6-10 years
   ☐ More than 10 years

4) Do you have science/technical education or background?

   ☐ Yes
   ☐ No
   ☐ Not applicable

5) Do you belong to any professional library organizations?

   ☐ Yes
   ☐ No (if no, skipped to question 17.)

6) Please indicate whether or not you are a member of each of the following organizations.

   ☐ ALA   ☐ Yes   ☐ No
   ☐ ACRL   ☐ Yes   ☐ No
   ☐ ACRL STS   ☐ Yes   ☐ No
   ☐ ASEE Engineering Libraries Division   ☐ Yes   ☐ No
   ☐ SLA (any division)   ☐ Yes   ☐ No
   ☐ MLA   ☐ Yes   ☐ No

7)   If you are a member of any other organization not listed above, please provide the name of the organization(s)

8)   Do you consider yourself an active participant (e.g., participate in committee work, attend conferences, hold office, etc.) of a professional organization?

☐ Yes
☐ No (if no, skipped to question 17.)

9)   For each of the following organizations, please indicate whether or not you are an active participant, e.g., participate in committee work, attend conferences, hold office, etc.

☐ ALA	☐ Yes	☐ No
☐ ACRL	☐ Yes	☐ No
☐ ACRL STS	☐ Yes	☐ No
☐ ASEE Engineering Libraries Division	☐ Yes	☐ No
☐ SLA (any division)	☐ Yes	☐ No
☐ MLA	☐ Yes	☐ No

10) If you are an active member of any other organization not listed above, please provide the name of the organization(s)

11) Please provide the name of the professional organization in which you are most active.

12) For this organization, please indicate whether or not your participation includes the following activities.

☐ Participate in committee work	☐ Yes	☐ No
☐ Attend conferences	☐ Yes	☐ No
☐ Hold office	☐ Yes	☐ No
☐ Contribute to organization's e-mail list(s)	☐ Yes	☐ No

13) Other activity not listed above, please specify.

14) How often do you attend the organization's conferences?

☐ I attend as often as conferences are held
☐ I attend irregularly
☐ I have never attended.

15) How has this participation been paid for?

☐ I pay
☐ My institution pays
☐ Combination of the two
☐ Not applicable

16) What do you gain most from your professional activity in this organization?

17) Is your participation in *any* professional organization a requirement for retention, promotion and/or tenure in your institution?

☐ Yes
☐ No
☐ Don't know

18) Have you *received* mentoring in your present position?

☐ Yes
☐ No (if no, skipped to question 21.)

19) Is/Was the mentoring part of a formal, structured mentoring program?

☐ Yes, sponsored by my institution	☐ Yes	☐ No
☐ Yes, sponsored by an outside professional organization	☐ Yes	☐ No
☐ Other, please explain in comment below	☐ Yes	☐ No

20) Comment on other mentoring programs.

21) Have you *acted* as a mentor to other science/technology librarians?

☐ Yes
☐ No (if no, skipped to question 24.)

22) Is/Was the mentoring part of a formal, structured mentoring program?

☐ Yes, sponsored by my institution	☐ Yes	☐ No
☐ Yes, sponsored by an outside professional organization	☐ Yes	☐ No
☐ Other, please explain in comment below	☐ Yes	☐ No

23) Comment on other mentoring programs.

24) Which of the following do you do when you have a question related to science/technology librarianship?

☐ I ask a peer at my institution   ☐ Yes   ☐ No
☐ I send a question to a professional organization's e-mail list   ☐ Yes   ☐ No
☐ I contact a colleague elsewhere   ☐ Yes   ☐ No
    (please indicate below how you came to know this person)
☐ Other (please specify below)   ☐ Yes   ☐ No

25) Explain how you met a colleague elsewhere or specify what other avenues you use when you have a question.

26 Please provide any other comments on the role of professional organizations in your work as a sci/tech librarian or about this survey in general.

Retention–After Hiring Then What?

Jodee L. Kawasaki

SUMMARY. This article will use the student retention model as a starting place for designing a new science librarian retention program. Retention programs are common in other areas of university life, especially for retaining first-year students. Retention programs demonstrate a commitment and interest by the institution; they send a message to the new students–you are important to us. Why not send the same message to new hires? In building a retention program for science librarians, these student retention programs can serve as models; they can be a good starting place. As with students, it is cheaper to retain library staff already on campus than to recruit new ones. The library saves money with less recruiting and training. The new science librarian becomes acculturated, learns the curricula, the faculty, and becomes a valuable team member with connections to the library and institution. doi: 10.1300/J122v27n01_15
[Article copies available for a fee from The Haworth Document Delivery Service: 1-800-HAWORTH. E-mail address: <docdelivery@haworthpress.com> Website: <http://www.HaworthPress.com> © 2006 by The Haworth Press, Inc. All rights reserved.]

KEYWORDS. Student retention program, acculturation, commitment, orientation, training, science librarians, training plans, employee attrition

Jodee L. Kawasaki is Information Resources Development Team Leader, Montana State University, Renne Library, P.O. Box 173320, Bozeman, MT 59717 (E-mail: alijk@montana.edu).

[Haworth co-indexing entry note]: "Retention–After Hiring Then What?" Kawasaki, Jodee L. Co-published simultaneously in *Science & Technology Libraries* (The Haworth Information Press, an imprint of The Haworth Press, Inc.) Vol. 27, No. 1/2, 2006, pp. 225-240; and: *Recruiting, Training, and Retention of Science and Technology Librarians* (ed: Patricia A. Kreitz, and JoAnn DeVries) The Haworth Information Press, an imprint of The Haworth Press, Inc., 2006, pp. 225-240. Single or multiple copies of this article are available for a fee from The Haworth Document Delivery Service [1-800-HAWORTH, 9:00 a.m. - 5:00 p.m. (EST). E-mail address: docdelivery@haworthpress.com].

Available online at http://stl.haworthpress.com
© 2006 by The Haworth Press, Inc. All rights reserved.
Digital Object Identifier: 10.1300/J122v27n01_15

INTRODUCTION

Many organizations spend a lot of time and money on finding the right person for a position, but often forget, or do not realize, that keeping them is as critical as hiring them in the first place. Are you keeping new hires once they arrive at your library? A few simple questions may help you analyze your library's situation. To assess your library's retention quotient, ask yourself these basic questions. Does it seem like there is a gap between new librarians and long-term ones? Is there a significant lack of librarians with some years of experience? This gap may vary; look at librarians with 3-6 years of experience, or, in some libraries, between 6-12 years. This analysis can only benefit your library–perhaps you do not need a retention plan. But if you do, a plan can help you develop a healthier library and meet the broader needs of the larger institution the library supports.

Another reason for implementing a retention program is more subtle. Your library may be retaining new hires but they may be developing negative attitudes shortly after arriving. If this is the case, library management needs to assess the situation and analyze how it developed. Investment in a retention program may prevent this disaffection from developing in the future and, depending on the current situation, may be able to improve it. Negativity affects not only the new hire and his or her likelihood of remaining and performing productively, but it has spillover effects on the morale of other library employees. Spending the time to help a new librarian feel a part of the library and the broader institution will benefit everyone involved.

This article will examine the problem of retention, particularly of science librarians, touch on the costs of not addressing the problem, and explain and apply the student retention program model as described by Montana State University's Amy Weatherhead; Oregon State University Student Orientation & Retention web site, University of Oregon Retention Program web site, SCSU web site, and others (listed in bibliography) for relevant components that might be used in a library-based model.

RETENTION AS A PERVASIVE PROBLEM

Corporate America and many of the industries are aware of and concerned with employee turnover. The Generation X workforce is 40% smaller than the Baby Boomers generation. There is fierce competition growing over employees, which may be instigated by one of the lowest unemployment rates in 30 years (Grimme, 2006). The literature is full of articles on employee turnover, searching Business Source Premier (EbscoHost) turned up over 57,000 articles on the topic. Corporations that institute a retention program, whether it is formal training or mentoring or informal activities generally seem to find their loss rates dropping and their cost of hiring and training lower (Klein and Weaver, 2000). The article by Hammers (2003) gives cost data related to the program she writes about, the retention program cost $2.5 million to launch, but the company saved $1.35 million by keeping employees longer than 3 months, they were 25% less likely to be absent saving another $306K, and sales have increased $3.7 million. By these figures launching an orientation and retention program was cheap. Another article (Gehring and Conner, 2002) looked at turnover costs of not just the interview time, negotiation of offers, salary and training time lost, but costs such as market share loss and productivity lost.

Industries have found that paying attention to employees, not just money, helps keep them around, ". . . job quality and workplace support have a combined 70 percent impact . . ." (Grimme, 2006). Two very recent articles provide good information about why developing an employee retention plan is a very good thing to have in place. The article, *Competing in a world market? Don't forget your people* talks about keeping people to give a company an edge in the global competition: "Today, however, there is fierce competition from all over the globe. If a U.S. firm wants to be competitive, it had better use all the brainpower it has available. Engineers and designers can be major competitive assets if they are both involved and committed. But they will only be assets if management shares key information with them, seeks their assistance, and acts on their recommendations. This sort of collaboration cannot be lip service once a quarter. To obtain the trust of your workforce and build commitment takes time.... But make a plan and start now. Don't wait" (Paris, 2006). The other very supportive article, *An American Crisis: attracting, retaining and motivating employees* on retention programs in the corporate sector from Grimme (2006) states: "Recent landmark studies confirm what theoreticians and management gurus such as Abraham Maslow, Frederick Hertzberg and Peter Drucker have maintained for decades:

- Money is a necessary, but not sufficient condition, to attract, retain and motivate good employees. You and I will go to work for a paycheck and benefits plan. But we won't really do work (at least our best work), unless something else is present.

- It is the quality of work itself and of our relationships with others at work that draws us to the best organizations and keeps us there, performing at peak effectiveness."

Colleges and universities have long been concerned about retention, particularly of minority and first year students (Swail, 2004; Noel 1985). Many universities have implemented formal, structured student retention programs–in fact this effort has evolved into a national focus on that first year experience or on building campus 'learning communities.' Many studies have tried to predict success by using prior academic achievement during high school, but Pritchard and Wilson (2003) looked at a set of different factors in their unique study. This article gives a good overview of factors used historically to predict student success and a new way of improving success. An article pushing the student retention model envelope by Betsy Barefoot (2004) is calling for the exploration of "the role of the college or university environment–especially the classroom itself–on student persistence . . . explore . . . the basic structure of higher education, especially the way instruction is designed and delivered." With all this said one only needs to search the ERIC database on student retention or student attrition to find a plethora of articles describing models for prediction of success or programs on first-year seminars, learning communities and such.

Across many university campuses, librarians participate in different ways within the campus wide student retention programs. The National Resource Center First Year Experience Center's website documents the close collaboration that has evolved between campus first year programs and librarians (http://www.sc.edu/fye/resources/fyr/bibliography1.html). Libraries, whose librarians actually participate in the many efforts of the colleges & universities to retain first-year students, should more readily recognize the value of applying these retention strategies to the new science librarian hires. Student retention models consistently discuss factors that predict student success and what the campus communities can do to promote these. "For decades, researchers have asserted that the more time and energy students invest in their college experiences, the more likely they will be to persist and succeed in college" (National Resource Center publications web site).

Has involvement in student retention programs prompted a more general recognition by libraries and librarians of the value of applying student retention models to staff retention, and in particular to science librarian retention?

RETAINING LIBRARIANS

There has been a great deal of study and writing about attracting and hiring librarians into the field as a large cohort of the profession 'greys' and moves towards retirement (Lenzini, 2002). The need to hire and train replacement librarians–particularly subject-specialized librarians such as science librarians–is well documented in the literature. Two good articles about recruitment of science librarians are Hackenberg, 2000, and Hallmark and Frances, 2003. Also, a webliography is available on this topic by Pellack (2006). Just the existence of this special issue of *Science and Technology Libraries* on recruitment and retention of science librarians is testament to the concern in the field. While the problems and challenges of recruitment are outside the scope of this article, a quick scan of the other articles within this issue show that recruiting science librarians is not an easy undertaking. The number of job postings for science librarians as well demonstrates this growing competition. Shouldn't, then, library administrators and supervisors wish to maximize the success of each hire?

A search of the library literature does reflect concerns with retention, although not as strong a concern as recruitment itself (Osif and Harwood, 1999). While much of the recent writing focuses on retaining minority librarians (Howland, 1999; Lippincott, 1997; Musser, 2001; U.C. Santa Cruz web site), there is some general concern expressed both about losing new hires because of low wages and high cost of living (North Carolina State University Libraries, 2005) and about losing new hires because of the kinds of lack of connection and lack of purpose and excitement (Stevens, 2003) that student retention programs were developed to fight.

DEVELOPING A RETENTION PROGRAM: MISSION AND GOALS

The resume, reference checks, and hiring process provide information about the past and present activities of the new science librarian. A retention program that includes orientation, professional development, and training will help predict the future success of the science librarian.

This article will use the student retention model as a starting place for designing a new science librarian retention program. Retention programs are common in other areas of university life, especially for students. Some universities have campus wide student retention programs, while others implement the retention programs at a lower level within the organization–colleges or departments. Retention programs demonstrate commitment and interest by the institution; they send a message to the new students–"you are important to us." Why not send the same message to new hires? When the library has a retention program, the new science librarian knows the organization is supportive, committed, and shows interest in them. It increases the employee's sense of belonging to the library. The information below is a synthesis of reading articles on student retention, the author's experience, and anecdotal evidence. The mission statement, goals, and various components to science librarian retention program are from the author's knowledge and experience.

In building a retention program for science librarians, student retention programs can serve as good starting models. Creating a program takes time and effort, but will be worth it in the long run. As with students, it is cheaper to retain those already on campus than to recruit new ones. The library saves money and time due to less recruiting, less time staff serving on search committees, and less time spent training by valuable, expensive supervisors and "senior" librarians. Besides the time and money savings to administration and the library as a whole, retaining new hires serves the university. Science librarians who stay can then build relationships with faculty and students, and build knowledge about curricula and the institution.

University of Alaska web site for the student retention program for the Alaska Native Science and Engineering program sets forth clear goals and examples. As does the Oregon State University web site.

A science librarian retention program needs a mission statement and goals. A mission statement explains the program's purpose to both library administrators and to library staff who may be asked to become involved. Goals give focus to the program and, when achieved, supply concrete reasons for supporting the program. An example of a mission statement (from the author) is:

> The Science Librarian retention program strives to support new hires in the transition process, as well as provide opportunities for success through orientation, training, and professional development.

Now you have the opportunity to define what equals success. Concrete, measurable and achievable goals are critical to any program's success but much more so when starting up a new initiative such as this. What problems have your initial analysis of turnover rates or staff morale shown that you wish to counteract? When creating goals, for either the program as a whole or for an individual new employee, it is important not to invent new requirements, but align the goals to existing needs and expectations. What does the new hire need to accomplish? What will he or she need to do to meet the requirements for tenure or annual reviews? Some sample goals from student retention programs that can be adapted to science librarians are:

1. Providing resources and services available on campus
2. Career development opportunities
3. Articulates and participates fully in the orientation program

And some goals that need to be developed to fit with the library's mission and the fact that this is a working, professional position rather than a student experience are:

1. Provide professional development and growth opportunities
2. Focus on serving the needs of the students
3. Transmits information, publications, and web & paper resources available to employees

Once you have the goals and outcomes for success defined, the next step is to build the components of the retention program. These components are what the organization provides for the new hires. They concretely inform the new hire, the supervisor, and the 'senior' colleagues participating in the program what training and orientation needs to occur to meet the requirements for success. Although the components are concrete activities tied back to the goals, each training plan should be tailored specifically to the needs of the individual position and to the existing training, skills and knowledge of the new science librarian.

DEVELOPING A RETENTION PROGRAM: THE STRUCTURED PLAN

Carrying the student retention model through for new science librarian hires, here are the components to implement for new hires. During the first six weeks the library needs to: (1) provide meaningful work, (2) provide appropriate tools to do the work, (3) participate fully in orienting new hires, (4) provide opportunities to make connections within the library organization and the institution, and (5) create an environment that provides elements for asking and seeking out information and professional development. Explanations for these components and elements that fit into the categories are listed below. These will build the necessary connections, allowing the new hire to be a part of the library and to want to be at work. Research from student retention indicates students that make a meaningful connection in the first 6 weeks of classes are more likely to stay committed to their education and stay at the institution (Noel, 1985). Just as students are trying to learn the ropes and figure out how college works, so are new science librarians in their new library.

The first component, that of providing meaningful work may appear surprising at first since one might wonder why hire someone if you *don't* have 'real' work for him or her to do? However, if you have just hired someone with 5 years reference desk experience, requiring this librarian to review the materials held in the reference area and observe at the desk for the first six weeks may be considered busy work and, of course, the effect on the new employee does set a tone about the department. The library needs to decide ahead of time what is meaningful work. The type of work may vary depending on the skills and experience of the new science librarian. Evaluate the new hire, gear the work to their skills and experience, and anchor it in the position description used to hire the person. The work may be simply handling the materials in the reference area for the science librarian with no prior library work experience. A project can get the science librarian involved in meaningful work or consider immediate involvement in collection management work for the science librarian with experience. A word of caution here, don't make a project an individual project; however, have the science librarian working with another librarian or a group of staff. An individual project can create isolation and upon completion the science librarian does not know anyone and nobody knows what project was just completed. It is important to make the work meaningful; do not belittle the new hire with simple busy work. The step of evaluating the skills and experience of the new science librarian is vital. Use the skills you hired; think through the work available and the reason you needed this science librarian. Match the work to the librarian based on the person's skills and experience; put them to use.

The second component of the training/retention plan, providing appropriate tools for the work, goes hand-in-hand with the first one. Tools can be interpreted in many ways. However, don't overlook some of the most obvious. For example, make sure the office area is clean, ready, and available immediately for the new hire. Would it not be an embarrassment to the organization to say we have an office space for you and everything is ready, but we don't have a chair or a computer or _____ (you fill in the blank)? Having resources, tools, or equipment available makes a powerful statement to the new hire–we have put thought and effort into both welcoming you and ensuring you have the basics tools needed to be successful (Morris, 2003). Of course, those basics are usually obvious such as a chair, phone, computer, desk, etc., but it is amazing what can be over-looked by the department. Here is where little things can be forgotten (campus phone book, paper clips, pens, etc.) but these send a clear message to a new hire. Remember the basic office supplies too, such as sticky notes, note pad, pens, pencils, phone book, file folders, paper clips, etc. Even if you can't put all these into the new work space/office, make sure the new science librarian knows where he or she can find these supplies, but do not forget the nameplate and business cards.

If time allows get the input from the new science librarian on preferences for the appearance of the person's name, whether a paper or electronic calendar is preferred, and other office supplies. Another tool needed by the new hire is the personal computer. If there is time and your supply budget or organizational computing support permits, contact the new hire before she or he arrives and ask them what they like to use for software, anything from what e-mail program they want and many other software preferences. The first impressions of the organization's flexibility and support make a lasting impression.

The third retention program component that of orienting the new hire is multi-faceted. The more confident you can make the new employee, the better for the library. Assessing the new science librarian's skills and experience will influence what orienting is necessary through the retention program besides what work to give her or him. It is important to use the knowledge and experience of the science librarian, those qualities which made the candidate the top choice. Communication between the supervisor and the science librarian will provide information to both about the orientation needed by the new science librarian. For example assuming the science librarian will have shifts at the reference desk(s), knowing the geography of the library, branch libraries, and the campus will build confidence in answering those types of questions. A tour of the library is as fine a starting point as any. Introducing the science librarian to everyone during the tour and explaining what they do is also helpful. Although this may have been done during the interview that may have been months earlier and so you should repeat the process, perhaps in more detail. For larger organizations tours may be done in segments by the obvious divisions of labor. Too much information at once may hamper the librarian's ability to remember important parts.

If possible during a campus tour, introduce the librarian to faculty members she or he will be working with. This provides the science librarian the opportunity to make meaningful introductions, along with showing that the library supports its employees. During a tour of the campus point out buildings, departments, places where events are held, and other popular spots students ask about. The librarian's confidence in assisting patrons will improve as local knowledge increases. In addition to a campus tour, the science librarian is well advised to make appointments with department heads that she or he will work with thus introducing her or himself before the first departmental visit with the entire faculty. Depending on the experience and comfort level of the science librarian, it may be prudent to have a senior librarian mentor the new hire when meeting the departmental faculty she or he will be working with. During these first months that mentor could be giving guidance on what requests from faculty are appropriate. The science librarian needs to learn what correspondence is required with the departments, how frequently, and in what way(s) (e-mail distribution list or paper newsletter) is this done. Partnering with a senior librarian will help keep communication ongoing within the retention program and within the department and/or library.

Another part of the third component of a retention plan is to orient the science librarian to policies and procedures of the Library and Institution both as resources for his or her own information and for when serving at the reference desk. The collection development policy gives guidance to the new hire on what materials to request or purchase. All policies need to be covered, both the formal written ones and the verbal standards of practice or policies. Possible items to cover are circulation and interlibrary loan privileges, library protocols for e-mail and scheduling appointments, handling or referring disgruntled patrons, public bulletin board policies, library suggestion box policy, and every thing related to Special Collections and/or Rare Book Room usage policy, hours open, etc. There are many unwritten polices, we all have them. Consider issues such as: can you ever make exceptions for the non-circulating materials to go out overnight, how does one make purchase requests if not a standard responsibility, how does upper management prefer to be communicated with–drop-in's or a more formal process?

These are just some ideas of the formal and non-formal policies that may exist at the library. All should be listed and the supervisor should have that list, which needs to be given to the new hire along with the full policies. Alternatively, have she or he investigate and discover all the policies listed, but either way discuss them together. Institutional policies and procedures are just as important as the library's. Again, develop a list of all the possible ones such as employee benefits, union membership (may apply in some libraries), the campus telephone system and voice mail, Internet usage policies, and hours for student services such as the computing labs are open. Knowing and understanding policies contribute to the potential for success of the science librarian.

One aspect of orientation that is easily overlooked may be called serendipity training. The resources he or she needs for personal information; cover anything from campus student clubs and staff/faculty groups to what recreation resources are available around the institution or community. Don't forget to show her or him where to find the list of campus activities and have the new hire read a history of the institution. Remember, being involved in the campus community builds meaningful connections. Give the new hire time and incentive to browse the web site of the library and the institution. The new science librarian will also be empowered to answer questions about institutional policies, benefits, etc. when he or she is familiar with the institution's web site. The student retention programs at Suffolk and South Carolina State University talk about newsletters and web sites with that information and/or links to insurance, benefits, local housing information, or what would help students better acculturate to college. To translate this into our model, the science librarian needs the equivalent of "a day in the life of the librarian" as a starting point for the new hire to "see into" the library. Consider how familiar the new librarian is with the area or region. Sometimes orientation needs to include history of the region or geography related to landmarks. As mentioned above, this will give the librarian working at a service point the knowledge of the local area and confidence in answering those questions when they arise. It is important for the new hire to be able to help patrons.

Another component of orientation is for the new hire to understand the evaluation system used in the library. The new hire must be given copies of the documentation for annual reviews, tenure reviews, and any other reviews that are done through out the organization and the timeline for these evaluations. Explain the process and supply information about what is important and what is not important to the new librarian. The library has a responsibility to new hires to give them the appropriate information and it should not be a secret. Ultimately, the science librarian has the responsibility to be successful or not, but can't do it without the necessary information.

Another aspect of importance is organizational politics. Every organization has politics of some sort. Acknowledging and explaining them is the best approach with new hires. Sharing knowledge of the work environment will always be a positive move by the department. Learning organizational politics isn't done in one session, but done over time, especially in the first 6 weeks to 6 months. As the new hire learns the organization's dynamics, then the politics will start making sense.

Another facet of orientation includes making sure the new hire is on all the appropriate library and institutional e-mail lists, receiving newsletters and publications (paper or electronic format), and getting invitations to the social events the library or institution holds. Does the department celebrate birthdays or work anniversaries? These can be good social events to bring the department together, help the new librarian learn about other members of the department, and show the collegiality of the department. There are other fun events to hold such as celebrating holidays or decorating for them or celebrating anniversary start dates for department members. Social events don't have to be fancy or formal, just social. Such events help build staff commitment to the library and help make connections within the first 6 weeks of starting the new job.

The discussion above has been about the orientation process, which inter-mingles with training needs. Training needs can't be neglected and need to be just as flexible as orientation aspects. This aspect in the science librarian retention program differs from a student retention program; the new hire brings knowledge, if not experience too, with them to the new work environment. Assessing the librarian's skills and experience is a must for recognizing appropriate training needs. Open a dialogue with the science librarian about their skills, identify and use their strengths, make note of their needs, attitudes and work habits based on what comes out of this conversation. Training each science librarian will vary, someone may need training on the e-mail system, while another will know it but need training on the database software most heavily used by the local patrons. The library and department need to recognize these differences and allow the retention program to keep communication open for the new hire; treat her or him with respect for it improves their self-esteem in handling the new position. Training needs must be assessed routinely during the first six months; these are not one size fits all. It needs to be a part of a retention program and have outcomes of expectations. If you have hired a science librarian with experience consider 'turning the tables,' have the new science librarian give a training session to the department on the science databases available.

Since it is a new position and library for the science librarian, some orientation and training is needed; even with lots of experience there are still things to learn about the new library and institution. Reviewing with the new hire their skills, knowledge, abilities, interest, and experience will provide meaningful retention program experience. These factors contribute to an employee's job satisfaction and commitment to the organization.

There are many other items that should be part of orientation and training. A few have been discussed, but keep an open mind, think of other policies or procedures that a new hire should know about. One not covered in this article, but vital is library professional development. There are many professional development opportunities for any librarian, these cannot be overlooked and can easily be a part of a retention program. Since library professional development is so prominent and readily available, the author felt there are enough articles discussing this option and its benefits that it need not be covered in detail here.

As noted, the fourth component of a retention plan is to get the new science librarian connected to the library within the first six weeks. This can be done through a variety of options mentioned above in this article for serendipity training. The main thing to keep in mind when developing a retention program is what can the department provide to get the new science librarian involved within the organization? Open communication will inform the mentor or supervisor of the interests of the new science librarian. The new hire wants to feel that she or he is apart of something and that they belong here. Other ways for the science librarian to make connections is through participating in institutional activities outside the library, meeting science faculty the librarian will be working with for instruction or collection development, getting on a campus-wide committee or becoming an advisor for a student club. A colleague within the department can also help get the new hire connected to community activities through contacts, clubs, or local groups. There are many other possibilities besides these few mentioned here.

A final component listed above, which has been discussed throughout the other components, is that the retention program needs to create an environment that provides elements for asking and seeking out information, and professional development opportunities. The University of Alaska's student retention web site suggests team-building meetings, saying "use these sessions to identify and mitigate problems before they jeopardize the student's academic success." Many people can have roles to play within the retention program just as is the case for student retention programs (Oregon State University, 2005). There will be a supervisor and a senior librarian mentor, yet all other members of the department can participate and should, since this will help the new hire make connections. If any colleague within the library sees a need or hears of an interest from the new librarian, they should be made aware that such a need or interest is a good opportunity to assist the new librarian. Having staff share these opportunities shows the library's support and interest.

CONCLUSION

Retention plans can be powerful tools for success for the new hire, the library and the campus it serves. In summary, a retention program needs to be flexible, have continual communication, and be able to be adjusted to fit the needs of the new hires based on their skills, knowledge, and experience. Create an environment where the new science librarian can ask, learn, and seek out information she or he needs. The whole department and/or library should be involved in orientation and training of the new science librarian. The best retention programs have a group of people with roles to play, information to provide, and support to be given to the new hire. The contributions by many employees give the science librarian diverse opinions, information, and opportunities to learn other points of view as well as affirming the organization's commitment to inclusiveness. When developing a new hire retention program, have a mission statement and write up goals and outcomes. These will provide guidance for each department within the library as well as creating a concrete plan administration can support. Any program must have a plan and must be supported by the library's administration for it to be successful.

REFERENCES

Astin, Alexander. 1999. Involvement in Learning Revisited: lessons we have learned. *Journal of College Student Development* 40(5): 587-98.

Astin, Alexander. 1999. Student Involvement: a developmental theory for higher education. *Journal of College Student Development* 40(5): 518-29.

Barefoot, Betsy O. 2004. Higher Education's Revolving Door: confronting the problem of student drop out in US colleges and universities. *Open Learning* 19(1): 9-18.

Boehman, Joseph. 2006. Affective, Continuance, and Normative Commitment among Student Affairs Professionals: executive summary. http://boehman.home.mindspring.com/jobo/ [February 22, 2006].

Gehring, John and John Conner. 2002. A strategic approach to employee retention. *Healthcare Financial Management* 56(11): 40-4.

Grimme, Don. 2006. An American Crisis: attracting, retaining and motivating employees. *Business Credit* 108(4): 67.

Hackenberg, Jill M. 2000. Who Chooses Sci-Tech Librarianship? *College & Research Libraries* 61(5): 441-450.

Hallmark, Julie and Mary Frances Lembo. 2003. Leaving Science for LIS. *Issues in Science & Technology Librarianship*. Issue 37 http://www.istl.org/03-spring/refereed1.html.

Hammers, Maryann. 2003. Quashing quick quits. *Workforce* 82(5): 50.

Howland, Joan S. 1999. Beyond Recruitment: retention and promotion strategies to ensure diversity and success. *Library Administration & Management* 13(1): 4-14.

Klein, Howard J. and Natasha A. Weaver. 2000. The effectiveness of an organization-level orientation training programming the socialization of new hires. *Personnel Psychology* 53(1): 47-66.

Lenzini, Rebecca T. 2002. The Graying of the Library Profession: A Survey of Our Professional Associations and Their Responses. *Searcher* 10(7): 88-97.

Lippincott, Kate. 1997. *Growing a Diverse Workforce in the Library and Information Science Professions*. ERIC Doc. ED411873.

Morris, Barbara. 2003. The cost to a bad start. *Marketing Magazine* 108(36): 29.

Musser, Linda R. 2001. Effective retention strategies for diverse employees. *Journal of Library Administration* 33(1/2): 63-72.

National Resource Center. 2002. *Strategies for Improving Teaching and Learning*. http://www.sc.edu/fye/publications/strategies/index.html [April 22, 2006].

National Resource Center. 2004. *The First-Year Experience and Academic Libraries: a select, annotated bibliography prepared by Scott Walter*. http://www.sc.edu/fye/resources/fyr/bibliography1.html [April 22, 2006].

Noel, Lee et al. 1985. *Increasing student retention*. San Francisco: Jossey-Bass.

North Carolina State University Libraries. 2005. *Annual Report 2004/2005*. http://www.lib.ncsu.edu/administration/annualreports/reportch05.html [April 22, 2006].

Oregon State University. 2005. *Student Orientation and Retention*. http://oregonstate.edu/soar/mission.html [January 24, 2006].

Osif, Bonnie Anne and Richard L. Harwood. 1999. Recruitment, selection, and retention: bibliographical essay. *Library Administration & Management* 13(3): 171-6.

Paris, Michael. 2006. Competing in a world market? Don't forget your people. *Machine Design* 78(7): 70.

Pellack, Lorraine. 2006. Careers in Academic & Science Librarianship. http://www.public.iastate.edu/~pellack/AcadSciCareers.htm [April 22, 2006].

Pritchard, Mary E. and Gregory S. Wilson. 2003. Using Emotional and Social Factors to Predict Student Success. *Journal of College Student Development* 44(1): 18-28.

South Carolina State University. date unknown. *Student Success and Retention Program.* http://www.scsu.edu/Services/StudentSuccess/overview.cfm [April 24, 2006].

Stevens, Jen and Rosemary Streatfeild. 2003. *Spec Kit 276, Recruitment and Retention.* Annapolis Junction, MD: ARL Publications Distribution Center.

Suffolk University. 2006. *Guide to Your Freshman Year.* http://www.suffolk.edu/ors/ freshmanyear.html [April 24, 2006].

Swail, Watson Scott. 2004. *The art of student retention, a handbook for practitioners and administrators.* Texas Higher Education Coordinating Board, Austin, TX. ERIC Doc ED485498.

University of Alaska and the Pacific Alliance Universities. 2006. *Alaska Native Science and Engineering Program University Retention Program.* http://soe.uaa.alaska.edu/ ansep/PA%20College%20Retention%20Program.htm [April 24, 2006].

U.C. Santa Cruz Library. date unknown. *Recruitment Advancement and Retention.* http://library.ucsc.edu/esln/recruit.html [April 22, 2006].

Yorke, Mantz. 2004. Retention, persistence and success in on-campus higher education, and their enhancement in open and distance learning. *Open Learning* 19(1): 19-32.

Weatherhead, Amy, First Year Initiative Coordinator Assistant Dean of Students. 2006. *Personal interview.* January 24 at Montana State University.

doi: 10.1300/J122v27n01_15

Competencies Required!
For Education, Recruitment, and Retention

Sara R. Tompson

SUMMARY. For a practice-based profession, librarianship has been slow to adopt competencies and standards for our practitioners in a majority of settings. Notable exceptions such as medical librarianship can provide some models, but science and technology libraries must go further if we expect the people in our operations to meet the needs of our users in this digital century. Recruitment and retention both should be based upon measurable performance standards and goals. This article discusses some sources upon which we can draw and from which we can adapt competencies and standards, as well as presenting some examples. doi: 10.1300/J122v27n01_16 *[Article copies available for a fee from The Haworth Document Delivery Service: 1-800-HAWORTH. E-mail address: <docdelivery@ haworthpress.com> Website: <http://www.HaworthPress.com> © 2006 by The Haworth Press, Inc. All rights reserved.]*

KEYWORDS. Competencies, hiring, recruitment, retention, sci-tech librarianship, standards, digital literacy, profession

---

Sara R. Tompson is Team Leader, Science & Engineering Library, University of Southern California (E-mail: sarat@usc.edu). Ms. Tompson was previously a physical sciences and/or engineering librarian for 19 years. She is past Chair of the Engineering Division of the Special Libraries Association (SLA) and current Secretary of the SLA Physics/Astronomy/ Math Division. She is also a licensed private pilot and has recently improved her flying competency by acquiring an instrument rating.

[Haworth co-indexing entry note]: "Competencies Required! For Education, Recruitment, and Retention." Tompson, Sara R. Co-published simultaneously in *Science & Technology Libraries* (The Haworth Information Press, an imprint of The Haworth Press, Inc.) Vol. 27, No. 1/2, 2006, pp. 241-258; and: *Recruiting, Training, and Retention of Science and Technology Librarians* (ed: Patricia A. Kreitz, and JoAnn DeVries) The Haworth Information Press, an imprint of The Haworth Press, Inc., 2006, pp. 241-258. Single or multiple copies of this article are available for a fee from The Haworth Document Delivery Service [1-800-HAWORTH, 9:00 a.m. - 5:00 p.m. (EST). E-mail address: docdelivery@haworthpress.com].

Available online at http://stl.haworthpress.com
© 2006 by The Haworth Press, Inc. All rights reserved.
Digital Object Identifier: 10.1300/J122v27n01_16

INTRODUCTION

> While competency development and implementation is not a fast or easy process, as part of a larger performance management system their use can help research libraries to recruit, hire, train, and retain valuable employees. In today's ever- changing and increasingly challenging environment, well-designed and implemented core competencies enable libraries and library staff to best meet the needs of the research library community. (ARL Spec Kit 270, Core Competencies. http://www.arl.org/spec/270sum.html)

It seems likely that discussions of competencies in the library *literature* far exceed the application of competencies in the library *workplace*. This article discusses ways in which competencies could be (and in some cases are being) more systematically applied to and used by science and technology (sci-tech) libraries and librarians to improve performance and service. Selected competency documents from other areas of librarianship and from sci-tech disciplines are examined as part of the discussion, since they provide some models that can be adapted to sci-tech libraries.

Librarians most frequently encounter competencies and standards when pursing a degree in librarianship. Competencies can come into play during the recruitment process as well. Competencies are used less often in evaluation and retention. If librarians are to continue to play a vital role for our organizations and for society–and there *is* a role for us to play–sci-tech librarians must continue to expand our competence in a broad array of practices and theories, and the organizations for which we work must provide us support and opportunities for doing so.

The Oxford English Dictionary[1] defines practice as "the carrying on or exercise of a profession or occupation, especially of law, surgery, or medicine." The Merriam-Webster Dictionary[2] defines a practitioner as "one that [sic: who] exercises an art, science, or profession (as law, medicine, or engineering)." Both definitions speak of professions. Librarianship is typically regarded as a profession because there are theories and knowledge behind what librarians do; the practice is more than simply another hands–on service industry.

Librarianship has been called a practice-based profession as it deals directly with users and resources and the services that connect the two. As one colleague has noted, "Librarianship is a practical discipline.

There is not a vast theoretical base, but there is a distinct and extensive body of applied knowledge."[3]

Librarians' application of knowledge happens, ideally, within a contextual framework built upon sound theories for organizing information resources to facilitate users' access thereof. There is a natural tension between theory and practice in librarianship. Competencies and standards for librarians must take into account both theory and practice. As noted in the LIS (Library and Information Science) Wiki, "A balance must . . . be struck between the education of theoretical knowledge and practical skills instruction."[4] Standards and competencies can resolve this tension between theory and practice and can be of enormous value in recruiting and retaining librarians who may have no science training into the specialty of sci-tech librarianship.

COMPETENCIES

In order to see how standards and competencies can be used, we must first understand the current state of competency development in the field. At present, there are three ways librarians encounter competencies: through their professional societies, through the broader organizations in which they are employed, and through their graduate education and training. Professional organizations to which some sci-tech librarians belong have developed professional competencies that could bear wider-spread use. Competencies documents from some large library organizations are compared and contrasted below. Several of these competencies sets will also be discussed further in the contexts of training, recruitment and retention.

American Association of Law Libraries (AALL)

AALL approved a set of competencies in 2001.[5] These include a rather lengthy list of core competencies, as well as specialized competencies divided into the traditional academic practice sectors of collection development, reference, teaching and management, as well as the addition of information technology, an increasingly important area of the profession. The AALL competencies are broadly enough defined that most could easily be adopted by sci-tech librarians, particularly in academic settings, where collection development, instruction and reference are commonly articulated areas of responsibility. "Science," "engineering" and more specific discipline terms could simply be substituted for "law" and "legal" in the AALL competencies.

American Library Association (ALA)

Various organizations within ALA have developed competencies for specific types of librarianship, though these tend to be more user- rather than librarian-focused. One example is the Reference and User Services Association's (RUSA) Core Competencies for Business Reference,[6] mainly a set of reference tools and resources. The ALA Intellectual Freedom Roundtable adopted a more skills-based document in 2002, Intellectual Freedom Core Competencies, that covers standards for library schools, for students (in any educational setting) and for working librarians.[7]

In 2000, the Association of College and Research Libraries (ACRL), a large division of ALA, adopted Information Literacy Competency Standards for Higher Education.[8] These useful standards for instruction have been applied by hundreds of academic librarians, and have been used, adopted, incorporated into, or served as a springboard for creation of, information literacy standards in a number of institutions. The California State (Cal State) Universities system established an information literacy working group in 1995 that has supported a number of projects, and has sparked the adoption of standards at some Cal State campuses.[9] For example, Cal State Los Angeles has established "Information Competence" as curricular policy.[10] Undoubtedly the adoption of information literacy standards for students has driven many librarians to hone their own information literacy skills, though none of these competencies explicitly require such.

Association of Research Libraries (ARL)

ARL surveyed its members in 2002 on the status of core competencies, particularly as related to performance measures. Of the 65 responding institutions, only 17 (largely state-supported, mid-sized institutions) had core competencies in place for library employees.[11] As the ARL authors note, "no clear consensus exists as to what the competencies should be or to whom they ought to apply." However, they go on to say, integrating competencies into performance management can benefit library customers, librarians, and their employers.[12] Academic libraries, the home organizations for many sci-tech librarians, lag a bit behind the more specialized libraries that belong to the organizations profiled in this section.

Medical Library Association (MLA)

MLA has promoted competencies for many decades, originally via their certification program and more recently via ongoing continuing education (CE) courses.[13] A variety of employers of medical information professionals have often recognized, and sometimes adopted, MLA CE credits as a competency measure. The MLA Educational Policy Statement, Platform for Change, advocates a collaborative approach, placing much of the responsibility for lifelong education on the individual librarian him or herself, as part of being a professional:

> Lifelong learning must be a cornerstone of every individual's professional development plan. Graduate programs of library and information science education, MLA and its chapters and sections, NLM, employers, commercial vendors and publishers, and other professional associations are all potential providers of educational opportunities, yet the ultimate responsibility for lifelong learning and professional development rests with the individual.[14]

The "Health Information Science Knowledge and Skills" section of the Platform document has a more specific list of competencies than those of many other organizations, particularly because clinical aspects of medicine are specifically addressed. But a number of these competencies could also be applied to sci-tech librarianship by simply substituting appropriate discipline topics in place of the medical areas.

Special Libraries Association (SLA)

SLA established a Special Committee on Competencies for Special Librarians in the mid-1990s, and that committee presented the SLA Board with Competencies for Special Librarians of the 21st Century in May 1996.[15] SLA defines competencies as: "... a combination of skills, knowledge, and behaviors important for organizational success, personal performance, and career development."[16] This definition captures both the theory and practice of librarianship. SLA competencies are demarcated as professional and personal. The competencies were revised substantially in 2003,[17] and now include two core competencies on which the professional and personal rest. These are:

> I. Information professionals contribute to the knowledge base of the profession by sharing best practices and experiences, and continue

to learn about information products, services, and management practices throughout the life of his/her career.

II. Information professionals commit to professional excellence and ethics, and to the values and principles of the profession.[18]

The 2003 competencies rely upon the revised SLA Research Statement which champions evidence-based practice,[19] an approach of growing importance in medicine. The redefined statement was driven by two significant changes wrought in the information landscape by the Web and pervasive search engines like Google. Information technology competency is more important than ever for librarians. And, users have the tools to do online research themselves. The new Research Statement asserts that increasing the evidence-based literature in librarianship's knowledge base, and then applying it, will keep librarians and information professionals viable in "an increasingly competitive world of information service providers."[20]

A 1999 article surveyed some SLA members who had improved their workplaces by application of the competencies, adapting them "to develop job descriptions, hire and evaluate staff, assess skills development, define continuous improvement goals and measure performance."[21] Three sci-tech librarians are among the interviewees. They reported applying the SLA competencies in a variety of ways, including as:

- Professional standards for teaching and research in academic science libraries
- A core philosophy for a software beta-testing project in a technology company
- A guideline for linking with the parent organization's strategic goals, and
- Concepts integrated into the organization's performance appraisal system.

Additional illustrations of the use of SLA competencies in training and retention are discussed below.

The concern professional associations are taking to define and promulgate standards and competencies is heartening. They have developed the best-rounded competencies addressing the "librarianship" side of the information professional's knowledge, skills and abilities. The areas of competency that are lacking—or at least less robust—in society-developed lists are the ones that address knowledge in the fields of science served and knowledge of developing information technology. As discussed below, these critical competency areas are also not yet fully addressed by library schools nor by employing organizations.

Science and Technology Organizations

Standards of the broader organizations employing librarians are sometimes used as competencies measures, and can be effective in assisting librarians to better serve their users in those arenas. Following are just a few examples of competency definitions in sci-tech organizations.

A research team studying software engineers defined job competency as "any attribute that contributes to doing a specific job well."[22] This team found some interesting differences in the competencies between outstanding engineers and their average-performing colleagues. "Star" software engineers exhibited these broad competencies, which have some relevance for librarianship: helps others; proactive role with management; exhibits and articulates strong convictions; mastery of skills and techniques; and, maintains a "big picture" view.[23]

The Foundation Coalition, an engineering education collaboration supported by the National Science Foundation and including a number of university partners, has developed a set of core competencies that are particularly focused on students and curricula, and that are being implemented at the participating universities.[24] "Active and cooperative learning" and "technology-enabled learning" are two that are especially suited for adaptation by sci-tech librarians.

An aviation writer has defined a profession as an endeavor requiring "specialized training, governed by standards, and the continued demonstration of competence."[25] By this definition, librarianship might be excluded from the professions! The wider use of required competencies would change that.

EDUCATION

A discussion of competencies would be incomplete without a brief examination of those used in graduate training in library schools because most, although not all, sci-tech librarians are graduates of accredited library and information sciences masters' degree programs. Accredited library schools have to meet and maintain certain competencies in their programs, faculty and resources. In the United States, ALA governs accreditation.[26] Library school students all have to maintain certain standards and demonstrate certain competencies to pass the courses. This can be the closest some librarians ever come to operating within a context of competencies.

One of the librarians interviewed by Scott and Kirby for their 1999 article[27] applied the SLA competencies in his teaching of information technology courses as an adjunct faculty member. The competencies can also be incorporated into library courses as themes or as previews of workplace requirements, and practicing librarians serving as adjunct faculty have done so. Both of the accredited library schools in Illinois have recently offered courses that incorporated the SLA competencies.

Lorri Zipperer, Rebecca Corliss and I incorporated key competencies into the syllabus as well as into the assignments for "Special Libraries Administration," which we taught at Dominican University's Graduate School of Library and Information Science for four semesters. Our 2002 syllabus states:

> The key objective of this course is to enable students to master Special Libraries Association (SLA) competency 1.7: [The special librarian] uses appropriate business and management approaches to communicate the importance of information services to senior management.[28]

In addition to structuring the principle assignment around the theme of communicating a library's worth to superiors, we incorporated illustrations of various SLA competencies into almost every class session.

Lian Ruan taught "Special Library Administration" at the University of Illinois Graduate School of Library and Information Science for two semesters. Ruan also incorporated SLA competencies into the syllabus, as noted in her course description: "An overall objective of this course is to prepare students to be able to achieve SLA competencies after they graduate and are working as information professionals."[29] Both Ruan and her guest lecturers frequently utilized one or more SLA competencies as themes in their discussion points, and the class project drew upon several of the organizational alignment competencies.

Zipperer and I have noted that as adjunct library school faculty we, "see librarianship [as] a dynamic profession of potential leaders, [and thus] a focus [is] placed on nurturing skills to aid the students to interact effectively in the field."[30] Introducing competencies in graduate school is a long-term approach to encouraging the adoption of competencies in the workplace, and to ensure future librarians' willingness to measure up to the challenges thereof.

Interestingly, a newly established Doctoral program in the Simmons College Graduate School of Library and Information Science is based in part upon a medical leadership competency document. The Simmons' Ph.D. in Managerial Leadership in the Information Professions adapted the Competency Model of the National Center for Healthcare Leadership as a key foundation for the curriculum as well as a tool for assessing students' progress.[31]

The competencies that have been developed by professional societies and by employing organizations, and that librarians have been exposed to during their graduate training, comprise a suite of tools that could be more systematically used throughout the life cycle of the professional librarian–first in recruitment, and then in several aspects of retention, as discussed below.

RECRUITMENT

Recruitment and retention are more important than ever in librarianship, in light of "the graying" of the profession,[32] as well as an increasing need for librarians to enable people to find what they need in the vast sea of always-accessible information. Sci-tech librarianship requires a triad of competencies–the professionally-focused competencies of librarianship, the subject-focused competencies of the scientific fields served, and the information technology competencies upon which so much of today's information access and delivery depend. A combination of MLS, scientific and technical competencies can broaden and ameliorate some of the problems facing sci-tech recruiting and retention.

Library managers report difficulty in recruiting professionals with any scientific background.[33] In addition, many of the articles in this issue suggest trying to recruit scientists who may wish a mid-career change into the profession. What better way to identify which theories, skills, and abilities are needed for each potential pool of candidates than through specific, thoughtful, competency development as part of the sci-tech library recruitment process?

The Medical Library Association's educational policy states the need for recruitment well:

> All partners in the educational process must actively forward strategies that ensure recruitment of promising individuals who demonstrate the basic skills and aptitude for achieving excellence in the field. Such candidates will evince analytic abilities,

interpersonal skills, self-understanding, willingness to take risks, persuasiveness, keen intellect, and an unquenchable desire to learn.[34]

Recruiting practices for sci-tech librarians in academic and special libraries settings do typically set standards for applicants in the job description itself as well as in the requirements, but many of these standards are quite broad. Admittedly, there is a balance required in position descriptions between too narrowly defined or too broadly defined advertisements; either end of the spectrum can yield ill-suited applicants or none at all.

Some academic position descriptions ask for proven capabilities, a move towards competencies. For example, a recent posting for a science and engineering librarian asks for:

- Demonstrated in-depth knowledge of one or more engineering or related science disciplines and of the research and publishing trends in these fields, as well as
- Demonstrated project management skills.[35]

Another recent posting, for a science librarian, also asks for proven competency: "demonstrated proficiency with both print and electronic information resources in sciences and/or engineering."[36] Both of these advertisements are typical of most job postings in also requiring broadly-defined traits, especially the ubiquitous "excellent communication skills." Presumably both employers utilize some criteria via which they can define excellence, a more nebulous trait than a demonstrable skill.

Competencies can be integrated into recruitment strategies. The University of Nebraska library developed core competencies in the late 1990s, and then built positions, and job interview questions, upon these competencies. This approach puts significant responsibility upon the interviewers, who must listen for the evidence of competencies in candidates' answers. Joan Giesecke (author of the ALA text Practical Strategies for Library Managers) and Beth McNeil discuss the Nebraska approach in a detailed article, from which the following illustration is taken:

Flexibility/adaptability is one of the most important core competencies in today's changing library environment. It can be very challenging to ask questions to determine a candidate's flexibility and adaptability. Answers to questions such as, "Tell me about an important project/task/assignment you were working on in which the specifications changed. What did you do? How did it affect you?" help the interviewer to determine how the candidate has adjusted to change. The nature of the "important project or task" can be very telling. How important does the project seem? Does the candidate's answer show that he/she adjusts well to less important changes and has trouble with bigger change?[37]

As illustrated by the examples above, competencies have the potential to assist library administrators facing a dilemma–how to turn partially-competent recruits into well-rounded, skilled sci-tech librarians. Competency-based recruitment strategies begin the process, but competencies must also be pivotal in retention strategies designed to foster ongoing learning.

RETENTION

Sci-tech librarians must maintain and expand their competencies once they are hired in order to continue to provide useful services to their clientele. The responsibility here is twofold: the librarian her/himself must be proactive in learning, and the organization must support development and expansion of relevant competencies.

In 1999, Giesecke and McNeil noted: "Little has been written that outlines library-wide competencies that are part of everyone's position, including both staff members and librarians."[38] This is still more the rule than the exception today. The ALA standards require accredited schools to "promote commitment to continuous professional growth." However, there are no absolute requirements for such growth.

Aviation writer Sheehan has averred, "All of the professions require continuing education of their members to ensure they not only stay abreast of the latest developments in their field, but also retain the basic lessons that enabled them to initially achieve their . . . status."[39] Librarianship could ultimately be strengthened as a true profession if it becomes more rigorous in requiring such continuous learning.

Evaluation

The use of competencies as both growth challenges and performance measures in the workplace is incumbent upon support from the organizations employing librarians–opportunities for continued learning in both theory and practice must be created, advertised and supported for the whole process to work.

One practice via which an employing organization can aim to retain the best librarians is to incorporate competencies into annual review processes (and provide librarians the support to develop and expand their competencies to meet these standards). Such a process was discussed above in the context of SLA examples. Three additional illustrations, one from academia and two from the corporate world, follow.

The ARL Spec Kit on Instructional Improvement Programs cites Kent State University's Liaison Librarian Performance Standards, which include both duties and responsibilities (e.g., "provide direct reference services . . .") and accompanying standards (e.g., "communicate effectively through listening and inquiring (i.e., allow patron to state need, clarify, avoid jargon, respond objectively").[40] The liaisons work specifically with academic departments, mainly on collection development. This model set of detailed and linked duties and standards is the core of the evaluation. The set can be used annually, with gains and areas for growth indicated in the evaluation, as the capability to prioritize focus on particular standards year. Furthermore, the liaison program, and thus the standards, are directly linked to the University Library's mission.

The original SLA competencies document includes several articles as well as the committee report and the competencies themselves. In one of the articles, Barbara Spiegelman presents a case study of her organization's move from management by objectives to a competencies-based system which includes the use of competencies for annual performance appraisals. One example from her technical library is this key job responsibility: "Search all technical and business databases/online services using cost-effective search techniques" which requires all of these competencies:

- Job knowledge
- Communication skills
- Strategic thinking
- Customer orientation
- Innovation
- Planning
- Results orientation, and
- Process orientation.[41]

Spiegelman makes the important point that the use of competencies in appraisals articulates demands and responsibilities, providing ". . . the clear knowledge of what is needed and wanted for growth within the company."[42]

At my previous position, my staff and I agreed to apply several SLA competencies to specific goals for our engineering firm library, goals that were also linked to the company's annual plan. One goal we developed read as follows:

> Special Libraries Association Competency 1.7 says: the special librarian uses appropriate business and management approaches. For 2002, the Library is focusing on 2 things that reflect this competency: (1) Customer survey to better understand and respond to our customers' information needs. (2) Refining our 'reference interview' techniques–how we talk with customers about what they need.[43]

We each defined specific tasks for ourselves that contributed to this goal. Introducing my staff to the competencies and "selling" them on the incorporation thereof into our goals was an almost surprisingly pleasant task. This experience illustrated one of Spiegelman's points: "Employees find it more acceptable to be rated on a variety of competencies and on a continuum of learning rather than to be slotted into a single rating [as some performance systems do] that does not necessarily recognize strengths."[44]

Using competencies in both retention and performance evaluation can help a developing sci-tech information professional fill in her or her knowledge or skill gaps. A competencies structure can also foster respect from the scientists and engineers as they observe (or are informed about) the ways in which sci-tech librarians and library administrators support continuous learning opportunities so that librarians stay up-to-date in the scientific fields they serve and in the information technology they use.

TRAINING

It behooves organizations employing sci-tech librarians to support training opportunities that support and expand the librarians' competencies, because the appropriate competencies should support the organization's growth. As Giesecke and McNeil have noted:

> To be useful, the competencies must relate to the organizational goals, objectives, and strategies. They are the knowledge and

skills that make the organization a success and help the organization change to meet a changing environment.[45]

Carla Stofle and colleagues at the University of Arizona, both a test-bed and a model for change management in academic libraries, state the need for training quite simply:

> We have not paid enough attention to providing continual development/learning opportunities. If we do not develop our staff, we will not have the staff with the skills that we need as our organizations change.[46]

They add that, furthermore, "Long term, this will not engender commitment to our organizations and will exacerbate our retention problems."[47]

Support of competencies training need not be excessively formal; a culture that supports ad hoc learning can be a powerful context within which its members find it easy to maintain and expand competencies. As noted by some computer scientists at a recent knowledge management conference:

> In knowledge intensive organizations . . . it is neither possible nor feasible to predetermine all possible 'learning paths' employees may be pursuing. In order to ensure a high degree of learning transfer in such knowledge intensive settings . . . the trend goes away from enforcing predetermined, general learning paths . . . towards supporting individual, work task related learning paths.[48]

FOR FURTHER STUDY

Sci-tech librarianship could benefit from further study of several competencies issues that lay a bit beyond the scope of this paper. Better understanding and application of competencies might help resolve one of the dilemmas now facing the profession–how to grow our replacements out of two potential populations: scientists wishing to make career changes, and trained librarians lacking sci-tech backgrounds.

Many academic librarians are on tenure or tenure-type tracks at their institutions, though this status has a complex history too long to cover here. The granting of faculty status to librarians can enhance their effectiveness within an academic setting, where working toward and achieving tenure indicates the approbation of one's peers, as it does for the teaching faculty.[49] Requirements for achieving tenure are typically fairly rigorous, but they can also be so broad as to be unclear. Competencies can be used to articulate the responsibilities required to achieve and retain tenure.

The library literature is not particularly robust in discussions of training, particularly as part of retention strategies. Our profession could benefit from additional focus on evidence-based training; determining more precisely where librarians have gaps in the skills required to meet library users' needs, and then implementing training programs to fill those gaps.

CONCLUSION

There is undeniably a role for librarians in the evolving information future. A recent University of Southern California (USC) library planning task force report noted: "As people seeking information contend with an expanding variety of content and a multiplicity of use environments, their need for point-of-need, context-sensitive assistance will persist."[50] The USC task force found the following competencies indispensable, noting that people working in libraries must be:

- Digitally literate
- Agents for positive change
- Managers of communication in learning spaces, and
- Supporters of a learning organization.

The use of competencies in education, recruitment and retention can help ensure that sci-tech librarians can stay efficient and effective in this time of rapid change. Competencies are demonstrably a key part of any profession. A comprehensive set of competencies can become a multipurpose tool, first used to recruit, then to train, and lastly to ensure both continuing competence and intellectual renewal.

NOTES

1. USC subscription consulted online January 2006.
2. http://www.m-w.com/.
3. David Fox, "Librarian-Scholars and the Boyer Model" *Teaching and Learning Bridges: Reflecting the Scholarship of Teaching and Learning at the University of*

Saskatchewan 1:1 (April 2002), http://www.usask.ca/tlc/bridges_journal/v1n1_apr_02/v1n1_librarians_boyer.html.

4. "Library Education" entry in the LIS Wiki, http://www.liswiki.com/wiki/Education.

5. Competencies of Law Librarianship http://www.aallnet.org/prodev/competencies.asp.

6. http://www.ala.org/ala/rusa/rusaourassoc/rusasections/brass/brassprotools/corecompetencies/corecompetenciesbusiness.htm.

7. http://www.ala.org/ala/ifrt/ifrtinaction/ifcompetencies/ifcompetencies.htm.

8. http://www.ala.org/ala/acrl/acrlstandards/standards.pdf.

9. http://www.calstate.edu/ls/Overview.shtml.

10. *Information Competency and Library Instruction Services for Faculty* http://www.calstate.edu/ls/1_brochure.doc.

11. *Core Competencies*. ARL Spec Kit 270 (Chicago: Association of Research Libraries, October 2002). Summarized here: http://www.arl.org/spec/270sum.html.

12. IBID.

13. Carla J. Funk, "What's Special about Special Libraries?–The Practice Environment of the Health Sciences Librarian,"INSPEL 32:4 (1998), 207, http://www.ifla.org/VII/d2/inspel/98-4func.pdf.

14. *Platform for Change, the Educational Policy Statement of the Medical Library Association*, (Chicago: MLA), http://www.mlanet.org/education/platform/index.html.

15. Barbara M. Spiegelman, editor, *Competencies for Special Librarians of the 21st Century* (Washington, DC: Special Libraries Association, 1997), 1.

16 IBID, ix.

17. *Competencies for Information Professionals of the 21st Century*, Revised edition, (Washington, DC: Special Libraries Association, June 2003), http://www.sla.org/content/learn/comp2003/index.cfm.

18. IBID.

19. *Putting OUR Knowledge to Work: A New SLA Research Statement June 2001–The Role of Research in Special Librarianship*, (Washington, DC: Special Libraries Association, June 2001), http://www.sla.org/content/resources/research/ rsrchstatement.cfm.

20. IBID.

21. Pamela J. Scott and Anne E. Kirby, "The SLA Competencies: Raising the Bar on Performance," *Library Journal* 124: 12 (July 1999), 46.

22. Richard T. Turley and James M. Bieman, "Competencies of Exceptional and Non-Exceptional Software Engineers," *Journal of Systems and Software* 28:1 (January 1995), 25.

23. IBID, 16.

24. Foundation Coalition Core Competencies, http://www.foundationcoalition.org/home/foundationcoalition/corecompetencies.html.

25. John Sheehan, "Are You a Pro?" *AOPA Pilot* 49:1 (January 2006), 85-86.

26. *Standards for Accreditation of Master's Programs in Library and Information Studies* (Chicago: American Library Association, 1993), http://www.ala.org/ala/accreditation/accredstandards/standard.html.

27. Scott and Kirby, 47.

28. *Revised Syllabus for LIS 774: Special Library Administration*, LIS 774–Spring Semester, 2002, Dominican University, Graduate School of Library and Information Science, http://domin.dom.edu/faculty/stompson/index.html.

29. *Special Library Administration LIS590SL Syllabus*, author's personal copy, cited with permission.

30. Lorri A. Zipperer and Sara R. Tompson, "Communicating Competencies and Collaboration," *Information Outlook* 6:9 (September 2002), 28.

31. Ph.D. in Managerial Leadership in the Information Professions, http://www.simmons.edu/gslis/academics/programs/doctoral/phdmlip/program/index.shtml.

32. Rebecca T. Lenzini, "The Graying of the Library Profession: A Survey of Our Professional Association and Their Responses," *Searcher* 10:7 (July/August 2002), http://www.infotoday.com/searcher/jul02/lenzini.htm.

33. See, for example, Barbara I. Dewey, "Science Background Required–Others Need Not Apply: A Study of the Science Librarian Hiring Crisis. *ASIS '86: Proceedings of the 49th ASIS Annual Meeting*, Sept. 28-Oct. 2, 1986, Chicago, IL, 64-68 and Mary Lou B. Jones, Mary F. Lembo, James E. Manasco and John H. Sandy, "Recruiting Entry-Level Sci-Tech Librarians: An Analysis of Job Advertisements and Outcomes of Searches," *Sci-Tech News* 56:2 (May 2002), 12-16.

34. Platform for Change, http://www.mlanet.org/education/platform/recommend.html#2.

35. San Diego State University Science & Engineering Librarian, http://bfa.sdsu.edu/ps/faculty.html.

36. California State University-Northridge Science Librarian, http://www.csun.edu/%7Efacacct/openings/position/0630.pdf.

37. Joan Giesecke and Beth McNeil, "Core Competencies and the Learning Organization," *Library Administration & Management* 13:3 (Summer 1999), 162.

38. IBID, 158.

39. Sheehan, 86.

40. *Instructional Improvement Programs: SPEC Kit 287*, (Washington, DC: Association of Research Libraries, Office of Leadership and Management Services, 2005), 87. The kit is summarized here: http://www.arl.org/spec/SPEC287web.pdf.

41. Barbara M. Spiegelman, "Using Competencies as a Performance Appraisal and Compensation Tool in Westinghouse Energy Systems: A Case Study" in Barbara M. Spiegelman, editor, *Competencies for Special Librarians of the 21st Century*, (Washington, DC: Special Libraries Association, 1997), 29.

42 IBID, 36.

43. Packer Engineering Knowledge Services Center, http://www.packereng.com/library.cfm, internal document.

44. Spiegelman, "Using Competencies," 35.

45. Giesecke and McNeil, 158.

46. Carla J. Stofle, Barbara Allen, David Morden David and Krisellen Maloney, "Continuing to Build the Future: Academic Libraries and Their Challenges." *Portal: Libraries and the Academy* 3:3 (July 2003), 374.

47. IBID.

48. Tobias Ley, Stefanie N. Lindstaedt, and Dietrich Albert, "Supporting Competency Development in Informal Workplace Learning." IN K. Althoff, A. Dengel, R. Bergmann, M. Nick & T. Roth-Berghofer, Editors, *Lecture Notes in Computer Science–Professional Knowledge Management: Third Biennial Conference, WM 2005* (Kaiserslautern, Germany, April 10-13, 2005), Revised Selected Papers Vol. 3782, 190.

49. Danielle Bodrero Hoggan, "Faculty Status for Librarians in Higher Education," *Portal: Libraries and the Academy* 3:3 (July 203), 431.

50. *Foundational Roles for Academic Libraries*. Report from the University of Southern California Information Services Division Dean's Task Force on Re-Envisioning the Mission of the 21st Century Information Services Environment. (Los Angeles, CA: University of Southern California, November 14, 2005).

doi: 10.1300/J122v27n01_16

Index

AALL (American Association of Law Libraries), 243-244

Accessibility-related issues, 174-175

"Accidental librarian" concept, 72-96

Accredited program accessibility, 174-175

ACRL (Association of College and Research Libraries), 1-4,13-14,31-32,108,113-118, 186-187,207-219

ACS (American Chemical Society), 9, 30-32

Action plans, 5-10
candidate identification parameters, 6-7
collaboration and, 8-9
"doing science" concept, 6-7
future perspectives of, 9
Generation Y and, 5-9
initiative-taking strategies, 8-9
Millennials and, 5-9
overviews and summaries of, 5-6

Advancement opportunities, 197-198

African countries (training-related issues), 159-171
ARCIS and, 166-170
background and historical perspectives of, 160-162
CASM and, 162-170
educational opportunities, 162-165
future perspectives of, 170
IAALD and, 165-167
overviews and summaries of, 159-162
professional status and, 165-166
reference resources for, 170-171
strategies for, 167-170
trends in, 162-170

African Regional Center for Information Science. *See* ARCIS (African Regional Center for Information Science)

Agnew, Shantel, 121-134

AGNIC-L, 138-156

ALA (American Library Association), 13,32-33,41-43,46-47,56-57, 59,73-74,165-167,244

American Association of Law Libraries. *See* AALL (American Association of Law Libraries)

American Chemical Society. *See* ACS (American Chemical Society)

American Library Association. *See* ALA (American Library Association)

American Society of Engineering Education-Engineering Libraries Division. *See* ASEE-ELD (American Society of Engineering Education-Engineering Libraries Division)

Appropriate coursework availability, 175-176

ARCIS (African Regional Center for Information Science), 166-170

ARL (Association of Research Libraries), 59-60, 117-118,244

Arnold, Tanya, 121-134

ASEE-ELD (American Society of Engineering Education-Engineering Libraries Division), 207-219

© 2006 by The Haworth Press, Inc. All rights reserved.